★

PRAISE FOR MISSION TRANSITION

"Matt Louis has created the *Ranger Handbook* of military transition guides. This book provides a concise pathway for service members to translate the skills and character they developed and forged in the military, so they can adapt to a new life mission and personal purpose after career service."

—GEOFF DAVIS,
Retired Member of US Congress, Former US
Army Ranger and Aviator, USMA Class of 1981

"I have read many transition guides and attended a host of transition seminars for military service members. All have value, but all fall short in some way. Matt Louis has captured the most important points of each of those experiences in one comprehensive guide. *Mission Transition* is thoughtful, well-researched, and extremely helpful not only to service men and women leaving the military, but for those veterans already in post-military careers who are seeking new opportunities."

—GUY C. SWAN III,
LTG (USA Retired), Vice President of the Association of
the United States Army (AUSA), Former Commanding General of
United States Army North (Fifth Army), and West Point Class of 1976

"As a veteran myself, I have long understood the many needs veterans have in making their transition from active duty. *Mission Transition* comprehensively addresses those needs in a practical manner and is a good book for our veterans leaving the military."

—ROGER STAUBACH,
Former Dallas Cowboy and Vietnam Veteran

"*Mission Transition* is not just a book, it is a life guide you'll return to again and again throughout your transition from the military to civilian success. As a veteran services organization leader who's assisted thousands of service members to a successful transition, I've never had a guide that covers all the bases. *Mission Transition* is easy to follow and is as applicable for a transition to New York City or a rural Midwest community. *Mission Transition* is a must-have guide for every government or non-government transition or training program."

—JIM LORRAINE,
CEO/President, America's Warrior Partnership, Former Special
Assistant for Warrior and Family Support to the Chairman of the Joint
Chiefs of Staff, Founder and Former Director of USSOCOM Care Coalition

"As someone that served for 25 years in the Marine Corps and now leads a military recruiting team, I can attest that the insights provided in *Mission Transition* are spot on. Transition is hard and having a plan is a critical element to making a successful transition. Matt has laid out an excellent framework of mostly common sense but often overlooked steps for maximizing your success in transition. I would highly recommend this to any transitioning veteran as it is never too soon to begin your planning for the next phase of your career."

—BEAU HIGGINS,
Senior Manager, Amazon Military Recruiting

"Occasionally a piece of work comes along that resets expectations in its field. It becomes the new standard. *Mission Transition* is that book for transitioning military personnel. Comprehensive, contemporary, and actionable, it is the indispensable tool and companion for anyone that has ever served and is trying to apply their character and experience in the civilian world. Whether your goal is that career-starting entry-level position or a capstone CEO role, *Mission Transition* is your strategic field manual to help achieve your objective."

—TED RUSS,
Author of *Spirit Mission*, Army Veteran

"As an advisor to senior US military leaders, I have seen what today's military and tomorrow's veterans can do despite the many obstacles of this turbulent age. This book helps remove what has historically been one of the larger obstacles to a veteran's lifetime success: their transition to full employment in civilian life. In doing so, it opens the door to an amazing talent pool that is poised to improve your organization's productivity and beat your competition. All military servicemen and women should digest its lessons; and organizations everywhere should process its learnings to capitalize on their expertise."

—ORI BRAFMAN,
New York Times Bestselling Author, Founder of Starfish
Leadership, Lecturer at the University of California, Berkeley,
Senior Fellow, Coach K Center on Leadership and Ethics (COLE)

"The next Greatest Generation is upon us as many of our heroes transition to private service. Most of these brave young men and women volunteered for military service *after* we were attacked on September 11, 2001, *after* the war started in Afghanistan and *after* the war started in Iraq. The qualities and experiences they possess, along with their high character, make them uniquely qualified for almost any position in the private sector. *Mission*

Transition is a tremendous resource for those seeking new careers as well as employers looking to improve their entities. This book will help our veterans understand how to convert their military experiences to meaningful careers when they take off the uniform."

—**PHIL MCCONKEY**,
President, Academy Securities, Navy Veteran, Super Bowl Winner

"As someone currently transitioning to civilian life after a career of almost thirty years in the military, I found *Mission Transition* to be *the indispensable guide* to this process. As the civil-military gap in the United States widens, fewer civilian employers understand the experience and attributes that veterans possess, and fewer veterans understand how to translate their experience and attributes into terms civilian employers can understand. While well-meaning, the military's own transition programs are little help here, as they tend to be one-size-fits-all seminars focused on helping veterans navigate the various assistance programs available to them. While important, this focus leaves little room for helping veterans identify and transition into a career field that can bring them professional fulfillment and financial security. *Mission Transition* does all this and more. Matt Louis has drawn on his considerable experience in both the military and the corporate worlds to produce the one book every soon-to-be veteran should read!"

—**BOB HAMILTON**,
Army Veteran, Associate Professor, US Army War College

"*Mission Transition* is bar none the best planning tool for service members who are tackling the daunting task of transitioning to the civilian workforce. It is a methodical handbook packed with clear and concise guidance, an exhaustive collection of outside references, and sage advice that you will not find elsewhere. Every veteran leaving the service should have this book—it should be standard issue. If there is a way to guarantee one's success outside the military, this book is it."

—**TIM KOPRA**,
COL (USA Retired), NASA Astronaut

"This is an incredibly powerful and important book. As someone who works with veterans in emotional and mental crisis, we have found a significant contributor to the challenges they face is an unsuccessful transition. *Mission Transition* has a higher purpose than just securing veterans jobs. It could save a veteran's life."

—**FRED JOHNSON**,
COL (USA Retired), Author of *Five Wars: A Soldier's Journey to Peace*

"Transition from the military can be challenging; I still remember the eerie silence after returning home from Iraq and the curious adjustments that come with returning to civilian life. We have made strides to better prepare our service members for their careers—in their service uniform, and the one that follows—but we can always do more. This book does just that; it is a guide containing real experience and practical steps for transitioning from the military to a successful civilian career."

—BRAD WENSTRUP,
COL USAR, Member of Congress

MATTHEW J. LOUIS

★ ★ ★

MISSION
TRANSITION

★ ★ ★

NAVIGATING THE OPPORTUNITIES
AND OBSTACLES TO YOUR
POST-MILITARY CAREER

HarperCollins
LEADERSHIP

An Imprint of HarperCollins

Published by HarperCollins Leadership, an imprint of HarperCollins Focus LLC.

Book design by Aubrey Khan, Neuwirth & Associates.

ISBN 978-1-4002-1476-1 (eBook)
ISBN 978-1-4002-1475-4 (HC)

Library of Congress Cataloging-in-Publication Data

Names: Louis, Matthew J., author.
Title: Mission transition : navigating the opportunities and obstacles to
  your post-military career / a book by Matthew J. Louis.
Description: Nashville, TN : HarperCollins Leadership, [2019]
Identifiers: LCCN 2019007471 (print) | LCCN 2019009383 (ebook) | ISBN
  9781400214761 (e-book) | ISBN 9781400214754 (hardcover)
Subjects: LCSH: Veterans--Employment--United States. | Career changes—United
  States. | Job hunting--United States. | Veteran reintegration—United
  States.
Classification: LCC UB357 (ebook) | LCC UB357 .L59 2019 (print) | DDC
  650.14086/970973--dc23
LC record available at https://lccn.loc.gov/2019007471

Printed in the United States of America

19 20 21 22 LSC 10 9 8 7 6 5 4 3 2

CONTENTS

To the members of the West Point Class of 1991—my classmates, my brothers and sisters in arms. You inspired me to write this book, and you inspire me every day with your outstanding achievements and incredible efforts in all facets of life. I pray this work is worthy of our heritage and meets the ever-growing needs of the sons and daughters of this great nation that we have all sworn to support and defend.

PREFACE

WHY WRITE THIS BOOK?

This book has been more than twenty years in the making. As a young army captain, I attended the Army Career and Alumni Program (ACAP) as a mandatory part of my leaving active duty to attend graduate school in 1996. Suffice it to say, it left a lot to be desired in terms of helping me get settled in the real world. So like every other veteran of my generation, I had to figure out for myself how to make the transition from the military. It was not an easy process.

It was then that I cobbled together the basic approach that has become the basis for this book. In the ensuing years, I have had several experiences that have inspired me to put pen to paper:

- I've worked with scores of veterans in applying my transition process and helping them make the same journey from the service. Much to my satisfaction, I found the diligent application of this process met with success at just about every turn.
- I've had the great pleasure of working with the wonderfully dedicated professionals who work in veteran collaboratives and related service organizations and observing the tactics they successfully use, many of which are featured in this book.
- I've witnessed the great frustration and difficulty that most veterans continue to experience in making their transition from active duty. This challenge has no limits;

achievements while serving, rank, or retirement status
matter not.

• I've read with increasing alarm the growing number of
studies and statistics that validate the ongoing issues this
talent pool faces.

Those experiences over many years have led me to a few
conclusions:

• Transition from the military is a multifactorial
conundrum and best approached as a process, with some
steps occurring in series and others taking place in
parallel.
• The transition process is equally applicable at all ranks
and levels. However, there are definite nuances in the
process that come with additional tenure.
• The difficulty experienced in transition usually increases
with time in service, short of achieving flag ranks.

Moreover, my experiences have led to a firm belief that veterans,
as a group, represent one of the most underutilized resources our
nation has to offer. They are hiding in plain sight and are separated
by a common language from 99.5 percent of the population that
hasn't served. For the benefit of all, we must *unleash the talent
within*.

This book is a first step toward doing just that. While there are
literally thousands of organizations in and outside of the government providing veterans support, I believe this work brings something unique to the conversation.

• This book details the transition process in a practical,
field manual–like manner, including lots of exercises,
templates, and how-to verbiage.
• The process mirrors commercial best practices advocated
in the job-hunting book *What Color Is Your Parachute?*

focusing on *who* (personal strengths) before *what* (the job market).

- It portrays a career decision tree and provides subsequent research on each of its branches.
- It spends considerable time focusing on the military-civilian cultural divide and the degree of change a veteran must address.
- It portrays how your ultimate financial needs in retirement will impact your financial goals in the civilian world.
- It provides nuances where applicable for the more tenured, field-grade veterans and retirees.
- This book also features an accompanying website (www. matthewjlouis.com) that provides voluminous templates, interactive tools, additional guidance and resources, and a repository for additional lessons learned by transitioning veterans—all of which are critical to your success. *Much of the content of the original version of this work is there. Please use it!*
- This work is also the outcome of exhaustive research. It references hundreds of sources; and you will find much of their detail in the endnotes. *Please do not ignore them.*

My aim and fervent hope are that this approach effectively enables successful employment outcomes for our nation's finest. They have earned that much, and that much we owe them.

On a personal note, I've had over twenty years of experience in the corporate world, which has enriched the details of the transition process for which I advocate. During a good portion of this time, I continued to serve in the reserves after my time on active duty, ultimately becoming a retiree myself. In total, I have spent twenty-five years in uniforms of some sort. Furthermore, I have audited the entire current Transition GPS curriculum (which includes the Soldier For Life–Transition Assistance Program [SFL-TAP]) to validate my approach.

I have a passion for helping people, especially those brothers and sisters in arms who have served and continue to serve our great nation, protect our freedoms, and enable the liberty we exercise every day. I'm eternally indebted to you for your ongoing sacrifices, and I hope this effort will in some way help ease your transition to the life you desire for yourselves and your families.

FOREWORD

Matt Louis and I are both West Point graduates with a heart for the military and veterans causes. We share a mutual friend and personal confidant, and we have all successfully made the transition from the military. Having done so, I think there are a couple of elements I believe are critical to demonstrating you are capable of positive change, which I call personal growth.

For a decade I have had the privilege to serve as the CEO of 7-Eleven. When I meet junior military officers and senior noncommissioned officers leaving the service and beginning their careers, I'm often asked two questions:

1. What do I consider to be the keys to building a successful career?
2. How did you grow in your career (and get to be CEO)?

Most leaders have their own answers to these questions, which are based on their experiences, philosophies, and perspectives. I want to share a summary of my experience and give my take on these questions.

The two essential talents that enable personal growth and success and allow individuals to take advantage of future opportunities are their capacity and their leadership.

- Capacity: an individual's intelligence and ability rooted in their knowledge and experiences.

- Leadership: an individual's capability to accomplish an organization's aims through the efforts of others. I believe in a unique style, upon which I will elaborate.

All readers of this book have demonstrated the first talent: capacity. Let's face it, you are serving in the greatest military the world has ever seen. You are gritty, ambitious, and intelligent with diverse experiences and capabilities. You will be in demand based on your capacity, and you will get opportunities to demonstrate it.

Having that solid capacity will be a base expectation. From where I sit, capacity is a bit of a commodity. That doesn't mean it's not important, but it's assumed you will have it and you will utilize it to grow and succeed.

What is not a commodity, and what will continue to be the real differentiator between individuals, is a person's leadership capability. Many of the most effective and successful people I've seen throughout my career are "Servant Leaders." I've seen servant leadership throughout my life and career, while playing youth and college sports, and while at West Point and in the army.

I saw it during my time in the military, in the organizations I've worked for, and in the organizations I admire today. Some of you may not have heard of servant leadership, but I promise all of you have seen it. I've been told the term *servant leadership* is an oxymoron, but I assure you it is not. If the term doesn't connect with you, look at it through the lens of a serving leader. They are the same.

Here's the exercise: I'd like you to think of a person in your life (living or dead) who had a positive influence on you, who took the time to support and improve you, who motivated and inspired you. This is a selfless person who put their organization and others ahead of themselves. It could be a teacher, a coach, a boss, a person for whom you'd knock down walls. Think of the qualities of character that person possessed or possesses.

I've conducted this exercise many times with a wide variety of groups around the globe. Inevitably they all come up with similar responses. They mention such qualities as:

- honest/trustworthy
- committed
- selfless/supportive
- humble
- good listener
- encouraging
- set standards
- believed in accountability
- appreciative
- good role model

Servant Leaders have that paradoxical mix of personal humility and strong professional will. They're ambitious for their organizations and others first, ahead of themselves. John Maxwell observed, "People don't care how much you know until they know how much you care."[1] That's where authentic leadership starts. If you can evolve your talents to lead in this way, you'll become that special person given permission by others to lead.

Now, combine that servant leadership approach with your undeniable capacity, and you'll continue to grow regardless of what direction or career path you take.

And so I suggest you strive to serve and support others and your organizations first, authentically. When you do, you will grow and attain success beyond what you imagine both personally and in your career.

Use this book as a resource throughout your transition, much like a field manual. It will enable you to form a new personal baseline from which you can spawn continued professional success by combining your newfound capacity with authentic servant leadership.

Good luck!

Joe DePinto
CEO of 7-Eleven Inc.
Dallas, Texas
July 4, 2018

INTRODUCTION

HOPE IS NOT A METHOD

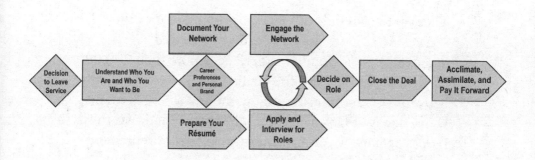

SOLDIERS, SAILORS, AND AIRMEN . . . !

You are about to embark on the Great Crusade, toward which we have striven these many months. The eyes of the world are upon you. The hopes and prayers of liberty-loving people everywhere march with you. In company with our brave Allies and brothers-in-arms on other Fronts, you will bring about . . . security for ourselves in a free world.

Your task will not be an easy one. . . .

But . . . I have full confidence in your courage, devotion to duty and skill in battle. We will accept nothing less than full Victory!

Good Luck! And let us all beseech the blessing of Almighty God upon this great and noble undertaking!

DWIGHT D. EISENHOWER,
ORDER OF THE DAY, JUNE 6, 1944 (D-DAY)[1]

Ike's heavily redacted order of the day could well apply to you, the transitioning veteran, as you enter the fray of the real world today. Given the monumental shifts in society and culture in the years since World War II, it is not a stretch to say the challenge you face today—overcoming the ever-growing military-civilian divide to secure full employment—is not all that different in stature from that collectively faced by the Allied Expeditionary Force in early June 1944. Does that sound far-fetched?

Well, consider the facts:

- There are thousands of you transitioning out of the service. After more than a decade of repeated deployments and combat experience, more than 200,000 of you matriculate into the civilian work sector annually.[2]
- Most of you are transitioning without a safety net. The Department of Defense tells us that more than two-thirds (70.7 percent) of you will transition short of retirement and without a pension.[3]
- Civilians—those who would hire you—do not share and thus do not understand your military experience. Approximately 99.5 percent of the American public has not served on active duty at any time since 9/11.[4] Only 8 percent of US adults are veterans, and that percentage is expected to decrease by a third by 2043.[5]
- A rapidly shrinking percentage of leadership in the corporate world shares your background. A study found a nearly 90 percent drop between 1980 and 2006 in the number of large publicly held corporations whose CEOs had a military background.[6] The *Wall Street Journal* reports this percentage to now be 2.6![7] Even if you expand that shot group to include all S&P 500 board members, the percentage with a military background is still less than 5.[8]
- Adding insult to injury, many of you enter the civilian world unprepared. Only a little more than half (51 percent) of veterans surveyed agreed or strongly agreed

that they were well prepared to successfully navigate the transition from military to civilian life.[9]

Consequently, every year there are tens of thousands of you entering the civilian marketplace without a safety net in a world that may not understand you, whose leaders likely don't share your background, and for which you may be unprepared. How does that strike you? The results speak for themselves:

- 53 percent of separating post-9/11 veterans will face a period of unemployment averaging twenty-two weeks.[10]
- 62.6 percent of your first jobs are *not* in your chosen career field, and the average time you spend in those roles is only 1.56 years.[11]
- While the time spent in subsequent jobs increases slightly (between two to three years in each job), almost half of you are still not in a job in your preferred career field by the *sixth* post-military job you hold.[12]

Most of you may take a job just to have *any* job, not necessarily the *right* job. And this, of course, tends to result in additional re-location, increased costs, repeated efforts, lost wages, and the corresponding inability to build wealth. That doesn't help you, your family, or your employer. You would think that such a record of false starts would compel efforts to find a role in your preferred career field. But that is obviously not the case. This is a signifi-cant—and sustained—failure rate.

★   ★   ★

DEFINITION OF A VETERAN

A veteran is defined by the Veterans Administration as "a person who served in the active military, naval, or air service, and who was discharged or released therefrom under conditions other than dishonorable."[13]

This confounding situation raises a couple of questions:

- Why are you, the transitioning veteran, systemically unprepared to enter the civilian workforce?
- Why does it seem to take veterans repeated attempts to find a job within a career field of their preference?

There are several reasons.

First, transitioning veterans don't seem to appreciate that "Americans don't understand military life. More than eight-in-ten post-9/11 veterans say the public does not understand well or at all the problems that those in the military face. That view is shared by 71% of the public."[14] This is problematic for two reasons: (1) While you have to be able to translate your skills to a prospective employer, an employer's lack of a common reference point puts you at a disadvantage, and (2) an employer's lack of understanding of the military hampers their ability to make an informed hiring decision and utilize your skills to their best use from the outset.[15]

★   ★   ★

TROOPS IN THE TRENCHES

"The best part of my transition was the opportunity to learn new things. Transition gives you a second chapter in your life—whether it's after four or thirty years. Most military people are self-starters and open to learning new things. So relish the opportunity; take advantage of it. Study new industries. Go out and ask questions. Gain a different perspective."

BRIAN HANKINSON, FORMER ARMY LIEUTENANT COLONEL

Second, while transition presents the opportunity to restart your career and the ability to capitalize on newfound freedom and possibilities, transitioning veterans typically fail to acknowledge what they are leaving behind. When you leave the military, you lose a real part of your identity. You lose your rank, the awards you wear on your chest, and the instant respect that comes with recognition of both. In losing your rank, you also lose whatever authority came with that rank; you no longer have UCMJ (Uniform Code of Military Justice) authority and are no longer able to give orders and expect those orders will be followed. You lose the camaraderie of peers that have experienced the same challenges of service, combat or otherwise. (In fact, the camaraderie of the military is often replaced by *competition* in the civilian workplace.) You lose the certainty that a chain of command poses for organizational hierarchy, which is often replaced by much more ambiguous environments in the civilian world. You lose the sense of community and built-in support network that comes with having your kids attend the same schools, shopping at the same BX/PX and commissary, sharing the same housing and other resources (hospitals, the club system, one-stop, etc.) at your respective duty station. Moreover, you lose the expectation that those resources and built-in support networks will reliably exist at whatever duty station to which you are assigned. You lose the structure of your work and your daily routine; there are no longer references, processes, manuals, and standard operating procedures for every aspect of your role. You also lose the training and common standards that come with the military experience.[16] Even more tangibly, you lose the tax-free nature of any allowances or combat pay. In short, the loss is significant, and you should expect to undergo the five stages of grief that most individuals experience when dealing with a significant loss.[17] You are entering entirely new communities with entirely new cultures with entirely new expectations—and you should adjust your approach accordingly.

★   ★   ★

TROOPS IN THE TRENCHES

"The most difficult part of my transition was the loss of the structure of the military. I went immediately to a job on post, working with troops, reporting to an officer. It took more than a few months to stop showing up early to work, not advising NCOs, even to quit saluting officers in the parking lot. Even today I still wonder why people don't adopt the structure of the military. Although I liked to challenge that structure, there was a certain comfort and reliability I find missing in work life now. Also difficult was the loss of camaraderie and feelings of guilt as people you know continue to serve and rotate through deployments."

PERRY JEFFERIES, FORMER ARMY FIRST SERGEANT

Third, existing transition support efforts of the military services often fall short of their well-intentioned goals. As Richard Nelson Bolles stated in *What Color Is Your Parachute?*, job hunts that start with doing research on yourself rather than the job market result in success 84 percent of the time. The current Soldier For Life–Transition Assistance Program (SFL-TAP) unfortunately starts with a focus on the job market, setting you up for a less than 28 percent success rate, at least by Bolles's accounting. Moreover, prior consideration of educational opportunities or industry-recognized certifications needed for a career of your choosing during and throughout your service tends to be an afterthought. Further, SFL-TAP also does not address the twenty-six Department of Labor competency models available for civilian industries.[18] These competency models outline the skills and abilities you need to be successful in a given industry and enable an employer to have a common basis for understanding your knowledge, skills, and abilities, as well as how they relate to potential openings within their organization.[19] SFL-TAP also assumes you have the self-awareness to identify your career interests at the point of transition.[20] This may assume too much; the reality is that more than half of you will pursue a different career than your military specialization.[21]

★ ★ ★

TROOPS IN THE TRENCHES

"You have to protect and prioritize yourself. Finding your new job should be Job #1. Your military role should be Job #2. You will get a middle-block evaluation regardless of how well you do your military role; so, your job search should be at least as important as your day job. No one will protect yourself but you. Also, don't ETS near the end of the calendar year. It turns out that the holiday season is not when companies are typically hiring. There is some seasonality to when they bring new people on-board."

DOMINIC LANZILLOTTA, FORMER ARMY CAPTAIN

Finally, the military organizations from which you are matriculating typically don't allocate sufficient time to prepare for transition. As you have likely experienced, most of the transition support available from the military services comes only at the tail end of your service. What should rightfully take one to two years is often rushed through in the waning days and weeks of your term in service. Because of this—and one example of its impact—most of you fail to maximize the education benefits available (Post-9/11 GI Bill benefits, Tuition Assistance programs) while on active duty, including opportunities to acquire industry-recognized certifications and licenses. There are many reasons for this, many of them justified, such as unplanned and untimely deployments, injuries, unanticipated reductions in force, remote duty locations, inflexible supervisors, family commitments, or lack of nearby institutions of higher learning. Post-military, you also tend to not utilize the existing state and federal resources available to you.[22] Of those of you who do utilize Post-9/11 GI Bill benefits, a significant number tend not to graduate. According to the Student Veterans of America National Veteran Education Success Tracker (NVEST), almost half of student veterans who enrolled in postsecondary education did not complete their degree.[23] Transition is a process, as this book will demonstrate, and you need time to think and work through that process to be optimally positioned for success in the civilian world.

Despite this, there is little doubt your military experience has provided you the building blocks that can ultimately enable success in the civilian world. As illustrated in the academic research summarized in "The Business Case for Hiring a Veteran: Beyond the Clichés," veterans draw from their unique and specialized military experience to apply relevant and market-connected knowledge, skills, and competencies within an organization (see the sidebar "The Value of a Veteran in a Competitive Business Environment").[24]

THE VALUE OF A VETERAN IN A COMPETITIVE BUSINESS ENVIRONMENT[25]

Veterans Are Entrepreneurial: Military veterans are twice more likely than nonveterans to pursue business ownership after leaving service, and the five-year success rate of ventures owned by veterans is significantly higher than the national average.

Veterans Assume High Levels of Trust: The military service experience engenders a strong propensity toward an inherent trust and faith in coworkers and a strong propensity toward trust in organizational leadership.

Veterans Are Adept at Skills Transfer Across Contexts/Tasks: Through their military training, service members and veterans develop cognitive heuristics that readily facilitate knowledge/skills transfer between disparate tasks and situations.

Veterans Have [and Leverage] Advanced Technical Training: Military experience, on average, exposes individuals to highly advanced technology and technology training. This accelerated exposure to high technology contributes to an enhanced ability to link technology-based solutions to organizational challenges.

Veterans Are Comfortable/Adept in Discontinuous Environments: Cognitive and decision-making research has demonstrated the military experience is positively correlated to the ability to accurately evaluate a dynamic decision environment and subsequently act in the face of uncertainty.

Veterans Exhibit High Levels of Resiliency: Military veterans exhibit high levels of resilient behavior, that is, because of their military experience. Veterans develop an enhanced ability to bounce back from failed professional and/or personal experiences more quickly and more completely compared to those who have not served.

Veterans Exhibit Advanced Team-Building Skills: Veterans are more adept regarding (1) organizing and defining team goals and mission, (2) defining team member roles and responsibilities, and (3) developing a plan for action. Further, research also suggests that those with prior military service have a high level of efficacy for team-related activities, that is, veterans exhibit an inherent and enduring belief they can efficiently and effectively integrate and contribute to a new or existing team.

Veterans Exhibit Strong Organizational Commitment: Research has demonstrated that military veterans bring a strong sense of organizational commitment and loyalty to the civilian workplace.

Veterans Have [and Leverage] Cross-Cultural Experiences: Individuals with military backgrounds (1) have more international experience, (2) speak more languages/more fluently, and (3) have a higher level of cultural sensitivity as compared to age-group peers who have not served in the military.

Veterans Have Experience/Skill in Diverse Work Settings: Those with military experience are (on average) highly accepting of individual differences in a work setting and exhibit a high level of cultural sensitivity regarding such differences in the context of workplace interpersonal relationships.

And there is more good news. A recent survey found that more than 90 percent of human resources (HR) managers said veterans are promoted faster than their nonveteran peers, and 68 percent said veterans performed either better or much better than their nonveteran peers. In short, "veterans bring a level of dedication and professionalism that promotes the bottom line while lower turnover increases institutional knowledge and cuts costs."[26]

Let's face it: Regardless of your rank or service, you undoubtedly have significant work experience leading teams, supervising and developing subordinates, planning and implementing projects and operations, and communicating to diverse audiences. You have hands-on experience, technical training, and in some cases licenses and certifications that have prepared you for the corresponding civilian certification.[27] You also demonstrate any number of soft skills, such as professionalism, teamwork, interpersonal and emotional intelligence, critical thinking, and the ability to solve problems.[28] In sum, thanks to skills developed during military service, you have the skills US employers say are needed for success in the workplace (see Figure I-1).

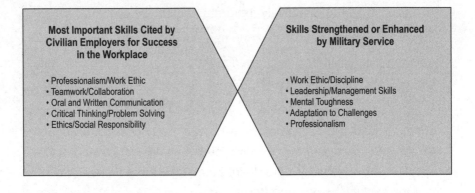

Figure I-1. Demand and supply of workplace skills.[29,30]

What you may lack is a clear-cut way to organize, translate, and demonstrate those skills and your personal strengths, your inner passion, allowing them to shine through to a civilian audience in a way they can understand. That's what this book intends to provide you. This book distinguishes between two separate audiences: those who have served less than ten years (junior military professionals—JMPs) and those who have served more than ten years (career military professionals—CMPs). Where applicable, separate guidance is provided for each audience.

The primary question this book aims to answer is: How can transitioning veterans realize their full potential by avoiding false starts and suboptimal career choices following active duty?

The answer to this question is realized via a detailed veteran transition process, and that process forms the basis for the organization of this book. Each chapter details a step or series of steps in the process. Highlighted icons indicate what part of the process is being discussed in that particular chapter.

This recommended transition process is detailed in Figure I-2.

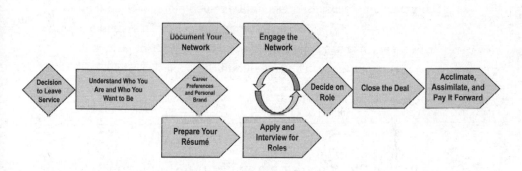

Figure I-2. The veteran transition process.

Upon completion, you should be positioned to effectively answer the basic questions every prospective employer has about you in a language they can understand:

- Who are you?
- What do you know?
- What can you do for us?
- How much will you cost us?

A complete transition must address multiple dimensions: employment, education, healthcare, and family support among them. While this book addresses all of these at some point, this effort is primarily focused on your employment since full employment tends to assuage issues related to many of the other areas.

★ ★ ★

TROOPS IN THE TRENCHES

"Start early and start with the big picture questions like: what do you personally value, what is important to you when it comes to work, what are the skills and interests that you excel at and that you want to keep doing. Don't think you are going to just go to the military TAP program and that will be sufficient. All TAP does is teach you to write a résumé and educates you on your VA benefits. The transition process is, or should be, much more involved than just writing a résumé and doing job searches online. This is a major life event and it needs to be treated accordingly if you hope to land in an occupation that you find meaningful and personally fulfilling."

CHIP COLBERT, FORMER ARMY LIEUTENANT COLONEL

You are about to embark on a major transformation, one that will be filled with much opportunity, joy, and rewards. But also one that comes with stress, questions, and doubts. Career change is not for the faint of heart. You will experience rejection, perhaps many times over and perhaps for the first time in your career, before you enjoy success. An abundance of persistence and courage will serve you well. Your perseverance will result in your success and position you to rightfully claim the title of the next greatest generation.

Finally, thank you for purchasing this book. My heartfelt intent is to help as many veterans as possible find productive roles in fulfilling careers as soon as they can upon leaving the service. The future productivity of your employers and a grateful nation depend on it. The future happiness and financial independence of your families depend on it. Let us begin . . .

KEYS TO SUCCESS

★ *Start early*. Taking this recommended approach a year or more prior to your transition is preferable. Optimally, service men and women should consider their exit strategy from the service as soon as they begin their service. Beginning with the end in mind will allow you to plan to acquire needed certifications, education, and expertise throughout your time in the service and better prepare you for the transition when it finally occurs.

★ This process equally applies to those of you who have already transitioned and are struggling with your career.

★ To borrow a phrase from Jim Collins: Confront the brutal facts. You are not entitled to a job, and no employer will simply give you one. Just as you earned everything you ever did in the military, the same will be true as you enter the civilian world. Get ready to get to work!

★ Don't succumb to frustration. This is hard work and will take time and effort. Your future and your family's future are worth your every effort.

★ Have an open mind. Give yourself the freedom to think in new ways. New thinking will be required; most hiring managers do not think like you do.

★ The future is yours for the taking. If nothing is ventured, nothing is gained. Go get it!

★ Follow the process recommended here in order, and don't skip parts of the process. You may want to jump to certain chapters, but I encourage you to read the book from front to back in order.

★ Use this book as a resource throughout the entirety of your transition, much like a field manual. Apply the crawl-walk-run approach to each process step. Read a chapter, apply it, and then come back to the next chapter.

★ This is a practical guide. This is not an exhaustive study on career change. I point to many references along the way (and on my website) that will allow you much further exploration of many of these areas. Please avail yourself of those. My purpose is not to boil the ocean. My purpose is to help you find the most direct route to your fulfilling future career by using the most effective and efficient process I know.

* * *

CHAPTER ONE

UNDERSTAND WHO YOU ARE

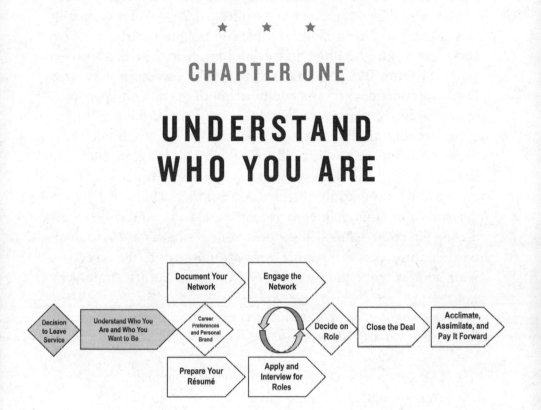

CONGRATULATIONS ON SERVING OUR COUNTRY AND FULFILLING YOUR TIME IN service. Your transition from the military may take different forms. You may be about to complete an initial mandatory service obligation or an entire twenty- to thirty-plus-year career. Retirees, your retirement pay is well earned. But you want more. At least I'll assume that, given that you're reading this book. Well, here's the good news: A grateful nation *needs* you. It needs the accumulated skills, experiences, and maturity your time in service afforded you. My hypothesis is your life mission is not yet complete. You have much more to do. You just need to transition your personal mission.

But mission transition is not as easy as it sounds. Successful career change, especially from the military, requires a significant amount of focus and work, similar to the same level of effort that made you successful in the military. In the words of Angela Duck-worth, it requires "grit." In her studies of West Point cadets in Beast Barracks, Army Special Operations Qualification Course survivors, Chicago public high school graduates, or Scripps National Spelling Bee contestants, the highly successful had grit. Duckworth defines grit as a combination of passion and perseverance. She found that those "highly successful had a kind of ferocious combination that played out in two ways. First, these exemplars were unusually resilient and hardworking. Second, they knew in a very, very deep way what it was they wanted. They not only had determination, they had *direction*."[1] You already have determination; this chapter aims to provide you that second ingredient—direction—that will support your resilience in the civilian world. But success will require your commitment to the objective: your success, your family's success, and your future employer's success.

In this chapter we will initiate the transition process by identifying who you are. We will discuss:

- The *who* portion of the self-discovery sequence
- Your strengths
- Your personality type and related career paths

The intended product of this chapter is your ability to articulate your strengths in a way that positions you as a fit for your chosen career path. This, combined with the output of chapter 2, will form the basis for how we will produce your résumé in chapter 4.

Let's start with a few questions:

- Did you know five years ago what you'd be doing today?
- Could you accurately predict what you'll be doing five years from today?
- Do you feel you have untapped potential that is not being utilized?

The typical answers are no, no, and yes.

Navigating a career is complicated. You've likely heard the phrase that a career is a marathon, not a sprint, and this is very true. You may well end up working in several positions over the course of this next portion of your career journey. And while that is typical, the goal of a successful transition is to enable your *first* civilian position to be as fulfilling and rewarding as possible. This is incredibly important, as research has shown that *finding an initial position in your preferred career field will nearly double the earnings, job duration, and rate of retention of transitioning veterans.*[2] Finding this initial position, however, takes some doing. So let's get to work.

Let's think through a few additional questions that are typical of veterans transitioning from the military. When you picked up this book, you likely asked yourself:

- What is available to me? What kinds of positions? What kinds of development opportunities, etc.?
- How do I attract recruiters and employers that I am interested in?
- What are companies looking for? Would they want me?
- How do I break out of the military mold I'm in?
- How do I move up in an organization?
- What are the risks of putting myself out there for a position and not getting it?
- How do I successfully transition to a new role? What will change?
- I just need a job, not a career. What should I do?
- I have family circumstances that make my home life a priority. How can I balance this?

Do these sound familiar? I remember asking these myself.

I'd encourage you to reframe these questions. To do so will change your perspective on the entire career search process to one that encourages you to leverage your strengths and exposes you to career opportunities based on those strengths. It's time to transition how we think about our entire approach!

★ ★ ★

TROOPS IN THE TRENCHES

"A mentor of mine early on in the process called me out as we were talking about various options I was considering and said, 'Chip, there is no doubt in my mind that you *can* do any number of things. What I am interested in hearing more about it is what you *want* to do, what is going to get you excited to get out of bed every morning?' That was an incredibly helpful distinction for me."

CHIP COLBERT, FORMER ARMY LIEUTENANT COLONEL

Consider the following rendering of the same questions:

- How can I do work that I am passionate about?
- How do I talk about what I am good at so people will notice?
- What can I look for in opportunities that will allow me to sustain my focus and energy beyond the initial job I select?
- How do I take control of the process and find what I really want?
- How can I be successful at anything that I choose to do?

What's different about the way in which these questions are posed? I would contrast them as follows:[3]

THE FIRST SET OF QUESTIONS	THE SECOND SET OF QUESTIONS
Done *to* me	Done *by* me
Follower focused	Leader focused
Structured	Open
Fear based	Opportunity based
Reactive	Proactive

The second set of questions changes the paradigm. It forces us to take control and be proactive! My own transition showed that I needed to shift my attitude toward this latter mentality. Over time, you should find yourself beginning to think the same way.

Who you are and who you want to be will be defined differently than how you define it today, even if you are pursuing a government position that directly leverages your military skill sets.

The first step down this path is to look within and get honest with ourselves. That is, to go all the way back and revisit who you are as a person and who you want to become. This may seem like a silly question ("Of course I know who I am"), but it is crucial to a successful transition. In fact, this is perhaps the most important step in the process. *Please do not skip this or skip ahead.*

★   ★   ★

TROOPS IN THE TRENCHES

"When I came out of the military, I felt that I had a great background and work ethic. But I had no idea what kinds of jobs might be available or what different industries entailed. It was like going to a restaurant and being unable to read the menu. I had an economics degree, but I initially went with an operations role in a paper mill—which was a mistake. I made the mistake of doing what I *could* do as opposed to what I *wanted* to do and ended up back in the same sort of structure I had in the military. I should have trusted my instincts. I should have been in sales and in financial services."

JON SANCHEZ, FORMER NAVY SEAL

Let's start with an analogy. As anyone who's ever been in the military can tell you, in order to orient your map, you must first find where true north is. True north, for our purposes, represents who you are and who you want to be, but in a language that a civilian hiring manager or executive will understand. These descriptions will sound very different than how you think and talk about them today. Never forget: You as a veteran represent 0.5 percent of the population. You are trying to be hired by the 99.5 percent of the population that has never served.

Understanding your true north will also help you understand how to relate to others. This is critical and necessary knowledge and likely something you may have never considered.

So how do we do this?

There is a process to everything, and this is no exception. Understanding who you are must come before consideration of what you might like to do. First *who*, then *what*. Our self-discovery sequence will follow the steps listed in Figure 1-1.

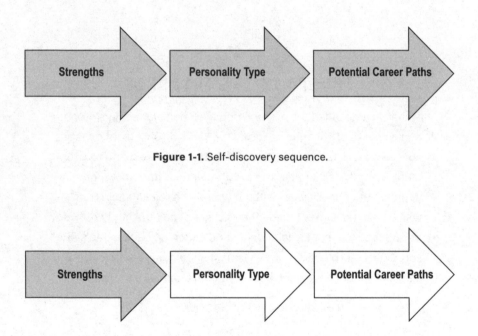

Figure 1-1. Self-discovery sequence.

Let's start with assessing your strengths.

People and organizations spend a lot of time, money, and energy trying to define a formula for career success. What most of them have found is that they can come up with a reliable way to predict only reasons for failure, not success. Why?

The simple reason is that success is as specific to the individual as the people who achieve it. There is no tried-and-true formula for how to be successful that will work for every single person. The closest you might come to a formula for career success is finding something to do that allows you to answer the question: How can I do what I love every day and still meet my job expectations and career goals?

★   ★   ★

TROOPS IN THE TRENCHES

"The hardest thing for me was understanding how to translate my skills in two senses. One, of course, related to résumé translation. But more important was identifying what you liked about the military and where you can find that same thing in the civilian world. Skills are a by-product of what you are passionate about. Understanding that frees you to pursue what gets you up in the morning."

BRIAN DICKINSON, FORMER AIR FORCE COLONEL

So what does this have to do with strengths, you might ask.

In his writing, Marcus Buckingham defines a strength as any activity that makes you feel strong.[4] The Gallup organization found that what differentiates high-performing teams and individuals from average or subpar performers is whether they have the opportunity to use their strengths every day. What Buckingham found was that only 20 percent of people used their strengths on a daily basis.[5] That alone may provide a basis for success.

So how do you go about identifying your strengths?

Let's start by considering what makes you feel energized, what makes you feel strong. Think of a particularly good day you have had. Consider your experiences at work, school, home, or other relevant settings. Consider different factors, such as environment, culture, people, structure, and mission. Think about what activities invigorate, motivate, or empower you.

What are some of those characteristics of your good day? How do you feel after a great day? Why is that so?

Conversely, think about a not-so-good day. Consider the same experience and factors as above, but also think about what tasks or responsibilities make you feel drained or exhausted.

What are the characteristics of your not-so-good day? How do those make you feel? Why is that?

Let's do a little exercise to help you identify your strengths.[6]

Review the list of verbs below. Circle those that you really love doing, those that strengthen you. Ignore those that don't make you feel particularly strong. If there is a verb missing that perfectly describes an activity you love to do, write it in one of the blank boxes. When you are finished with the list, put a star next to the five most important activities you've identified. (If you find yourself struggling with this, enlist the perspective of a spouse, partner, or family member—someone who knows you well.)

Connecting	Developing	Managing	Planning
Strategizing	Organizing	Networking	Mentoring
Coaching	Consulting	Writing	Troubleshooting
Testing	Teaching	Studying	Streamlining
Selling	Scheduling	Revising	Reviewing
Recurring	Pricing	Presenting	Persuading
Navigating	Measuring	Maintaining	Developing Leads
Influencing	Illustrating	Forecasting	Explaining
Evaluating	Editing	Drafting	Documenting
Designing	Defusing	Debating	Dancing
Counseling	Comparing	Communicating	Cold-calling

Table 1-1. Table of strengths.

Building	Budgeting	Brainstorming	Assessing
Analyzing	Creating	Interviewing	Advising
Reporting	Calculating	Examining	Facilitating
Negotiating	Arranging	Directing	Training
Solving	Leading	Following	Supporting

Table 1-1. Table of strengths (*continued*).

Now that you've identified your strengths, let's turn them into statements that a prospective employer would understand and appreciate.

★   ★   ★

TROOPS IN THE TRENCHES

"The feeling of uncertainty made transition difficult. I found myself for the first time in nearly twenty-six years not knowing precisely what my next duty station and job position would be. I also did not have a clear picture of the industry, company, or culture I would become part of. It's akin to a movement to contact, but in this case your objective is to gain and maintain contact with a job opportunity."

DAN HODNE, FORMER ARMY COLONEL

For each strength you have identified, write a strength statement that describes how you most enjoy that activity. For example:

- I feel strong . . . planning
- subject or topic of the activity . . . athletic teams

- who the activity is with/to/for . . . for my community athletic association
- objective of the activity . . . allow kids to experience team sports

Result: *I feel strong planning athletic teams for my community athletic association to allow kids to experience team sports.*

Try to be as detailed and specific as you can in pulling these statements together.

Statement 1: _____
_____
_____

Statement 2: _____
_____
_____

Statement 3: _____
_____
_____

Statement 4: _____
_____
_____

Statement 5: _____
_____
_____

There you have it. You've now defined your strengths! You should now be able to:

- Identify what energizes you at work
- Talk about yourself naturally, from a place of passion and genuineness

- Describe to a prospective employer how you can leverage those strengths
- Target specific jobs and industries that are best suited for you

This process of identifying our strengths begins to help us look within ourselves and understand what makes us tick as human beings. It enables a more accurate output from a personality test, which is our next exercise. The importance of the personality test is that it will identify specific career options that tend to match your personality type.

★ ★ ★

TROOPS IN THE TRENCHES

"The most difficult part of my transition was determining what type of industry and role I would be happiest in pursuing. I surely wanted to find a company with values similar to my own, but I was not completely sure about what types of roles would give me the most satisfaction. In order to pare down my options, I took a strengths finder survey as well as a Myers-Briggs assessment to better understand my strengths and weaknesses in order to pair them up with industries and roles that would fit my skill set."

MALISSA GALLINI, FORMER ARMY CAPTAIN

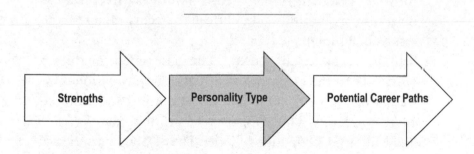

There are many of these types of tests or assessments on the market today. I'll preview four of them, but I urge you to complete at least two of them. Consistent outcomes from more than one source will help with your confidence level. I can't stress the importance of this exercise enough. The insights you glean will benefit you immensely in understanding what first career field and position may best match your personality type. There are some costs associated with each, but all are well worth it.

1. CareerLeader.[7] This assessment consists of questions focused on three areas: a business career interest inventory, a leadership motivations profile, and a leadership skills profile. Through a series of questions, they are able to help you pinpoint both an optimal career field that aligns with your strengths as well as a corporate culture that will be most accepting of your personality type. You may find this last point to actually be more important than the first. The late business management guru Peter Drucker said, "Culture eats strategy for breakfast." The point is that culture, defined as how organizations as a group behave, can have far more impact on the trajectory and success of your career than any strategy an organization is following. Keep your radar up to detect the cultural nuances of organizations as you network for opportunities (more on this in chapter 10).

2. Myers-Briggs Career Test.[8] It uses the Myers-Briggs Type Indicator® (MBTI®) personality assessment to find the twenty-four most popular careers (and ten least popular) for your personality type. The Myers-Briggs career test has ninety-three questions, takes fifteen to twenty minutes, and results in a nine-page report.

3. Self-Directed Search® (SDS).[9] This assessment enables a crosswalk to the Department of Labor's Occupational Information Network (O*NET) career options and required education levels. The SDS site refers to it as the Veterans and Military Occupations Finder. The SDS asks a series of questions about your aspirations, activities, competencies, interests, and other self-estimates.

4. iStartStrong™ Report,[10] which is based on the Strong Interest Inventory® assessment. This personalized report

presents results as general themes and specific interests using engaging four-color graphics, paints a clear picture of how one's interests and themes link to various jobs, work settings, and career fields, and provides hyperlinks to related O*NET occupations.

★   ★   ★

TROOPS IN THE TRENCHES

"Don't worry about trying to find the perfect job. Find the right *fit*. Few civilians feel they have the perfect job. Find the culture that best fits you. Find people who you want to be around."

JON SANCHEZ, FORMER NAVY SEAL

Upon completion of your chosen personality tests, you will have successfully defined the *who* part of the self-discovery sequence. Chapter 2 will focus on the *what*.

KEYS TO SUCCESS

★ Don't skip this.

★ Take the time to do it thoroughly.

★ If you don't know where you're going, any road will get you there.

★ Do what works for you, not someone else (friends, spouses, etc.). You are unique. You have unique experiences and strengths that will translate into a career path that is best for you alone.

* * *

CHAPTER TWO

UNDERSTAND WHO YOU WANT TO BE

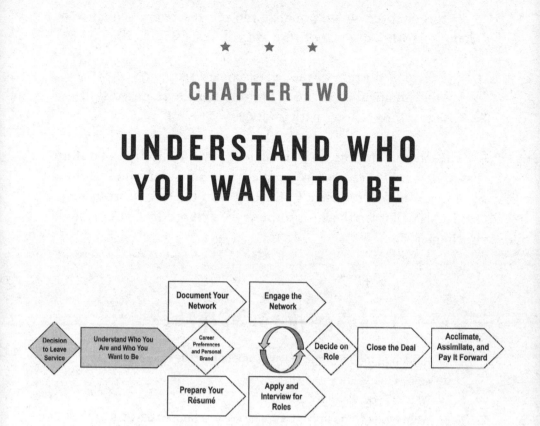

RECALL THE SELF-DISCOVERY SEQUENCE FROM CHAPTER I. THE FIRST TWO elements, strengths and personality type, represent the *who* portion of the sequence. As stated in the introduction, it is critically important to define this portion first. Only after having this understanding can you properly orient yourself toward a viable career path. Understanding those potential career paths and identifying those that might be best fits for you are the subject of this chapter.

• • •

In this chapter we will finalize the self-discovery sequence by identifying who you want to be. We will discuss:

- The *what* portion of the self-discovery sequence
- Your practical career path options and the required skill sets of those career path options

The intended product of this chapter is your selection of a short list of potential career paths, coupled with an understanding of the required skill sets for each. Combined with the output from chapter 1, this will form the basis for how we will produce your résumé in chapter 4.

★   ★   ★

TROOPS IN THE TRENCHES

"Every time I tried to engage with someone, I was asked questions to which I didn't know the answer:

What do you want to do?

What type of industry or company are you targeting?

What size company are you looking for?"

FORMER ARMY COLONEL

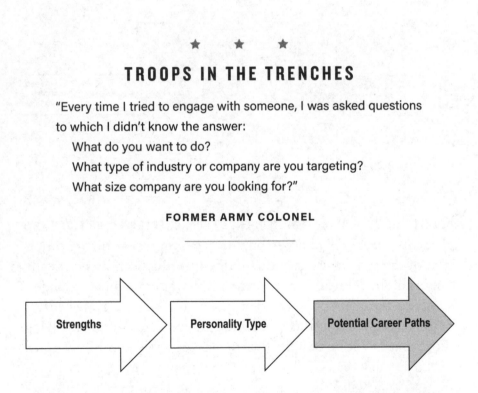

Your answers to the strengths exercise and the personality tests will point you in the direction of one of a few possible occupations. Hopefully you will find these outputs to be incredibly enlightening. Some of you, however, may still be questioning their findings. To *all* of you, I suggest one last confirmatory exercise. Before settling on a specific occupation, let's ponder the typical career alternatives available to you upon leaving the service. This exercise—and your resulting preferences—have proven to be critical in the wealth, happiness, and career longevity of transitioning veterans. As I said earlier: *Finding an initial role in your preferred career field will nearly double the earnings, job duration, and rate of retention of transitioning veterans.*[1]

Figure 2-1 represents the practical career alternatives available to most transitioning veterans and the percentage of veterans that choose them.

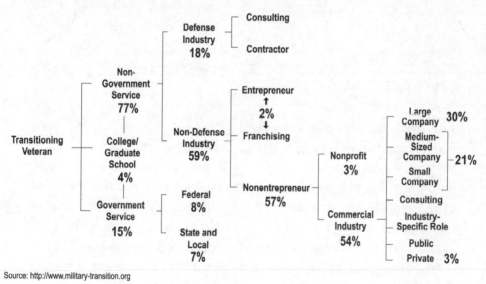

Source: http://www.military-transition.org

Figure 2-1. Practical career alternatives and percentage of veterans choosing them.[2]

Let's review the decision tree to understand the logic behind the options. We will then review the specific Department of Labor competency models for various industries to better understand where your strengths, transferable skills, and experiences might offer an ideal match.

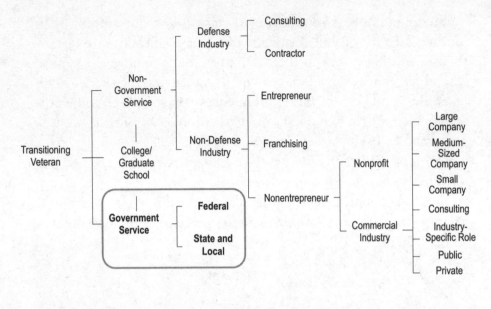

GOVERNMENT SERVICE

The first decision point involves consideration of whether you want to continue a career in a government service capacity. Surveys tell us that 8 percent of you will matriculate into federal government roles.[3] That continued government service could take one of many different directions. At the federal level, professional or wage-grade roles are available in nearly every department or agency (see the sidebar "Federal Occupation Designations").[4]

Most of these agencies have a Veteran Employment Program Office, which is responsible for promoting veterans' recruitment, employment, training and development, and retention within their respective agencies. Veterans can contact individuals within these offices for specific information on employment opportunities in those agencies.[5]

FEDERAL OCCUPATION DESIGNATIONS[6]

Occupations in the federal government are designated professional (general schedule or GS) or trade, crafts, or labor (wage grade) and are further categorized and defined by series and/or grade.[7]

Professional occupations require knowledge or experience of an administrative, clerical, scientific, artistic, or technical nature and are not related to trade, craft, or manual labor work.

Trade, craft, or labor positions involve the performance of physical work and require knowledge or experience of a trade, craft, or manual labor nature.

The federal hiring process is fairly straightforward (but can be lengthier and more difficult than its civilian counterpart), and available roles are centralized (see www.usajobs.gov). In-demand positions are annotated (see the "Explore Opportunities" portion of the website) and regularly updated. Under certain conditions, you as a veteran—or your spouse—could earn a five- to ten-point preference on your application score (except for senior executive service roles).[8]

Keep in mind, there may be a post-service restriction that applies to you. The National Defense Authorization Act of 2017 enforces a 180-day hiring restriction of retired service members as Department of Defense (DoD) civilians. This removes a previous provision of DoD Directive 5500, which allowed the immediate hiring of retirees as DoD civilians in the case of a national emergency.[9]

At the state and local level, available roles vary by governmental agency and geographic location, as do their hiring processes. However, many of the same federal occupations exist at the state and local level. Seven percent of transitioning veterans end up working for state or local government.[10] See your state's government jobs website for details.[11]

•   •   •

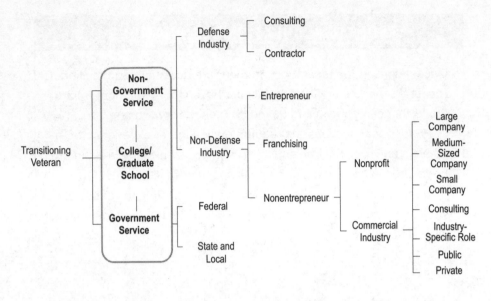

COLLEGE OR GRADUATE SCHOOL

In leaving the military, many service members find the allure of college campuses to be significant—and for good reason. College (including technical college) or graduate school (business school, law school, medical school, etc.) offers transitioning veterans some time and space to adjust to civilian life while picking up additional skills valued in the civilian world, all the while surrounded by peers who have spent their careers to date working with the 99.5 percent of people who have never served on active duty. It's a great opportunity to gain lots of intelligence on how your civilian peers have succeeded while plotting your next career move. Surveys show that 4 percent of transitioning veterans will choose this path.[12]

★　　★　　★

TROOPS IN THE TRENCHES

"Although I didn't know what I wanted to do with my life, I knew I wanted to do something in the sciences and I knew an advanced degree was needed to give me the knowledge and credibility to pursue this path."

FORMER ARMY CAPTAIN

The benefits to this approach are many. Because you'll have taken the time to more finely tune your targeted career path, there will be an even greater likelihood your eventual landing spot will be more rewarding, your tenure will be longer at your eventual employer, and your earnings will be higher. This was the path I chose, and I wouldn't have done it any other way. I found that I needed that two-year period in graduate school to deprogram, as I called it at the time. And even then, there was still some adjustment needed at my initial employer after graduation. To enable your own personal deprogramming, I encourage you to register for Columbia University's free massive open online course (MOOC) that prepares you for the transition to higher education.[13]

For those who have served at least ninety days on active duty after 9/11, there is even more good news.[14] You are eligible for the Post-9/11 GI Bill, which pays for a percentage of your tuition, provides a monthly housing allowance, and grants a stipend for books and supplies. You'll find several resources regarding this and other potential support vehicles on my website (www.matthewjlouis.com):

- The Veterans Administration provides a fact sheet on the Post-9/11 GI Bill on their website.[15]
- Beyond the GI Bill, there are a host of other financial aid programs at the federal level. See the veterans portion of the SmartStudent™ Guide to Financial Aid at FinAid .org.[16]

- Benefits at the state level vary widely. Military.com has consolidated all of them on their website.[17]
- Try to qualify for in-state tuition, which provides a substantial discount at most colleges. State residency requirements vary widely, but a general rule of thumb is to establish residency at least one year ahead of enrollment in the state of your school choice to qualify. If you begin your transition sufficiently early and plan accordingly, you may benefit handsomely.[18]

In preparing to return to college, the National Association of Veterans' Programs Administrators (NAVPA) provides ten tips for transitioning veterans.[19] You can find it on my website (www.matthewjlouis.com).

★ ★ ★

TROOPS IN THE TRENCHES

"Perhaps the most challenging thing for me to adapt to in grad school was the never-ending debate about the how or why to do something. This constantly perplexed me as I wanted to make a decision (right, wrong, or indifferent) and take action! Alas, that is not the academic way, and I quickly learned that fostering debate and inclusion were the approved solution in this new world—a good lesson to learn before I took my first job in consulting."

FORMER ARMY CAPTAIN

Some periodicals regularly rank schools that are deemed to be more receptive to veterans. GI Jobs produces an annual list of military-friendly schools.[20] Military Times also produces an annual best for vets list of four-year, two-year, and nontraditional colleges you can find on their website.[21]

Short of a full-blown degree, you may find the acquisition of a license or certification to be invaluable in the marketplace. Licensing and/or certification may play a key role in initiating or advancing your career in jobs such as a mechanic, medical technician, therapist, computer network engineer, website developer, and many others. A license or certification may also be required for jobs that are subject to state or other government regulations. The Department of Veterans Affairs explains on their website how they may reimburse a portion of the cost to obtain such licenses or certifications.[22] Also well worth reviewing is the VA's web page that collates a host of non-VA resources for student veterans and school administrators.[23]

★   ★   ★

TROOPS IN THE TRENCHES

"Don't be afraid to pursue a technical occupation. Do you want to be an architect? A professional engineer? A scientist? These fields need leaders too. If these require you to withstand a bit of short-term sacrifice for long-term personal reward, don't be scared off. It's worth it down the road, and you won't regret what you didn't do when you had the chance to do it."

FORMER ARMY CAPTAIN

Here's a final word on this topic for those of you who may be lacking sufficient education for the career you seek or, for whatever reason, eschewing upping your skills by going back to school. A recent survey by the Center for a New American Security (CNAS) found that among veterans entering the workforce who had a master's degree, 53 percent found a job within three months while the same could be said of just 36 percent of those who had only a high school/GED diploma. Regarding retention, veterans with bachelor's degrees are more likely than those without degrees to stay in their first post-transition job for ten or more months.[24]

The numbers speak for themselves. Assuming you need it, an investment in higher education is an investment in yourself—one that usually pays off in measurable ways over the course of your new career, whether that is in continued service to the government or not.

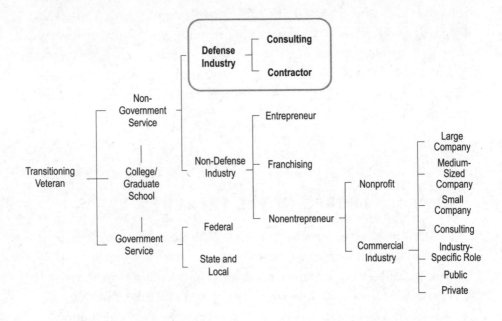

DEFENSE INDUSTRY

If you decide an ongoing career working for the government is not for you, the next decision you'll want to make is whether you desire a career serving the Department of Defense (DoD) in a civilian capacity. Having just served in the military, your experience and skills acquired therein easily translate in that space. The two primary options for serving the Department of Defense in a civilian capacity are as a consultant or a contractor.

DOD CONSULTANT

Consultants work for professional service organizations and provide expert advice to other professionals in the Department of

Defense. Consulting roles can be challenging, but they do have their rewards. You will be busy, likely working longer hours than your government clients. Travel is typically less significant when serving federal (as opposed to commercial) entities, as most of the work tends to be local. We will explore this career path in more detail when we ponder the potential career paths in commercial industry.

CONSULTING CAREER BACKGROUND

For more information on this career, the Bureau of Labor Statistics' Occupational Outlook Handbook provides a thorough overview of this profession.[25] For more on the nature of consulting work and the personal strengths required, see the Resources section of my website at www.matthewjlouis.com.

If becoming a consultant (the federal government calls them management and program analysts) *within* the federal government is of interest, information is available from the Office of Personnel Management (OPM) through USAJOBS (www.usajobs .gov/), the federal government's official employment information system.

Remember, for both consultants (above) and contractors (below), there may exist some post-service restrictions that limit, delay, or forbid your civilian employment.[26] Make sure you do your homework first.

Surveys tell us that up to 18 percent of you may transition into a defense industry role of some sort.[27]

DOD CONTRACTOR

Contractors exist to allow the DoD to effectively outsource its needs. Those needs may be temporary or ongoing. Temporary needs tend to occur during overseas contingency operations. Examples from some of our latest conflicts include base support (such as food service), security details, or translation services.[28] The DoD's needs may also be of an ongoing nature. Contractors include those organizations that produce weapon systems, for example. Defense News produces an annual list of the top DoD contractors, which you can find online.[29] The strengths and skill sets required to be successful in these roles would most closely align with several of the industry competency models maintained by the Department of Labor, which you can find online.[30] We will also explore these competency models in more detail when we ponder the career paths in commercial industry.

★   ★   ★

TROOPS IN THE TRENCHES

"Deciding what I wanted to do was easily the most difficult part about my transition. I had so many options, I didn't know what I wanted to do. I also had no idea what types of jobs I was qualified to do. As a career military officer, I had limited knowledge on corporate and business structure. For example, operations and sales in the business world are completely different in the military. Trying to correlate the two industries and the job types was hard. To do that, I spent a lot of time seeking advice from family, friends, and classmates."

KEVIN BERRY, FORMER ARMY COLONEL

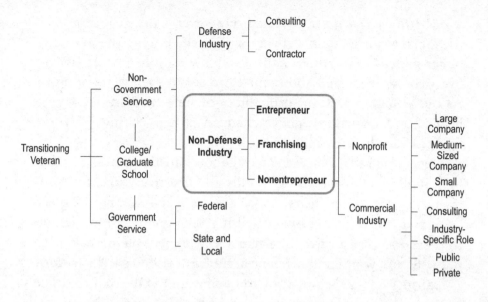

NONDEFENSE INDUSTRY

If you've decided that work in the defense industry is not for you, that opens a whole new world of potential opportunities. Let's consider each in turn. The first decision to consider in nondefense industry occupations is whether you are inclined to entrepreneurial roles, of which I would define two: entrepreneurship and franchising.

ENTREPRENEURSHIP

Entrepreneurship involves starting your own business, being your own boss. For some of you, this may seem like a dream career, given your immediate past spent serving lots of bosses in the military. You've likely seen *Shark Tank* on TV and may believe you have the next best thing in mind to lure that kind of financing and support. You may have heard the story of a veteran buddy who started a business and sold it to a huge conglomerate in short order and made a hefty sum in the process and thought, *How hard can it be? If they can do it, so can I.* However, I urge caution here. Although reported numbers vary widely, the Bureau of Labor Statistics tells us that "about half of all new establishments survive five years or more and about one-third survive ten years or more. As one would expect, the probability of survival increases with a firm's age. Survival rates have changed little over time."[31] These findings vary little by industry.

Think about that. The Bureau of Labor Statistics is telling us that half of all new businesses fail within the first five years, and two-thirds fail within ten years. Those are the facts. Among the questions you will want to ask yourself if you're going to consider entrepreneurship as a career alternative is whether you are willing to put your and your family's financial future at risk in such a venture.

Statistics tell us that many of you will want to take that risk. The US Small Business Administration and the US Census Bureau tell us that veterans own about 10 percent of US firms, and only 20 percent of these firms have paid employees.[32] Said differently, 80 percent of all US-based, veteran-owned businesses had zero paid employees. So there is an 80 percent chance you won't be drawing a salary. Let that sink in for a moment. As John Adams said, "Facts are stubborn things."[33]

If you're still undeterred, let's discuss the nature of entrepreneurship. It certainly has its benefits. Most lists of the benefits of entrepreneurship include:

- *Control*: You're in charge. You get to do what you want, what you love. It is a direct outlet for your strengths and passions. With that comes gratification.
- *Learning and growth*: Few days will be the same as an entrepreneur, and since you are likely to be among the very few employees in the enterprise, you will be forced to take on much of the responsibilities for running it. Typically, that comes with an incredible amount of lessons learned and great satisfaction.
- *Flexibility*: As the boss, you get to decide how long to work and when to take a vacation. You get to decide how

much to work and when to bring on additional employees. Much freedom and independence come with that.

- *Financial*: For starters, there are many tax deductions available to business owners that are not available to individuals. Add to that the fact that you get to decide how much to pay yourself. Finally, consider the possibility that, after much time, effort, and commitment, there is an outside chance of outsized financial rewards. With that comes security, personal fulfillment, and the ability to give back to others or charitable causes of your choice.

Keep in mind, starting and running a business takes a ton of work. Plan on spending sixty to eighty hours a week or more getting your idea up and running. To improve your chances of success, I urge you to thoroughly educate yourself on what it takes to plan, start, and grow a business. Here are some resources to help:

- Bunker Labs is a national nonprofit organization built by military veteran entrepreneurs to empower other military veteran entrepreneurs. They have local chapters in several cities and provide educational programming, mentoring, and networking to help military veterans start and grow businesses.
- The Kauffman Foundation is also a great resource for budding entrepreneurs.
- Visit the Small Business Administration website for guidance on how to start and grow your business.
- The Service Corps of Retired Executives (SCORE) offers free business education and mentorship. Visit their website.
- Visit my website (www.matthewjlouis.com) for links to the Department of Labor's Small Business Development Centers[34] and other specialized services for veteran entrepreneurs. These services include the following:
    - ▸ The SBA offers fifteen organizations that serve as Veterans Business Outreach Centers.[35] These sites

provide entrepreneurial development services such as business training, counseling and mentoring, and referrals for eligible veterans owning or considering starting a small business.

▶ The Department of Veterans Affairs also sponsors resources for veterans who want to start or develop their own businesses. Their Veteran Entrepreneur Portal makes it easier for small businesses to access federal services and quickly connects veteran entrepreneurs to relevant best practices and information on topics such as accessing financing, business growth strategies, federal government contract opportunities for businesses, and more.[36]

▶ Women veterans with a business interest will find resources at Veteran Women Igniting the Spirit of Entrepreneurship (VWISE), which provides training, networking, and mentoring to women veterans to help them become successful entrepreneurs.[37]

▶ The SBA enables set-asides for government contracting programs if you certify under one of SBA's contracting assistance programs (women-owned small business, service-disabled veteran-owned small business, etc.).[38]

Many programs and additional support also exist at the state level, so please research your state's small business website as well. Many of those have specific programs targeted at veterans.

FRANCHISING

Closely related to entrepreneurship is franchising. The difference here is that, rather than founding your entire business on your own idea, you are buying into the business concept that someone else germinated. According to the International Franchise Association,

"A franchise is the agreement or license between two legally independent parties which gives a person or group of people (franchisee) the right to market a product or service using the trademark or trade name of another business (franchisor)."[39] In a practical sense, franchising is a way to reduce your risk in going into business for yourself. As the International Franchise Association puts it, franchising is "how to be in business for yourself, not by yourself."

Think about owning a McDonald's restaurant or a Sport Clips haircut shop or a Planet Fitness gym facility. These are all franchises, and there are many more like them. Here's how they work: (1) You find a franchisor with whom you'd like to do business, (2) you agree to pay them a onetime franchise fee to establish your business, (3) and you also sign a franchisee agreement, a contract that specifies the geographic territory in which you may operate as well as the terms of business (licensing details, operating methods, branding guidelines, etc.) to which you and the franchisor will commit. The franchisor will help your business get up and running, will provide ongoing assistance, and will ensure your business stays in compliance with the terms of the agreement. In exchange, you pay the franchisor ongoing royalties for the use of their trade name and operating methods. You run the day-to-day business, hire and train employees, and benefit or risk loss based on the performance of your business.

Owning and operating a franchise does have its advantages. For starters, you are typically buying into an established brand and customer base, which normally take years to establish. Because the franchisor is typically providing you proven products and methods, there is a certain level of quality and consistency enabled by the franchising agreement. At a tactical level, the franchisor will normally help with preopening support (things like site selection, design, construction, financing, training, and a grand opening) and typically provides some amount of ongoing support (training, national and regional advertising, operational assistance, ongoing supervision and management support, and increased spending power via access to bulk purchasing). The franchisee (you) realizes a level of independence in running the business.

Relative to entrepreneurship, this all adds up to a reduced level of personal risk and increased chances of business success.

On the other hand, you as a franchisee are not completely independent. You are bound by the terms in the franchise agreement, which usually dictate which products or services can be offered, their pricing, and the geographic territory in which you can offer them. Also, by the nature of the franchise, you are indirectly linked to any number of other franchisees around the country or around the globe. If some of them behave badly and bring down the franchise, your business may go down with them. And then there are the fees. In addition to the initial franchise fee, franchisees must also pay ongoing royalties and advertising fees. Finally, the terms of the franchise agreement may limit your exit scenario options.

As with entrepreneurship, I urge you to thoroughly educate yourself about franchising and franchisors before diving into this career alternative. The International Franchise Association offers a free download of their introduction to franchising article.[40] The Small Business Administration offers an introductory course to franchising as well.[41] Some franchisors are viewed to be better business partners than others. *Forbes* publishes an annual list of the best and worst franchises to own.[42] Also, the Federal Trade Commission has a number of resources to help you spot potential business opportunities and investment scams.[43] Finally, the Veterans Transition Franchise Initiative (VetFran) was developed to help the transition to civilian life. To date, more than six hundred franchise companies have participated in the program. On the VetFran website, you'll find their company profiles as well as the financial incentives they offer to veterans.[44]

If you choose to pursue this career alternative, your military training should serve you well. The International Franchise Association has produced a helpful list of keys to franchising success that will resonate with you.[45] On a final note, please realize franchise rules vary from state to state. So, once again, do your research. As the Small Business Administration reminds us, "You could lose a significant amount of money if you do not investigate a business carefully before you buy. By law, franchise sellers must disclose certain information about their business to potential buyers. Make sure you get all the information you need first before entering into this form of business."[46] In other words, buyer beware.

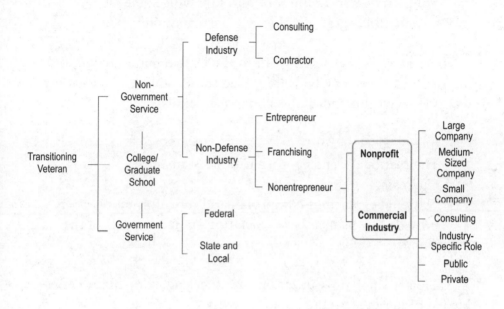

NONENTREPRENEUR

If you've decided any form of entrepreneurship is not for you, have no fear, there are plenty more career options to ponder. Of the nonentrepreneurial options, I'll focus on the nonprofit space and for-profit industry roles in variously sized organizations.

NONPROFIT

Nonprofit organizations exist to benefit communities, not make profits for their owners or shareholders. The Johns Hopkins University Center for Civil Society Studies defines nonprofit organizations as:

- Organizations—institutionalized to some extent
- Private—institutionally separate from government
- Nonprofit-distributing—not returning profits generated to their owners or directors
- Self-governing—able to control their own activities
- Voluntary—noncompulsory and involving some meaningful degree of voluntary participation[47]

To learn more about this work in the United States, the following organizations may be helpful (see the Resources page on my website—www.matthewjlouis.com—for details):

- Independent Sector
- The National Center for Charitable Statistics
- Guidestar
- National Council of Nonprofits and the information provided by its member associations in many parts of the country

There are similar organizations in other countries, but no reliable list of national umbrella bodies exists.

Included within this career path option is the opportunity to become a teacher. Surveys show that 3 percent of you will choose this path. Those that do might consider the Troops to Teachers program if you want to make a difference in young people's lives, use your experience to bring subjects to life, help students realize their potential, and positively impact your local community. The background on the program is found on the program's website: "Troops to Teachers was established in 1993 to assist transitioning service members and veterans in beginning new careers as K–12 school teachers in public, charter, and Bureau of Indian Affairs schools. The program provides counseling and referral services for participants to help them meet education and licensing requirements to teach and subsequently helps them secure a teaching position. Since 1993, more than 20,000 veterans have successfully transitioned to a career in education."[48] The website speaks to the teacher certification process, financial assistance, career assistance resources, and teaching opportunities in every state in the nation.

A final option in the nonprofit arena involves volunteering to work through AmeriCorps. AmeriCorps is a service organization where people of all ages help solve complex challenges within their communities while gaining job skills in a new career field, expanding social networks, and gaining a deeper connection to the community. Members receive a flexible education award that complements your GI Bill benefits. Full-time members receive a modest living allowance, healthcare benefits, and childcare assistance. Nationwide, there are nearly four hundred Employers of National Service that prioritize hiring AmeriCorps alumni. Some members may also be eligible for hiring into federal government roles.

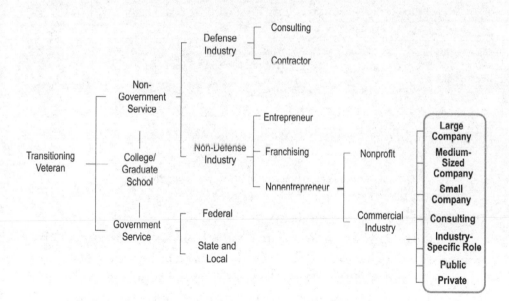

COMMERCIAL INDUSTRY

Commercial industry is the career option where most (54 percent, according to surveys[49]) transitioning veterans will eventually find themselves. But herein lie several options. Roles in commercial industry will vary by, among other things, industry sector, size of organization, type of work (consulting versus direct industry work), and type of organization (public or private).

Table 2-1 portrays these typical commercial industry career path options.

Industry Sector (per 2017 NAICS codes)	Large Companies				Medium-Sized Companies				Small Companies	
	Industry Work		Consulting		Industry Work		Consulting		Industry Work	
	Public	Private	Public	Private	Public	Private	Public	Private	Public	Private
Agriculture, Forestry, Fishing, and Hunting										
Mining, Quarrying, and Oil and Gas Extraction										
Utilities										
Construction										
Wholesale Trade										
Information										
Finance and Insurance										
Real Estate and Rental and Leasing										
Professional, Scientific, and Technical Services										
Management of Companies and Enterprises										
Administrative and Support and Waste Management and Remediation Services										
Educational Services										
Healthcare and Social Assistance										
Arts, Entertainment, and Recreation										
Accommodation and Food Services										
Other Services (except Public Administration)										
Public Administration										

Table 2-1. Typical commercial industry career path options.[50]

Let's review the components of Table 2-1.

First, the industry sectors listed come from the North American Industry Classification System (NAICS), which the Office of Management and Budget (OMB) developed as the standard for use in describing the US economy. NAICS groups organizations into industries according to similarities in the processes they use to produce goods or services. The table reflects the highest level of industry sector groupings.[51]

★ ★ ★

TROOPS IN THE TRENCHES

"My advice would be to educate yourself about various careers in the civilian sector. Be an avid reader of business books. Reach out to vets who are in those fields and get their input. Don't go into a field for the money. Understand your strengths, career, and personal goals to help select your field."

FORMER ARMY CAPTAIN

The Department of Labor has produced competency models that define the skills and competencies needed to be successful in many of these industries.[52] These models provide a common framework that:

- Identifies specific employer skill needs
- Develops competency-based curricula and training models
- Develops industry-defined performance indicators, skill standards, and certifications
- Develops resources for career exploration and guidance

These models can be exceptionally helpful in identifying the knowledge, skills, and abilities you gained during your time in the military and how they translate into the civilian world. They can also help identify the additional knowledge, skills, or abilities you will need to acquire to be successful in a specific industry or sector.

See Figure 2-2 for the *generic* building blocks competency model. Please visit the website for competency models for *specific* industries. The models for specific industries will have blocks populated in accordance with the needs of that industry or sector. Each competency model also comes with gap analysis worksheets to identify specific knowledge, skill, or ability gaps you may have (see the "Download the industry model and worksheets in several formats" link in each industry competency model section).

MANAGEMENT COMPETENCIES	OCCUPATION-SPECIFIC REQUIREMENTS
Staffing Informing Delegating Networking Monitoring Work Entrepreneurship Supporting Others Motivating and Inspiring Developing and Mentoring Strategic Planning/Action Preparing and Evaluating Budgets Clarifying Roles and Objectives Managing Conflict and Team Building Developing an Organizational Vision Monitoring and Controlling Resources	

TIER 5 — INDUSTRY-SECTOR TECHNICAL COMPETENCIES

Competencies to be specified by industry representatives

TIER 4 — INDUSTRY-WIDE TECHNICAL COMPETENCIES

Competencies to be specified by industry sector representatives

TIER 3 — WORKPLACE COMPETENCIES

Teamwork	Customer Focus	Planning & Organizing	Creative Thinking	Problem Solving & Decision Making
Working w/ Tools & Technology	Scheduling & Coordinating	Checking, Examining & Recording	Business Fundamentals	Sustainable Practices	Health & Safety

TIER 2 — ACADEMIC COMPETENCIES

Reading	Writing	Mathematics	Science & Technology	Communication	Critical & Analytical Thinking	Basic Computer Skills

TIER 1 — PERSONAL EFFECTIVENESS COMPETENCIES

Interpersonal Skills	Integrity	Professionalism	Initiative	Dependability & Reliability	Adaptability & Flexibility	Lifelong Learning

Figure 2-2. Generic building blocks competency model.[53]

Second, industry career paths can be segmented by employer size, which may be one of your career search criteria. Companies are segmented by the relative size of their market capitalization (cap), which is simply the number of their outstanding shares multiplied by the share price. There tend to be three size groupings:

1. Larger companies are known as large-cap companies. These are companies with market capitalization greater than $5 billion.[54] That is what it takes to get onto the S&P 500, the most widely followed large-cap index in the world.[55] There are roughly seven hundred of these companies in the United States. These companies tend to be household names and are the kinds of companies you hear mentioned on most business news reports. *Importantly, these companies are sufficiently large to afford the veteran support infrastructure (training, veteran communities, support groups, etc.) you may desire in transitioning from active duty.* Mid-cap and small-cap companies, while they are economically incentivized to hire veterans, may not have the internal infrastructure to support veteran transitions in the same manner as some large-cap companies.

2. Medium-sized companies are known as mid-cap companies. These companies tend to have market capitalizations between $1 billion and $5 billion. And although the middle market represents just 3 percent of all US companies, midsize companies account for about one-third of all private-sector jobs and one-third of the private-sector gross domestic product.[56]

3. Small companies are known as small-cap companies. In the United States, you must meet the defined requirements of the Small Business Administration to be officially considered a small business. Why? The federal government offers all sorts of programs to help small businesses because they are responsible for 42 percent of new job growth.[57] This definition varies by industry and by either the number of employees or the amount of annual

revenue.[58] Small businesses tend to have market capitalization of less than $1 billion.

Third, industry career paths include roles in both consulting and those doing industry work. The above Department of Labor industry competency models identify the required skill sets for industry work. As for consulting roles, the Bureau of Labor Statistics Occupational Outlook Handbook provides a thorough overview of what those roles entail.[59] Consultants work on a contractual basis to help senior client leaders improve their organization's efficiency or make them more profitable through reduced costs and/or increased revenues. The Occupational Outlook Handbook highlights the skills critical for success in this profession:

- Analytical skills
- Communication skills
- Interpersonal skills
- Problem-solving skills
- Time-management skills

To those I would add leadership skills, business development skills, and networking skills. Building and maintaining relationships—both inside and outside your organization—will be critical to your success (there's much more on this in chapters 5 and 6).

The profession certainly has its upsides and downsides. Compensation, breadth of work opportunities, and the ability to directly impact organizational outcomes are usually noted as the benefits of being a consultant. Travel, stress, and long hours, however, tend to be among the complaints from these professionals.

To enter the consulting profession in commercial industry (as opposed to the above-noted DoD consulting option), you may need to pick up some additional skills coming out of the military. If you lack a bachelor's degree, this will entail earning one to attain an entry-level role. If you lack a graduate degree (e.g., an MBA), this may entail earning one to attain a mid-level role. While a certification is available (the Institute of Management Consultants offers the Certified Management Consultant designation),[60] it is no substitute for additional formal education.

Lastly, industry career paths exist at both public and private companies. Note some of their differences:

	PUBLIC COMPANIES	PRIVATE COMPANIES
Ownership	Owned by shareholders in the form of shares of stock that are listed on a public exchange	Owned by their founders or a group of private investors or managers
Reporting Requirement	Usually required to file quarterly earnings reports with the Securities and Exchange Commission (SEC), which are available to shareholders and the public	No requirement since they do not trade on a stock exchange

These differences can have a huge impact on the culture and management behaviors within an organization. Public companies are, in effect, beholden to the quarterly earnings projections they make to shareholders.

This tends to drive a certain short-term mind-set potentially at the cost of longer-term goals. Private companies, although they may not take advantage of it, at least have the relative luxury of not being beholden to these short-term requirements, and thus can focus more on longer-term goals.

There are pros and cons to each ownership model that impact the skills required to succeed in each. Public companies can use financial markets to raise capital (i.e., cash) for business needs by selling stock (equity) or bonds (debt).

Management of private companies, on the other hand, doesn't have to answer to shareholders and isn't required to file with the

SEC. However, a private company must rely on private funding, which can increase the cost of capital and limit growth. At the entry- and middle-management levels, the skills needed to succeed vary little between similarly sized public and private companies in identical industry sectors. Variability in required skill sets does enter the picture at senior-management levels, however, when the expectations of the differing ownership models comes into play. Senior managers must make decisions regarding the financing of and capital allocation within their organizations, and they are held accountable for the organization's performance based on those decisions. So skill sets needed to assess business opportunities and make corresponding decisions become critical.

Whereas the largest public companies are in the S&P 500, *Forbes* magazine annually ranks the largest private companies.[61] A recent list includes 223 companies that have combined revenues of $1.62 trillion and employ over 4.5 million people. *As it relates to your transition from the military, these large private companies have the same advantages as their public peers in perhaps being better able to afford the infrastructure needed to support your transition efforts.*

★ ★ ★

TROOPS IN THE TRENCHES

"Transitioning from the military is the curse of the blessing. You can do anything, which is a blessing; but you need to figure out what 'anything' is first, which is the curse. Learn to follow your passion and your heart. Learn to trust your gut."

JON SANCHEZ, FORMER NAVY SEAL

By now, you should suspect that one of a couple of career paths might be the right one for you. Research those options that appeal most to you. Focus on your life mission. Leave salary and other nice-to-have criteria to the side for now. What's more important now is alignment with your optimal career field, your *direction*. If you're still struggling between a few options, that's okay. The next steps in the process will add clarity and help you to narrow your focus.

PRIORITIZATION MATRIX

If you're still struggling with prioritizing a career path, try this alternative way to narrow your focus:

- Make a list of criteria, ranking the criteria from 1 to 5 (1-less important, 5-most important).
- List your options and score them using the following scale (1-not a good fit, 3-good fit, 9-best fit) with input from your family.
- Multiply the criteria rankings by the score of each career field option and sum those products. This will produce an emotionless direction for you. In theory, the highest scored option will best match the relative importance of your stated criteria. In Figure 2-3, Career Field B is the clear winner. See www.matthewjlouis.com for a downloadable template.

Sample Criteria	Ranking	Career Field Options			
		Field A	Field B	Field C	Field D
Strengths Match	5	3	9	9	1
Geographic Location	3	3	3	1	3
Industry Match	4	9	9	3	9
Lifestyle Match	2	1	3	9	1
Role Match	5	3	9	1	3
Growth Potential	4	9	9	3	9
Etc.					
	Outcome	113	177	95	103

Figure 2-3. Sample prioritization matrix.

Good work. Your life map is now properly oriented.
Well begun is half done. Now, on to the next step.

KEYS TO SUCCESS

★ Consider all practical career alternatives.

★ Research and prioritize potential career fields based on your
strengths and personality type.

★ A simple prioritization exercise can take the emotion out of
decision-making.

CHAPTER THREE

DEFINE YOUR CAREER PREFERENCES AND PERSONAL BRAND

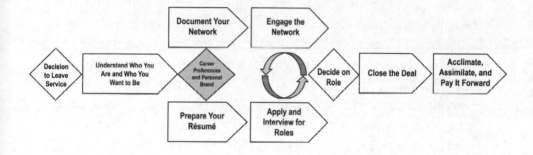

YOU HAVE IDENTIFIED YOUR TRUE NORTH AND SOME POTENTIAL CAREER alternatives. But before we can start drafting a résumé or reaching out to potential employers, we need to identify some preferences and lifestyle factors that will help us to narrow our focus. Anyone who's done a career search can tell you it is better to take a rifle shot at the target rather than a shotgun approach. This chapter will help you set the scope on that rifle and enable you to engage that eventual target.

In this chapter we will discuss:

- Identifying industry, geographic, and role preferences
- Recognizing lifestyle factors that may narrow your focus
- Defining your personal brand

The outcome of this chapter should be the prioritization of your career preferences and identification of your personal brand, both of which will help you narrow your target set and position you to build your personal story for engaging with that eventual target. *Studies have shown your success in identifying your preferred career field and finding a role within it will effectively* **double** *the perceived readiness for transition, the retention rate in, and the longevity of your first post-military role.*[1] *Early identification of your career preference also results in higher salaries, increased ability to build wealth, and greater perceived quality of life.*[2]

As you work to identify your career preference, understand there are several factors that may influence that decision. We have just identified your strengths. That will be a huge determinant of the outcome. But there are several others as well, and these include the role or function you will play within your chosen employer, the industry in which you want to work, the geography in which you want to live, and other lifestyle factors. You should understand that priorities in these areas will also play a part in determining your ultimate career decision—and they will change over time. Your preferences today may not be your preferences five to ten years from now. Finally, understand that decisions made regarding these areas are interdependent; a decision made today in one area will impact your future flexibility in other areas.

★

ROLE PREFERENCES

As you ponder the career path that most appeals to you, consideration of the kind of role you would play may help you identify potential targets. What do we mean by role? For starters, let's define it as a position in one or more corporate functions. And what do we mean by a corporate function? Corporate functions are generally composed of core business processes and support business processes. What follows is a handy reference that will give you a flavor for the kinds of activities performed in each. See if you can find a match with any of your strengths.

★   ★   ★

TROOPS IN THE TRENCHES

"If I had it to do over again, I would take a different approach—one focused on opening the aperture of potential career choices, taking advantage of learning opportunities, having fun, and reducing stress. I would leverage my military and college alumni networks to schedule exploration meetings with industry leaders in any field that might interest me (i.e., car enthusiast? Find someone you know who knows someone working at BMW). Rid yourself of pretense and expectation by arranging a visit to ask questions, learn, and seek advice . . . with no expectation for a job offer. Chances are, if you are prepared and an engaging, interested fan of the business, you'll learn something new (at worst), confirm or deny your career interest in that field (good), and/or be referred to a potential opening or employer (at best). This is the best way to convert your transition from a fishing trip into a hunting trip—where you have more control of your prospects and higher odds of finding the right job."

GRANT HESLIN, FORMER ARMY CAPTAIN

★

CORE BUSINESS PROCESSES

Strategic Management: Those activities carried out at the highest managerial levels. Included are the formation, implementation, and evaluation of cross-functional decisions that enable an organization to achieve its long-term objectives. Among such operations are the following:

- Setting product strategy
- Identifying new investments, acquisitions, and divestments

Procurement, Logistics, and Distribution: Those activities associated with obtaining and storing inputs and with storing and transporting finished products to customers:

- Buying, loading, packing, shipping
- Receiving, transporting, warehousing

Operations: Those activities that transform inputs into final outputs, either goods or services. In most cases, business functions categorized as operations will equate with the industry code of the establishment or the activity most directly associated with that code. Operations activities include:

- Producing goods, providing services
- Managing production or services
- Controlling quality

Product or Service Development: Activities associated with bringing a new, improved, or redesigned product or service to market:

- Analyzing markets
- Researching, designing, developing, and testing products or services

Marketing, Sales, and Customer Accounts: Activities aimed at informing existing or potential buyers:

- Advertising, marketing, branding, or managing products
- Managing accounts, selling
- Processing orders, billing, collecting payments

Customer and Aftersales Service: Activities, including training, help desks, call centers, and customer support for guarantees and warranties, that provide support services to customers after purchasing a good or service:

- Providing customer relations, service, or support
- Installing, maintaining, or repairing products
- Providing technical or warranty support

★

SUPPORT BUSINESS PROCESSES

General Management and Firm Infrastructure: Corporate governance, accounting, building services, management, and administrative support activities:

- Providing general management, administrative support, legal and regulatory support, investor relations, facility or maintenance services, security services
- Managing contracts, finances, fraud, or government relations

Human Resources Management: Activities associated with recruiting, hiring, training, compensating, and dismissing personnel:

- Managing human resources, labor relations, payroll and compensation
- Recruiting, training, hiring and firing personnel

Technology and Process Development: Activities related to maintenance, automation, design or redesign of equipment, hardware, software, procedures, and technical knowledge:

- Developing, engineering, and maintaining computer systems
- Managing data, designing processes

- Developing, testing, and managing software and information technology services[3]

If, after reading these options, you find you are struggling with narrowing your choices to more than a few, consider a few points:

- Some larger organizations, recognizing your lack of experience in these corporate functions, have designed internships or rotational programs that expose you to several functions over the course of the program. This allows you to experience these functions firsthand and decide about your proper fit. Rotational programs tend to be geared toward junior military officers (JMOs) or noncommissioned officers (NCOs) with at least a bachelor's degree.
- Consider an apprenticeship.[4] An apprenticeship combines on-the-job training and specialized classes to help workers enter highly skilled occupations. Workers may earn a salary while gaining valuable skills.
- Consider short-term training. Having a certificate, license, or certification in your career field can help you qualify for a job, get a promotion, or earn more money.[5]
- Consider formal transition programs such as BreakLine or Deloitte's CORE Leadership Program.[6]
- Your role will likely evolve over time. As you are successful in one role, most organizations will attempt to utilize your strengths in other areas as well. This provides you with greater knowledge and breadth of experience as your career progresses.
- Don't expect to begin your career in general management (yes, even retirees). Experience in multiple roles over the course of many years is a basic requirement for entering general management. This may well be your career destination; just don't expect to start here.

★

INDUSTRY PREFERENCES

Another helpful way in which you might narrow your career path is to consider the industry in which you might prefer to work. For our purposes, I'll refer to the North American Industry Classification System (NAICS), the standard used by federal statistical agencies in classifying businesses for the purpose of collecting, analyzing, and publishing statistical data related to the business economy.[7]

At its highest level, NAICS groups the economy into the following groups:

- Agriculture, forestry, fishing, and hunting
- Mining, quarrying, and oil and gas extraction
- Utilities
- Construction
- Wholesale trade
- Information
- Finance and insurance
- Real estate and rental and leasing
- Professional, scientific, and technical services
- Management of companies and enterprises
- Administrative and support and waste management and remediation services
- Educational services
- Healthcare and social assistance
- Arts, entertainment, and recreation
- Accommodation and food services
- Other services (except public administration)
- Public administration

A visit to the NAICS website, however, will identify more than two thousand industry segments within the above groups.[8] Download the most recent NAICS to begin your search. As in our review of potential roles, try to identify a potential match with your personal strengths.

Although the industry groupings don't align perfectly, the Bureau of Labor Statistics tells us that veterans find employment in private industry in the ratios portrayed in Figure 3-1:

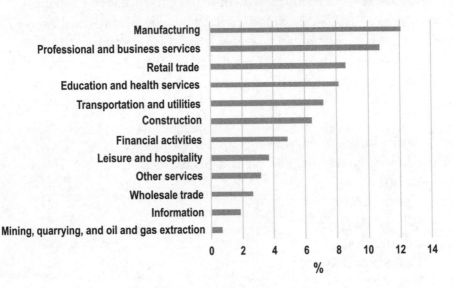

Figure 3-1. Veteran employment by industry.[9]

★

GEOGRAPHIC PREFERENCES

Another way in which we can narrow our career path focus is by considering our geographic preferences—those areas of the world in which we prefer to live. This factor is often weighed together with industry preferences. Industries often tend to be clustered in certain geographic locations. The headquarters of most oil and gas organizations, for example, are in Houston. Most technology companies would call Silicon Valley in California home. The headquarters of many banking organizations tend to be clustered in a few cities around the country: New York, Chicago, Charlotte.

These facts don't necessarily mean you have to move, but your willingness to do so may be an advantage in a competitive field of candidates.

A related geographic consideration is the differing cost of living in various communities. As we will review in chapter 9, you should be entering your transition with some idea of your annual budget needs. With that in mind, apply one of many available cost-of-living-comparison tools to your situation. Consider the table below, which highlights one aspect (housing) of various costs of living (100 = US average, less is cheaper than average):[10]

	HOUSTON, TEXAS	LOS ANGELES, CALIFORNIA	DIFFERENCE
Cost to own a home	94.0	358.4	LA is 281.3 percent more

Isn't that good to know? It is precisely these sorts of facts that you want to uncover before pulling the trigger on any specific location.

Another geographic-related consideration is your relationship status. If you are single and unattached, you may find that your geographic options are limitless, and this consideration does not narrow your choices at all. On the other hand, if you are married and/or have children, this may be a significant consideration. A typical scenario might include consideration of you or your spouse's extended family locations, especially if children are involved and there is a desire for a support network.

Keep in mind, the civilian communities into which you're moving will be very different from the military communities you have experienced. Chances are, your neighbors will have little idea what you've been through and what expectations you have in communing together—i.e., helping watch kids, helping with chores, helping when spouses are out of town, etc. Remember, your neighbors are part of the 99.5 percent. They haven't been through what you have. For the most part, they are used to keeping to themselves and expect you to do the same. This may well factor into your decision on where to locate professionally. If you choose a location without a built-in support network, do so with the knowledge that the experience you will have with your new neighbors, schools, and communities in general will be different than the experience you had in the military. The expectation will be that you will adjust to their norms and not vice versa.

Where most veterans live may also interest you. A recent survey found that most veterans live in the populous states of California, Texas, Florida, Pennsylvania, and New York. "Older veterans tend to concentrate in large cities and concentrated retirement areas such as Southern California, Arizona, Texas, and Florida. Working-age veterans are more dispersed, with clusters around major military bases, as well as major urban areas and job centers."[11] The VA's National Center for Veterans Analysis and Statistics provides demographic data on the population of veterans across all states and territories.[12]

For additional help, you might consider any of the many studies that list the largest employers in each of the fifty states (a simple online search will turn up several). I recommend you combine any of these studies with a reliable "best for vets" employer study. One example is the annual list comprised by the *Military Times*.[13] In reviewing their list, I urge you to pay attention to the ratings of the respective companies for their onboarding training, their willingness to accept military experience in lieu of a certification for some roles, their company training about the military, and their military spouse policies. It's also important to note their survey methodology includes consideration of the employer's support of the National Guard and Reserve as well as their willingness to make up any pay differentials if an employee is deployed.[14] Please see my website (www.matthewjlouis.com) for additional guidance.

A final note on geographic location: Don't be discouraged if the headquarters location of your preferred employer is in a location you do not prefer. Assuming it is a large corporation, they will likely have offices in other parts of the country, some of which may be more suitable for your preferences. You may be able to find this information on their website or by engaging with your network (more on that in chapter 6). Consider also that some roles such as sales or consulting may require travel on a regular basis. This will enable you to see many parts of the world, easily providing variety in work location. Finally, consider that many organizations are allowing their professionals to operate virtually. While this may not seem like a desirable option, especially if you desire a close-knit team environment like your military experience, it is nonetheless an increasingly available option.

★   ★   ★

TROOPS IN THE TRENCHES

"Follow your instincts, but do your research. Don't blindly follow the masses to the next hiring event. I saw too many peers take the first good offer they received (industry or career-path be damned) and end up jumping ship to an entire new industry, field, or job type in less than two years and sometimes again and again and again. In most cases, they did it for the money (which helps), but they were miserable."

FORMER ARMY CAPTAIN

★

LIFESTYLE PREFERENCES

A final set of factors to consider are lifestyle factors. Some of you may find these factors to be your most important criteria, and as a result, these will help you to narrow your career choices. There are surely many others beyond the following short list you might consider. The good news is that many online resources have proliferated in recent years that will help you to research these. However, I argue that the best way to confirm your research is to engage with your network (more on that in chapter 6). To give you a sense of how to approach them, let's consider each in turn:

- *Job Security*: In transitioning from the military, you would like to have some degree of confidence that the job you are taking won't evaporate within a short period of time. Some will tell you your job security is in your own hands, meaning an organization would not lay off a highly productive, valuable employee. But that is only partly true. While I certainly encourage you to give your best efforts to your new employer to become an invaluable employee, the ways and waves of today's global economy—and your eventual employer's reactions to them—are hardly under your control. You should do some homework to understand how your prospective employers have approached these economic waves in the past. And you should go deeper in your research than simply referring to *Fortune*'s annual "100 Best Companies to Work For" list (although that is a good indicator, because the ratings come from the employees). Some online resources to check out include:
    - ► Glassdoor.com
    - ► Indeed.com
    - ► Vault.com
- *Flexible Work Arrangements*: If you have children or other familial commitments, you may find the option to work from home or have a flexible hours schedule to be appealing. Not all companies allow for this. *Fortune*'s annual list speaks to this, as does *Working Mother* magazine in its annual "100 Best Companies" list.[15] Your personal network can also act as a confirmatory source of firsthand information on this topic.

★   ★   ★

TROOPS IN THE TRENCHES

"I had a lot of anxiety about the amount of responsibility I placed on my family in getting out. They were used to security, and transition creates uncertainty. They were used to a steady paycheck, and now there wasn't one. We weren't sure where to live or where the kids were going to go to school. In fact, I doubled my family's pain by moving twice within just a couple of years. The bottom line is that you need to do your due diligence on where you want to plant roots for this next phase of your life, and make sure your family is part of that discussion. Do you want to live close to your extended family? What region of the country do you like? Knowing these things up front can help you address some of this uncertainty and help relieve some of the stress the family feels. Knowledge is power."

BRIAN HANKINSON, FORMER ARMY LIEUTENANT COLONEL

- *Competitive Compensation and Benefits*: As you transition from the military, you must understand this topic is treated very differently than how you're used to treating it. In the military, pay tables and many benefits are public and common knowledge. This is not the case in the civilian world. Details around this topic are largely kept private. What one person earns and the benefits he/she has is no one else's business. So don't expect a lot of transparency in this area. Moreover, you should understand you will need to make decisions on a larger number of benefits than you were typically afforded in the military. Some benefits are mandatory, as specified by either federal or state law:
    - ► COBRA (Consolidated Omnibus Budget Reconciliation Act)
    - ► Disability

▶ Family and Medical Leave Act
▶ Minimum wage
▶ Overtime
▶ Social Security disability insurance
▶ Unemployment benefits
▶ Workers' compensation

Beyond the mandatory benefits, many employers offer some combination of a range of additional benefits to attract and retain talent (see chapter 9 for details). This list can be voluminous and would include such things as health insurance, dental insurance, vision care, life insurance, paid vacation leave, personal leave, sick leave, child care, fitness subsidies, tuition assistance, a retirement plan, leaves of absence for military and other matters, and other optional benefits such as long-term care policies or legal plan coverage. This is far from a complete list, and all of these are treated differently by each employer, so you will want to compare benefits packages from each.

Laws regarding benefits and trends within those that are offered change over time, and since the nonmandatory benefit packages are not public knowledge, you'll need to do some homework in this area. For starters, the organization's website will typically mention what benefits they offer. Another way to research this topic is to review the same online resources highlighted in the "Job Security" paragraph above: Glassdoor.com, Indeed.com, and Vault.com. The final way in which you can secure specific information is at the appropriate time in your interviews with a prospective employer (more on this in chapter 8). You should be prepared with a list of unresolved questions to thoroughly understand what is being offered and be able to accurately compare one employer's benefits package to another's. TheBalance.com provides a sample list of questions.[16]

- *Business Travel Requirements*: The nature of the role to which you are applying will largely dictate the amount of time you will need to travel in your career. Roles in sales and consulting typically come with hefty amounts of travel, with many requiring well above 50 percent of your time. If you really enjoy travel, the tourism or travel industries will enable frequent travel. For some roles, the amount of time you spend on the road is a negotiable item you can discuss with your prospective manager. To get a sense of what expectations might be at a given employer or for a specific type of role, I direct you to Glassdoor.com, Indeed.com, and Vault.com. Again, all information should be confirmed by engaging with your personal network.

  One final note on business travel requirements: What might work for you may not work for your spouse. I urge you to make decisions on this and all other criteria after discussion with your partner. If I've learned nothing over the course of my career, it is that spouses weigh these items differently than you do, and they want to weigh in on them. As your family grows, you will want to be proactive about this to ensure alignment with your family's priorities and head off any potential disagreements.

- *Opportunities for Professional Growth*: No one wants to hire into a dead-end job and face yet another job search because no opportunity to advance existed in the organization. Ideally, the organizations you are considering offer additional training in your career field, which supports upward mobility, as well as the opportunity to move into other areas of the organization, which provides diversity of career paths and potential for future growth. Leverage your network and do your research using the same websites as above to better understand the nature of your target.

By now, you should have identified several preferences that should have helped narrow the number of potential employers. We are almost ready to begin the process of composing a résumé for use in initiating a discussion with these targets. To do so, however, you must first define your personal brand, which will help you guide the creation of its content.

FOCUS ON YOUR LONG-TERM SUCCESS

A common pitfall of many transitioning veterans is to jump at the first opportunity you see without considering and weighing all the criteria discussed in this chapter. While finding a *job* is important in meeting your *short-term* financial obligations, finding a *career* that enables *long-term* success should be your goal and is the aim of this book. Critical to this task is identifying what is important to you and matching available jobs to those criteria.

★   ★   ★

TROOPS IN THE TRENCHES

"Don't settle for the first shiny thing you find. Go for what you want."

DOMINIC LANZILLOTTA, FORMER ARMY CAPTAIN

★

PERSONAL BRAND

Your personal brand has two dimensions. The outside-in dimension of your personal brand is that for which you are known. It is how the world sees you, and as such, it is what differentiates you from your peers. The inside-out dimension of your personal brand is that unique set of qualities and passions that drive you at work and in life. It is what you talk about when an opportunity presents itself to give your elevator speech to the decision makers you are trying to influence during your transition. You leverage the inside-out dimension to influence the outside-in dimension. Because of your military background, you are viewed a certain way today by the outside world, but you can change this over time and with practice. We will get into the characteristics of an optimal personal brand statement (i.e., elevator speech) shortly. Let's first define in a bit more detail the primary attributes of a personal brand, of which there are three:

1. *Who you are*: This includes your strengths and how you use them every day. This includes the unique values and skills you bring to a prospective employer, and your ability to contribute by leveraging those values and skills.
2. *How you present yourself*: This includes your dress, your behavior, and your body language. These are the key things that drive first impressions and are critically important.
3. *How you communicate*: This includes the words you use, the way in which those words are said, and nonverbal cues in how meaning is interpreted.

Albert Mehrabian, a professor emeritus at UCLA, conducted a study on the way we communicate. He found that the visual aspects of communication (body language, eye contact, gestures) account for 55 percent of the impact a communication opportunity has on an audience. Second in importance are vocal elements (tone of voice, pace, and volume) at 38 percent. Finally, only accounting for 7 percent of a communication's impact, were verbal elements (actual content, choice of phrases).[17] Keep this in mind when relating your personal brand to others.

So let's create your personal brand statement (aka, an elevator speech—something that you could share with a busy professional during a thirty-second elevator ride). This brand statement should include a few basic points:

- Your primary strengths or skills
- Your past or current job description
- A brief description of your future goals
- What makes you unique

An effective personal brand statement has the following characteristics:[18]

- *Concise*: Your statement should be no more than one or two sentences in length and between thirty and sixty seconds in duration. It should be brief and compelling.
- *Clear*: Your statement should use language anyone could understand. Avoid acronyms, jargon, or fancy words.
- *Powerful*: Your statement should use strong verbs (remember your strength statements from the previous chapter) and language that creates a memorable visual image in the mind of the listener.
- *Unique*: Your statement should describe you and only you. Don't use generic terms like rank, military organization, or unit of assignment.
- *Authentic*: Your statement should feel honest and genuine, not rehearsed.
- *Tailored*: Your statement should speak directly to the audience you are engaging. You must know your target audience (military, civilian, recruiter, networking opportunity) and be able to pull from several versions of your statement to directly engage with that audience.

These personal brand statements can also double as an answer to the typical interview question, "Tell me about yourself." Here are some examples to ponder:

- "I am a transitioning naval officer with experience in managing logistics in multiple geographies and complex environments. I'm trying to leverage those strengths in a *Fortune* 100 construction or oil and gas organization in the Midwest. I feel my insatiable desire for continuous improvement would add significant value to any organization."

- "I'm a former army aviator with strengths in managing dozens of personnel in high-risk situations in many parts of the globe. I'm seeking a product development role in an aviation-related business in the eastern United States. My hands-on experience with most active aircraft in the service would enable me to assimilate quickly."

- "I'm a marine in the process of transitioning from the service. Although I worked in supply operations in the service, I have a strong passion for craft brewing. I've brewed a few dozen batches of my own and have even won some medals in a local contest. I'm seeking a role with a craft brewer on the West Coast. My passion for brewing and experience in supply would add a lot of value to a prospective employer."

- "I'm an air force technician with experience in cyber. I'd like to leverage this strength in a professional services organization serving clients with these same challenges. I have no geographic preferences, just a passion for using this skill set for which I was presented multiple awards by my superiors."

I recognize this little exercise is potentially off-putting to you. As a veteran, you've been indoctrinated to work as a team and focus on mission first. Selfless service has been your hallmark since you put on the uniform. Well, this is different. Civilian organizations don't hire teams; they hire individuals. And those individuals—you—need to sell those organizations on their (your) unique qualifications. The only way you do that is to get comfortable talking about yourself. It may seem selfish. It may feel boastful. If may even feel unpatriotic. It will certainly feel unnatural. That's okay. It is something, however, with which you'll need to get comfortable. And this only comes with time, patience, and practice.

Take the time to thoughtfully create your personal brand statement and practice it with a friendly audience. Rehearse it until it becomes natural and you can confidently present yourself to an audience that knows you less well.

By now you should have been able to narrow your career options and potentially some target employers. You should also have your personal brand statement at the ready for that next opportune elevator ride with a busy professional. Our next step is to formalize the document whose translation of your skills and experiences will get you that desired interview with a target employer: your résumé.

KEYS TO SUCCESS

★ Do not jump at the first job opportunity you see. Focus on your long-term career success by identifying what is important to you and matching available jobs to those criteria.

★ Recognize that your career path preferences will change over time.

★ Include your spouse or partner in prioritizing your career preferences.

★ If you can't narrow your focus, you will need to identify a corporate culture that allows for some flexibility in roles over time. Consider corporate rotational programs.

★ Your personal brand is a living thing. It will change over time. Keep it updated.

★ Time. Patience. Practice. It's a new world. It requires your adjustment. But don't expect too much of yourself too soon.

★ ★ ★

CHAPTER FOUR

GET YOUR RÉSUMÉ INTO FIGHTING SHAPE

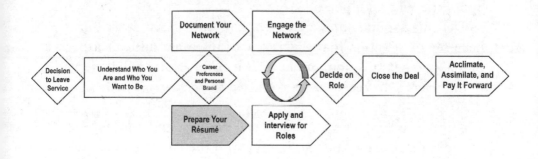

A RÉSUMÉ IS THE BASIS FOR ANY DISCUSSION WITH AN EMPLOYER ABOUT A potential role. It is table stakes. If the prospective employer can't understand it, you are dead in the water. The intent of this chapter is to help you begin to translate your strengths, skills, and experiences into something a civilian hiring manager can understand.

In this chapter, we will discuss:

- The basics of building your résumé
- How to translate your strengths, experiences, and skills into something a prospective employer would understand and appreciate
- The primary goal of for-profit entities and why that should matter to you

The outcome of this chapter should be (a) a résumé that accurately and favorably describes how your experiences and skill sets would best match a civilian or government hiring manager's job opportunity in a language the hiring manager can see as matching a current need of theirs and (b) an accompanying cover letter that effectively introduces your value proposition to a prospective employer.

With your true north identified, your next challenge is to translate your strengths, skills, experiences, and preferences into concepts and language that a civilian hiring manager (one of the 99.5 percent) can both understand and appreciate. Your goal—the whole goal of the résumé—is to secure an interview: a face-to-face discussion with a potential employer about your candidacy and appropriate fit for a possible role.

That may sound simple enough, and on its face, it is. But it's been my observation that this is one of the more difficult aspects of making the transition. But keep at it. Your efforts will be repaid in full. Here's the reason why you need to persevere:

- If the civilian hiring manager can't understand your résumé, there will be no interview. If there is no interview, there will be no job—no career.
- If you are lucky enough to secure an interview, and you revert to military speak during the interview, there will likewise be no job or career.

In a real sense, you must learn a new language, and you'll need to learn to both write and speak in that new language consistently. It took you time to learn to speak in military three-letter acronyms, and it will take time to likewise learn how civilian managers and executives communicate. They have their own set of terms and acronyms.

Given the practical scope and intent of this book, we will focus on a subset of career paths for résumé examples and types. For a broader scope and more voluminous examples, see the additional resources on my website (www.matthewjlouis.com). Table 4-1 presents the practical types of tailored résumé applications. Many variants on this list exist, as any online search will quickly confirm. My advice is to tailor your résumé as much as you possibly can for the specific opportunity you are considering. The practical reality is that most of you reading this book will be applying for civilian or government roles at middle and senior levels. Moreover, while there are several résumé types available (including the curriculum vitae [CV] for medical, education, or legal fields and narratives for government role vacancies), we will keep it simple and focus on the chronological, functional, and combination examples for civilian opportunities and outline examples for government opportunities. For mid-level civilian opportunities, I recommend a narrow focus on the chronological format. (The shaded boxes are addressed herein.)

Employment Type	Résumé Type	Entry-Level Roles	Mid-Level Roles	Senior-Level Roles
Civilian	Chronological			
	Functional			
	Combination			
Government	Outline			

Table 4-1. Practical types of résumé applications.

★   ★   ★

TROOPS IN THE TRENCHES

"The sooner you get your résumé together, the better. Everyone will offer their opinion on its content, and some of that will be conflicting. The key is to just get comfortable with what you have."

DAVE USLAN, FORMER AIR FORCE SENIOR MASTER SERGEANT

Before we get into the specifics of government and civilian résumés, let's review some general guidance that applies to both.

Quantify Your Accomplishments: Use numbers, percentages, or dollars to quantify your accomplishments. You can find this information in things like your performance reviews, previous job descriptions, awards, and letters of recommendation. When explaining your accomplishments:

- Include examples of how you saved money, earned money, or managed money.
- Include examples of how you saved or managed time.

Customize Your Résumé: You should tailor your résumé to the job announcement rather than sending out the same résumé for every job. Customizing your résumé helps you match your competencies, knowledge, skills, abilities, and experience to the requirements for each job. Emphasize your strengths and include everything you've done that relates to the job you're seeking. Leave out experience that isn't relevant. We will discuss the application process in more detail in chapter 7.

Address Every Required Qualification: Your work experience needs to address *every* required qualification in the job announcement. Not addressing every required qualification is a surefire way to have your résumé eliminated from further consideration.

Use Keywords: Keywords are important terms (they could be nouns, abbreviations, or acronyms) or phrases in the job announcement that are critical to what the hiring manager is seeking. They should be used not only in your résumé but also in your cover letter and during your interview. Their use becomes critical in the age of résumé scanning technology, which organizations will use to eliminate those applicants they perceive to be unqualified based purely on the word selection in their résumé.

Organize Your Résumé to Make It Easy to Understand: You need to organize your résumé to help organizations evaluate your experience. If you don't provide the information required to determine your qualifications, you might not be considered for the job.

- Provide greater detail for experience that is relevant to the job for which you are applying.
- Show all experiences and accomplishments under the job in which you earned it. This helps organizations determine the amount of experience you have with that skill.
- Use either a bullet or paragraph format to describe your experiences and accomplishments.
- Make sure your accomplishments emphasize what *you* did—how you personally enabled the accomplishment—not simply what the team did.
- Use plain language. Avoid using acronyms and military terms that are not easily understood. Remember, those hiring you are part of the 99.5 percent of the population that have never served on active duty. See the civilian section below for some translation examples.
- Use active voice. Structure your accomplishments in a format that stipulates the SCAR: the Situation you faced, the Challenge that situation presented, the Action you took to address the challenge, and the quantifiable Result of those actions.

Be Concise: Organizations receive dozens or even hundreds of résumés for certain positions. Hiring managers quickly skim through the submissions and eliminate the candidates who clearly are not qualified. Look at your résumé and ask yourself:

- Can a hiring manager see my main credentials within ten to fifteen seconds?
- Does critical information jump off the page?
- Do I effectively sell myself on the top quarter of the first page?

Review Your Résumé Before You Apply: Check your résumé for spelling and grammatical errors and have someone else, with a good eye for detail, review your résumé.

★

GOVERNMENT RÉSUMÉS

Let's say after reviewing the career fields in chapter 2, you've decided that a role in federal government service is for you. Great! (State and local government roles are certainly an option as well. See my website [www.matthewjlouis.com] if that is of interest. We will focus only on federal roles for our purposes, but many of these guidelines should apply to your situation too.) You've created your personal brand in chapter 3 and now you are ready to pull together that résumé. The first thing to understand about government résumés is that they are significantly different from their civilian counterparts. Please note the major differences in Table 4-2.

GOVERNMENT RÉSUMÉS	CIVILIAN RÉSUMÉS
Specific names of bases, posts, locations	No specific names of posts, locations
Detailed accomplishments noted	Accomplishments can be generalized
Detailed description of technical work	General description of work performed
Military terminology is sparingly used, avoid acronyms	Military terminology is translated
Security clearance is listed	Security clearance is listed
Training is described, including location, number of hours, course titles, and certifications (if applicable)	Training and certifications may or may not be included (career path dependent)
Average length: 3–4 pages	Average length: 2 pages

Table 4-2. Major differences in federal government and civilian résumés.[1]

The good news for those applying for federal government roles is that the résumé requires somewhat less translation than their civilian counterpart. Also, these résumés do not require cover letters (although you may upload one, which I recommend, to distinguish your application) and are only accepted online at www.usajobs.gov. It will still take some work to pull it together, however. You will need to start by pulling together several career documents:

- Your separation papers
- DD-214: Certificate of Release or Discharge from Active Duty
- Current Leave and Earnings Statement (LES)
- Performance appraisals
  - Coast Guard: performance reviews
  - Navy: fitness reports (officers) or performance evaluations (enlisted)
  - Army: evaluation reports (officer or noncommissioned officer)
  - Marine Corps: fitness reports (E-5 and above)
  - Air Force: officer performance evaluation report or enlisted performance appraisal
- DD-2586: Verification of Military Experience and Training (VMET)[2]
- Military Training Record
  - Coast Guard: educational assessment worksheet (CGI 1560/04e)
  - Navy: electronic training record
  - Marine Corps: basic training record (BTR)
  - Army: education and training section of the OMPF
  - Air Force: training business area (TBA) or air force training record (AFTR)
- Training certifications and forms
- Previous résumés or employment forms
- Award citations
- Letters of commendation and letters of appreciation

- Articles or letters concerning military activities
- List of publications
- List of speaking engagements
- Official orders
- Professional organization memberships or conference attendance materials
- College transcripts
- Military transcripts
  - ► Coast Guard: joint services transcript (JST)
  - ► Navy and Marine Corps: sailor and marine transcript (SMART)
  - ► Army: Army/American Council on Education Registry transcript (AARTS)
  - ► Air Force: community college of the air force transcript
- Course descriptions for courses taken relevant to your objective
- Specialized training (include joint or other training that may not be listed elsewhere)[3]

With those documents pulled together, we can start to get to work. There are two ways to produce your résumé: Build it online at www.usajobs.gov (after creating an account and user profile) using their résumé builder app or produce it offline and upload it to www.usajobs.gov. All offline application forms (OF-510 or OF-612) are now obsolete. Visit my website (www.matthewjlouis.com) for guidance on how to use the résumé builder. I recommend using the résumé builder as not all agencies accept uploaded résumés or documents from www.usajobs.com. However, if you persist in an offline approach, I will walk you through how to pull that together. Those using the résumé builder app will still gain from reading the tips in this section.

Although there are several styles, I recommend you produce your federal government résumé in an outline format, which features small paragraphs, keywords, and accomplishments. Features of the outline format include:[4]

- Use ALL CAPS to highlight keywords and important skills for the job
- No formatting, no indentations or centering of text
- No bold, italics, bullets, underlines
- Flush left, ragged right (no justified copy)
- Small paragraphs (four to eight lines max)
- Use ALL CAPS to highlight headers
- Add accomplishments at the end of each job block
- Feature the last ten years of work experience

The table below speaks to sections of the résumé and what you should include in each.

FEDERAL RÉSUMÉ SECTION	WHAT TO INCLUDE
Contact Information	• Name • Address • Phone • Email address
Work Experience	For each work experience, include: • Start and end dates (the month and year) • The number of hours you worked per week • The level and amount of experience (e.g., whether you served as a project manager or a team member) • Examples of relevant experiences and accomplishments that prove you can perform the tasks at the level required for the job as stated in the job announcement Also include any volunteer work and roles in community organizations that demonstrate your ability to do the job.
Education	For colleges from which you have earned a degree: • College name • City, State • Major • Month and year degree was earned

(continues)

Table 4-3. Contents of a federal résumé.

FEDERAL RÉSUMÉ SECTION	WHAT TO INCLUDE
References	For each personal or professional reference: • Name • Job Title • Employer • Phone number • Email address
Job-Related Training	For each course taken: • Name of course • Organization that trained you • Year of course completion
Language Skills	For each language in which you claim fluency (novice, intermediate, or advanced levels): • Level of spoken fluency • Level of reading fluency • Level of writing fluency
Organizations/ Affiliations	For each organization/affiliation: • Organization/affiliation's name • Role within the organization/affiliation
Professional Publications	Name any items you have published that might be relevant to the role for which you are applying. For each, list the title and date of publication.
Additional Information	List any job-related honors, awards, leadership activities, skills (professional licenses, certifications, or computer software proficiency), or any other information requested by a specific job announcement.

Table 4-3. Contents of a federal résumé (*continued*).

Federal jobs often require that you have experience in a type of work for a certain period. You must show how your skills and experiences meet all the qualifications and requirements listed in the job announcement to be considered for the job. Here are some additional tips for standing out from the crowd:[5]

Use Keywords: You will spot these keywords in the duties, key requirements, and qualifications sections of the job announcement. (For senior-level/SES roles, you will find these in the executive core qualifications [ECQs] and mandatory technical qualifications [MTQs] areas.) You should use those exact terms or phrases throughout the application process, including your résumé, cover letter, and during your interview.

Make Your Résumé Searchable: Making your résumé searchable adds it to the USAJOBS résumé mining collection. Résumé mining helps HR specialists and hiring managers from federal agencies look for applicants for their job announcements. Note there are a few limitations to this:[6]

- Only one of your résumés can be made searchable at a time.
- Only certain formats are searchable, including Word, text-based PDFs, text files, and résumés created using the résumé builder tool.
- Your résumé will only remain searchable for eighteen months unless it is renewed.

There are also items you should *not* include in your federal résumé:

- Classified or government sensitive information
- Social Security number (SSN)
- Photos of yourself
- Personal information, such as age, gender, religious affiliation, etc.
- Encrypted or digitally signed documents[7]

See www.matthewjlouis.com for sample résumés for mid-level and senior-level federal opportunities and how to upload them to USAJOBS (you may upload up to five).

Separate from the résumé, USAJOBS allows you to post other documents to enable you to claim your justly earned veteran's preference, if applicable, and to provide a cover letter. Here is your chance to stand out from the crowd. I recommend you take full advantage of this opportunity *if the agency permits it*. Rule number one in this case is to follow the instructions the hiring agency provides under the required documents section of the vacancy announcement. If the agency says, "Do Not Submit Any Additional Information," do not submit any additional documentation. If, however, the hiring agency permits it, these additional documents could include your DD-214, SF-15, SF-50, OF-306, a transcript, or a cover letter. All these documents must be less than three megabytes and in one of the following formats: GIF, JPG, JPEG, PNG, RTF, TXT, PDF, or Word (doc or docx). See Figure 4-1 for a visual of the web page for entering that data.

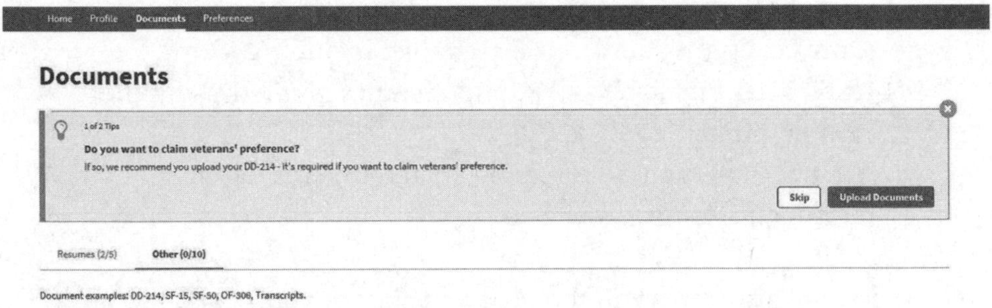

Figure 4-1. Veterans preference documentation page at the USAJOBS website.

In the interest of overcoming résumé scanning technology, a well-written, error-free cover letter has the potential to distinguish your application and secure an interview. Your cover letter should act as a one-page sales pitch that demonstrates why you are the right person for this opening. It should be tailored to the agency and the opening to which you are applying. It should be in the same style and format as your résumé, but it should do more than regurgitate a summary of the facts in your résumé. It should contain three paragraphs:

- An opening: An energetic introduction of your background and how your strengths not only fit the role description but will further the organization's stated mission.
- A middle: A table that summarizes how your qualifications directly satisfy, if not exceed, the requirements for the role.
- A closing: A sentence or two expressing your thanks for being considered and your anticipation of being contacted regarding the next steps of the application process.

My website (www.matthewjlouis.com) contains a sample cover letter. Please note in the additional resources on my website that there are entire books written on this topic that go into much greater detail on the subject.

With your completed résumé and draft cover letter, you now have a basis for tailoring it for specific opportunities that we will address in chapter 6.

Let's now turn to civilian résumés.

★

CIVILIAN RÉSUMÉS

So you've decided to pursue opportunities outside of the government. Congratulations! While this may at first seem like a tougher road, given the amount of work you will need to put into translating your experience, the rewards may be well worth the cost. Some good news is that you'll have much more flexibility in producing a civilian version of your résumé. As you'll see, there is much more to consider and upon which to decide.

Your immediate challenge and task are to recognize what civilian business leaders understand and then speak in those terms. The individuals who will be hiring you understand the language of business. They studied it in school and have been working in it on a full-time basis since they themselves were first hired. Don't let that intimidate you. You don't need a two-year MBA to get this (although that is a fine option). To understand the basic motivations of business, I'll provide you with the following five-minute MBA.

For starters, you should understand that for a commercial (for-profit) enterprise to exist as a business, it needs to have two things: (1) a product or a service of value and (2) a paying customer. The objective measure by which that business is judged is its bottom line, also known as net income or profit. This measure drives other metrics (such as share price) that are outside of our scope. Let's keep it simple. The simplified income statement below (see Table 4-4) demonstrates how an organization arrives at net income (profit) and the goals a typical organization would have to continually grow net income year over year.

INCOME STATEMENT	GOAL	SAMPLE COMPANY GOALS
Revenue = Price x Volume	Increase ↑	↑ 10% per year
– Direct Costs (labor, material, etc.)	Decrease ↓	
= Contribution Margin	Increase ↑	
– Indirect Costs (travel, overhead, etc.)	Decrease ↓	
= Operating Margin	Increase ↑	↑ 12% per year
– Taxes	Decrease ↓	
= Net Income (profit)	Increase ↑	↑ 10% per year

Table 4-4. Simplified income statement and sample company goals.

So what?

1. Most commercial organizations are judged by their ability to produce a positive and gradually increasing net income.
2. The above equations demonstrate that, to succeed, organizations must either increase revenue (by either increasing volume and/or price) and/or decrease costs (including taxes) in any legal way possible.
3. To the extent you can help an organization do either of those, you are an asset to that organization.
4. And so the content of your résumé must speak to your strengths that might enable an organization to do either of those. Those strengths might be direct (sales, marketing) or indirect (finance, operations), but their outcomes must still result in a positive impact to the bottom line (profit). It will be critical that you make that connection based on your own unique background, strengths, and experiences.

Now, upon reflection, you may find your military experiences to date don't directly speak to those exact terms or concepts. You may not have sold anything in your entire life. You may know nothing about marketing or finance. That's okay. Take a breath. You've done more than you think you have, and what you've done relates more to these terms and concepts than you might think. Let me explain.

All organizations are composed of people—individuals like you, individuals with their own set of skills, experiences, issues, and challenges. All are unique and not as unlike you as you may think. Ultimately, the skill sets of all individuals in a successful organization must be brought to bear at the right time and place to move the needle on revenue and costs. If you think of increasing revenue and decreasing costs as the mission, it's not so different after all. Haven't you been spending your time in the military bringing the strengths of those you have managed to bear at the right time and right place so your organization (unit) would accomplish its mission and be successful?

Of course you have. Those are exactly the strengths you have been exhibiting in the military. You have been leading. You have been managing. You have been training. You have been coaching. You have been organizing, creating order from chaos. You have been accountable. You've exhibited integrity, courage, and bravery. You've overcome challenges from your competition. You've demonstrated flexibility. You've learned quickly. You've developed self-confidence. You're dependable and enthusiastic. You've demonstrated loyalty, initiative, unselfishness, and endurance.

See. You've done a lot! And those are exactly the kinds of strengths and character traits that successful organizations are desperately seeking to improve both their top and bottom lines.

Recall from the introduction that the Institute for Veterans and Military Families (IVMF) at Syracuse University found ten characteristics that are generally representative of military veterans.[8] These characteristics were found to enhance organizational performance in a competitive business environment. The ten characteristics cite that veterans . . .

- Are entrepreneurial
- Assume high levels of trust
- Are adept at skills transfer across contexts/tasks
- Have and leverage advanced technical training
- Are comfortable/adept in discontinuous environments
- Exhibit high levels of resiliency
- Exhibit advanced team-building skills
- Exhibit strong organizational commitment
- Have and leverage cross-cultural experiences
- Have experience/skill in diverse workplace settings

We call those strengths *transferable skills*. Focusing on those transferable skills will enable you to speak the language of civilian business people and help you land your next role outside of the military.

There are some great resources available to help you translate your military skills into something a prospective civilian employer can understand.

- O*Net Online provides a handy military crosswalk that, upon entering your military occupational classification, will provide a civilian-friendly reading of the knowledge, skills, abilities, and other details related to that role.[9]
- You might also consider using the Department of Labor's competency models (see chapter 2), which define the skills and competencies needed to be successful in many industries.[10]
- For a tool that matches your military experience to a number of possible civilian job openings, check out the skills translator at Military.com.[11] Upon entering your branch of service and military occupational specialty, a list of related civilian positions and job openings appears. My caution would be, as a commercial site, the output of this tool certainly does not comprise the totality of available civilian roles. In fact, I would guess your eventual career will be found through other means. But the novelty of the tool is useful in that it demonstrates *possible* roles that might be a match.
- Several large corporations, including Google, have developed skills translators.[12] Some are tailored for their own purposes whereas others are agnostic in their approach. An internet search for "military skills translator" will reveal several.
- Lastly, for former army and Marine Corps enlisted personnel, the RAND Corporation has documented the soft skills obtained through military courses that you have attended throughout your career.[13]

So let's get to work. You have your life mission on the line, and we have some work to do to get your strengths and experiences successfully translated into something a civilian business leader can understand. We need to get this translated compilation—your résumé—into fighting shape.

There are two main topics to review:

- The construction of the résumé itself
- The appropriate translation of your background into its content

★

RÉSUMÉ BASICS

Let's first talk résumé construction. There is an entire industry focused on job searches (you've likely come across a few of these companies offering you their services), and the résumé is one of its primary focus areas. Because of the résumé's recommended composition and content, it is very subjective and unique to every instance in which you use it. There are as many opinions on this topic as there are people in the industry.

We're going to keep it simple and practical. Let's start with the primary purpose of the résumé, which is to secure you a follow-on interview with a hiring manager at your targeted company. Nothing more, nothing less.

Here are some basic guidelines (keep in mind the visual aspect of communication accounts for 55 percent of its potential impact):

- Your résumé should be no longer than two pages (even for retiring colonels or navy captains).
- Try to use a font no smaller than ten points. If you expect the résumé to be subject to scanning software, use nothing smaller than eleven points.
- Font size should only vary between various indentation levels of the document, but even then, only by one degradation. Within a given indentation level, use the same font size and type throughout. Throughout the entire document, limit the total indentation levels (and corresponding font size changes) to no more than three.
- Unless you are applying for a role in the arts, maintain a consistent font type throughout the document. There have

been lots of studies on this, but most professional writers recommend at least one of the following fonts: Arial, Calibri, Garamond, Times New Roman, or Verdana.

- Unless you are applying for a role in the arts, use one font color—black—throughout the document.
  - ▶ One exception would be a hyperlink added to an electronic version of your résumé (e.g., to reference an impressive article about you or a report you wrote). In standard word processing software, the hyperlink will automatically appear underlined and in a different color. This is fine, as it will draw the reader's attention to the fact that additional information is accessible via the link.
  - ▶ If you insert a hyperlink, however, spell out the web address in hard copy versions of the résumé; otherwise the reader will only see underlined text and have no way of accessing the important information you want them to see.
- For hard-copy versions of your résumé that might be used in a formal setting, use professional résumé paper, not standard white copy paper. Any local stationery or office products store offers several options. As a rule, use neutral colors (almond, ivory, light gray, or light blue) and between 25 percent and 100 percent cotton or linen.

We will consider three civilian résumé formats: the chronological format, the functional format, and the combination format. The latter two are primarily recommended for more senior-level roles.

Chronological Format: The chronological format is widely used and applies to all levels of civilian opportunities. What distinguishes a chronological format from a functional format is that in the work experience portion of the résumé, it lists employers and dates first and responsibilities and accomplishments—which speak to translatable skills—second. I recommend this format because it provides the prospective employer quick and easy identification of some of their basic questions: What did you do for whom and when, and how does that translate into helping us accomplish our goals?

At a minimum, a chronological résumé should contain the following:

- Your contact information, which should be at the top of the first page.
- A short statement that either states your objective (which should align with the potential employer's opportunity) or summarizes your strengths and translatable skill sets in an abbreviated fashion. This should be just below your contact information.
- Your work experience in reverse-chronological order, highlighting specific strengths or translatable skills that are relevant to the position to which you are applying. I recommend placing this before the education section. As an experienced hire, you want to highlight your more recent accomplishments first, which in most instances will be your experience, not your education.
  - ► Career military professionals with twenty or more years in service may find it difficult to list all their work experience. With all the assignments they have had, it becomes nearly impossible to list the complete details and responsibilities carried out and the results of all those roles. And so I suggest spending more space focusing on more recent experiences. Earlier experience can be summarized, but please enumerate those years of experience. Try to avoid leaving what appears to be an employment gap on your résumé. A phrase such as "Successive noncommissioned officer assignments of increasing responsibility, 1995–2000" would do the trick. You could even enumerate especially noteworthy accomplishments beneath that phrase to help round it out.
- Your education in reverse-chronological order, which tends to place the highest degree received at the top of the

list. For the same reason noted above, I would place your education level after your experience.

- Your security clearance level, assuming it is active (you will want to renew it if it is about to expire). This can be an asset in a civilian organization. The nature of the role to which you are applying will determine where it might best be placed on the page. For roles that require it, you should include it near the top of your first page, perhaps in your summary. For roles where it may not be required, I would place it toward the bottom of the résumé.

Regardless of the résumé format, and depending on the opportunity you may be considering, your résumé *may* also contain several additional pieces of information. This information, in most instances, should follow the above information (experience, education, etc.).

- Any honors or awards that speak to your eminence in activities relevant to the specific needs of the prospective employer.
- Any certifications that may be relevant to the industry in which you are seeking employment. This could include your security clearance if you are applying for a role where it may not be used.
- Any professional associations or affiliations that are pertinent to the prospective employer.
- Any specific language or technical skills that might be relevant to your candidacy.
- Additional education or fellowships that might be relevant to the prospective employer.
- Any relevant publications you may have written or relevant appearances in websites or other media.

Like government résumés, there are some things you should not include in your civilian résumé. I suggest your résumé avoid statements such as "References available upon request." A prospective employer will ask for references if they are needed. The phrase itself is not needed and only takes away from the white space on the page that you could better use for other purposes. Also, unlike government résumés, you should not provide your salary history or salary expectations. Finally, you should avoid including any information that could potentially lead to bias on behalf of the reader, e.g., political affiliation, religious beliefs, medical data, your race, or even your picture.

Again, you can drive yourself silly referencing a plethora of additional guidance online. But if you stick to these basic construction guidelines, you should be in good shape.

See www.matthewjlouis.com for sample chronological résumés for mid-level and senior-level roles.

Functional Format: The functional format differs from the chronological format in that the work experience portion of the résumé lists skills and accomplishments first and employers and dates second. I recommend this only for senior-level civilian opportunities, where the proven performance of specific, executive-level skill sets becomes more critical than the specifics of who you worked for and when.

At a minimum, a functional résumé should contain the following:

- Your contact information, which should be at the top of the first page.
- A short statement of your objective (which should align with the potential employer's opportunity) or summary of your strengths and translatable skill sets in an abbreviated fashion. This should be just below your contact information.
- Your primary professional strengths related to the prospective employer's opportunity, supported by detailed descriptions of duties, responsibilities, and accomplishments that highlight those chosen strengths.
- Work or employment history in reverse-chronological order.
- Education and training in reverse-chronological order.
- Your security clearance, assuming it is active.

The functional résumé may also contain the additional information noted above in the chronological format section, depending on the available space on the page. And the same rules regarding what *not* to include that are noted above apply here as well.

See www.matthewjlouis.com for a sample functional résumé for a senior-level role.

Combination Format: The combination or hybrid format brings together elements from both the chronological and functional formats. Whereas the chronological format more heavily weighs the employee and date data, and the functional format more heavily weighs the duties and responsibilities data, the combination format provides a balance. For similar reasons stated above, I recommend this only for senior-level civilian opportunities.

At a minimum, a combination résumé should contain the following:

- Your contact information at the top of the first page.
- A short statement of your objective (which should align with the potential employer's opportunity) or summary of your strengths and translatable skill sets in an abbreviated fashion. This should be just below your contact information.
- Your primary professional strengths related to the prospective employer's opportunity, supported by detailed descriptions of duties, responsibilities, and accomplishments that highlight those chosen strengths.
- Work or employment history in reverse-chronological format. This will usually follow the strengths section, but unlike the functional format, this should include additional details on your accomplishments in each of the roles noted.
- Education and training in reverse-chronological format.
- Your security clearance, assuming it is active.

As with all formats, the combination or hybrid résumé may also contain the additional information noted above in the chronological format section, depending on the available space on the page. The same rules regarding what *not* to include that are noted above apply here as well.

See www.matthewjlouis.com for a sample combination résumé for a senior-level role.

One alternative to the standard résumé for career military professionals (I advise against using this if you have served less than twenty years) is an alternative combination résumé for civilian executives that is one part single-page biography and one part chronological summary. This would be supplied to senior (C-suite-level executives) civilians who are very limited on available time. The first page explains in simple facts what you do for a living, giving factual examples. It also presents some conversational hooks that highlight your experience. There's also a picture of you in civilian executive attire (more on appropriate civilian attire in chapter 8), probably taken one day before you get your haircut. The first page should be enough to generate interviews and facilitate introductions, but the second page of executive highlights provides more facts and figures if they want to keep reading. See www.matthewjlouis.com for a sample alternative combination résumé.

★

RÉSUMÉ CONTENT

I contend the most important part of the résumé is the appropriate translation of your strengths and experience, that is, the actual content on the page. Every word that goes into your résumé should highlight those transferable skills and experiences that we previously discussed. They will help prospective employers understand how you can meet their specific needs and challenges.

OVERCOMING APPLICANT TRACKING SYSTEMS (ATS)

Applicant tracking systems (ATS; aka robots) provide employers an automated way of keeping track of applicants for available roles throughout the hiring process. They also help keep employers in compliance with applicable regulations. ATS systems exist to help employers, not you. They are not your friend. While their stated purpose is to better facilitate the hiring process, an unspoken part of their purpose is to screen out candidates. They do so by focusing on keywords in résumés. If a résumé does not contain the words or combination of words sought by the employer, that résumé may be rejected before being read by a human being. There are two approaches to overcoming these robots:

- Identify the keywords used in the job description. Tailor your résumé to include those keywords multiple times throughout the document.
- Submit a cover letter (see www.matthewjlouis.com for a sample) along with your résumé that likewise leverages the keyword approach.

See Jobscan as a possible means to apply this guidance.[14]

For starters, put yourself in the shoes of a civilian executive with no military background (99.5 percent of the population). How would you react to the following statement?

"Flew over fifty combat missions in the UH-60 A/L Black-hawk in support of OIF and over a hundred combat ISR sorties in the RC-12 N/P Guardrail in support of OND."

The likely reaction from a civilian executive might be:
- What does this have to do with the vacant position? We aren't hiring pilots.

- Other than being a pilot and perhaps able to operate under pressure, what skills does this demonstrate that I could utilize?
- Are fifty missions and a hundred sorties impressive? I have no idea.
- What is a US-60 A/L Blackhawk? A RC-12 N/P Guardrail? OIF? OND? ISR?

"Army lieutenant colonel and cybersecurity professional with extensive executive leadership and management experience and over ten years of experience in computer and network security."

The likely reaction from a civilian executive:
- You're not applying to be in the army, so why does that matter?
- I don't understand your rank (is that a high rank?). It holds no sway in my organization. Does this person have a superiority complex? Will he be able to adjust to life in the real world?
- Why list both management and leadership? Does this person understand the difference?
- Does this person understand what executive leadership entails in the real world, much less extensive executive leadership?

"Second in command of a forward-deployed, European-based tank battalion consisting of 44 M1A1 main battle tanks, 150 tracked and wheeled vehicles, and approximately 600 soldiers."

Likely reaction:
- With a few exceptions, we don't command anyone in the civilian world to do anything. Can this person adjust his style?

- Is this supposed to be impressive? To what is this relative? Were his peers responsible for more than this? I can't tell.
- What does all of this translate to in dollars and cents?
- Was this person truly the primary person responsible or was this accomplished as part of a team?
- What skill sets were required to be successful here? How do they relate to the role to which this person is applying?
- What is an M1A1 main battle tank? A tracked vehicle? A wheeled vehicle? A tank battalion? Forward-deployed? Second in command?

Now ask yourself: Are those the kinds of reactions that you want? Are those the kinds of reactions that will get you an interview and an opportunity to land a role at a prospective organization?

The obvious answer is an emphatic no!

Now, let's revisit those same statements after they've been translated into a language that resonates with the intended audience:

"Recognized by the organization's CEO for performing admirably and exceeding expectations under pressure on repeated occasions in my assigned role."

This not only sounds different, it should garner quite a different reaction:

- This person goes beyond basic requirements. We need that.
- Recognition by a senior leader says a lot about how this person stands out in a crowd or among peers. We need leaders in our organization.
- Performing under pressure is not an issue. That's great; we're always operating under pressure.

"Experienced cybersecurity professional with over ten years of organizational leadership experience in computer and network security."

Better reaction: This person has cyber skills and leadership experience, with a specialty in computer and network security. We can use both of those, the technical skills and the leadership skills.

"Chief of staff of a leading-edge overseas organization with primary responsibility for $600 million in equipment and six hundred personnel."

Better reactions:
- Wow! I want to learn more about that.
- This person knows how to manage. That's the kind of responsibility this person will have here as well.
- This person has been overseas. That's good, because we operate in a global economy.

★ ★ ★

TROOPS IN THE TRENCHES

"The most difficult part of my transition was translating my military skills and experience into civilian terms. When I first began job hunting, I assumed civilian employers would understand what I had done in the army, and, in fact, I assumed the burden was on them to do the translating. After a few failed interviews, I realized I needed to put far more effort into telling my story in ways that made sense outside of the military. When I was able to do that, I was able to paint an accurate picture of what I might bring to a company."

JULIA ALDRICH, FORMER ARMY CAPTAIN

Now you're getting somewhere. Now you're making sense to the reader or listener. Now you've opened the door for yourself. Now you have an opportunity for further discussion.

Besides that, what else do you notice? We used fewer words to get across our points. How great is that? We now have more space on the page to include our quantifiable accomplishments in a language that actually means something and highlights our strengths and transferable skills!

Let's keep at it. Here are some additional examples. You may be used to representing your experience in these kinds of terms:

- "Hand-picked from a XX-person military force."
- "A special team of the highest caliber special assistants."
- "Charged with leading an army of over 1.3 million soldiers and their family members."
- "A team of twenty-three high-caliber military and civilian strategists."
- "Implementation plan to sustain army dominance in land warfare."
- "Developed a war plan to deter and if necessary defeat threats to US interests."
- "Three-star leader."

Translated, the rest of the world communicates and understands this same experience in a very different way:

- Hand-picked from a 2.1-million-person organization.
- A team of highly capable specialists.
- Assigned to lead over 1.3 million professionals.
- A team of twenty-three highly competent strategists.
- Implementation plan to sustain operational dominance.
- Developed an operations plan to address competitive threats to national interests.
- Executive leader.

To you this may sound incredibly strange. In fact, it may even represent an entirely new language. Well, welcome to the rest of the world and to the rest of your life. Don't believe for a moment that using a boatload of military-specific jargon and acronyms makes you sound accomplished, savvy, smart, or clever. It does not.

It may result in the entirely opposite reaction from a civilian reader, and this you want to avoid.

Here are some more examples of how to better translate your experience:

Original: "Served additionally as an arms room officer, over-seeing security, maintenance, and accountability of weapons, optics, and restricted hardware within a weapons storage facility; scored in top 10 percent of units for security and efficiency of armory."

Improved: "Oversaw the security, maintenance, and accountability of all organizational weapons, optics, and restricted hardware; scored in top 10 percent of similarly sized peer organizations for security and efficiency."

Lesson: Translate terminology. Be succinct with your quantifiable results.

Original: "Top platoon leader in company and third out of twenty-six in battalion in evaluations; promoted to first lieutenant."

Improved: "Top team leader in the organization and number three out of twenty-six in the enterprise; promoted to manage more complex teams."

Lesson: Emphasize skills, not ranks. Translate terminology.

Original: "Graduated in top 10 percent of class at Infantry Officers Course and Northern Warfare Training Center; Airborne School."

Improved: "Graduated in top 10 percent of class at two army officer basic leadership courses."

Lesson: Translate military terminology.

Original: "Overcame long-standing structural issues within the section by bringing personnel from various functional groups together to build a unified team and establish processes to ensure timely repairs of critical equipment; raised the readiness rate of water purification assets from less than 50 percent to 91 percent in two months' time, restoring Hawaii's ability to deploy teams in support of humanitarian assistance and disaster relief missions."

Improved: "Personally raised the readiness rate of water purification assets from less than 50 percent to 91 percent in two months' time, restoring the organization's ability to deploy teams in support of humanitarian assistance and disaster relief missions."

Lesson: Be succinct with your quantifiable results.

Original: "Integrated a highly independent staff and modernized office practices in order to showcase the best aspects of the company to foreign visitors and senior military leaders."

Improved: "Improved protocol processes of a diverse five-member staff, resulting in thirty-four successful visits by foreign dignitaries and senior military leaders."

Lesson: Quantify your accomplishments.

Original: "Lieutenant, United States Navy, Amphibious Squadron 5, US Pacific Fleet."

Improved: "US Navy officer."

Lesson: Dispense with detailed ranks and units.

Original: "Company executive officer, anti-tank company."

Improved: "Chief of staff."

Lesson: Focus on skills. Translate terminology. Avoid military specifics, especially those dealing with lethality.

Starting to get the hang of it? Here are some reminders:

- Quantify your accomplishments as much as you can. How you perform against peers or against the norm is important. This tends to indicate a trend to a prospective employer. Use percentages (top 5 percent) or relevant ratings (fifth among fifty peers) wherever possible. You might be able to say, for example, you were rated first among peers (had a 1-block NCOER). Or you were awarded a Meritorious Service Medal (perhaps the only one in your brigade). Or you scored in the top 5 percent on a given task. Some examples:

- ▶ "Set two records for maintenance army-wide."
  - This is good but becomes much more meaningful if you would be able to specify the relative nature of the task. How many others were competing for this outcome? What was your specific role in enabling this outcome? Were you the leader or just part of the organization?
  - ▶ Better: "Directly supervised a one-hundred-person maintenance organization whose annual readiness performance bested fifteen hundred other equivalent organizations."
- Order your experience ahead of your education on your résumé (if you are transitioning directly from the service). You are considered an experienced hire. The latest and greatest things you have done—and those transferable skills you have gained via that experience that would appeal to employers—are far more compelling. Put them up front. (If you are using college or graduate school as your transition vehicle, you may want to put that up front.)
  - ▶ In enumerating specific details in each instance of your experience, attempt to separate your responsibilities (which speak to what you were charged with doing) from your results (which speak to what you accomplished). For example, the first line under a given role would speak to the scope and nature of your requirements (responsibilities); the bullets following the first line would speak to the quantifiable accomplishments you realized in executing against those requirements (results).

- Avoid formal military ranks. The roles for which you are interviewing do not have ranks. Moreover, civilians don't understand your military rank. It will confuse them (at best) or annoy them (at worst). They may see your use of the rank as an attempt to assert your authority (which you no longer have) before you even walk in the door. What's important are your strengths, your transferable skills, not rank. Civilians aren't hiring corporals, captains, or colonels; they're hiring professionals with skill sets who can help them solve their toughest challenges.
  - ► Bad example: "Ranked number one of four lieutenants by my company commander and in the 95th percentile by my battalion commander."
  - ► Better example: "Rated by CEO in top 5th percentile among twenty-four peers."
  - ► Exceptions would include instances in which you may be applying for government contracting roles in your identical career field. These employers have the military as their client, and they want to ensure an apples-to-apples relationship with those clients.
- Avoid naming specific military units. Again, civilians will not understand or appreciate who these organizations are or what they represent.
  - ► Bad example: "160th Special Operations Aviation Regiment (Airborne)."
  - ► Better example: "Covert aviation operations organization."
  - ► Exceptions again include instances in which you may be applying for government contracting roles in your identical career field. Another exception might be those elite units whose name would be broadly known to the public, for example, SEAL Team Six.
- Avoid naming specific individuals in referring to your accomplishments. Civilians will likely have no idea who you're referring to, which doesn't help. What's possibly worse is that the individual's record may not be spotless

(witness several very senior military leaders exposed in the media in recent years for unbecoming behavior) and may reflect poorly on you as well.

- ▶ Bad example: "Hand-selected by Chief of Naval Operations, Admiral John Smith."
- ▶ Better example: "Hand-selected by the chief of naval operations."
- ▶ Exceptions may include the president of the United States or other obviously recognizable names. However, even then you run the risk of politics entering the discussion if your audience leans one way or the other. The safe bet is to use generic terms to refer to the leader in question.

- In referring to your commanders or leaders, use equivalent civilian terminology, for example, terms such as organizational leader, first-line supervisor, CEO, president, vice president, boss.
  - ▶ Bad example: "Rated as the best commander in the Joint Staff Directorate by a two-star admiral."
  - ▶ Better example: "Rated as best among five peers by our supervisor."
  - ▶ Exceptions again include instances in which you may be applying for government contracting roles in your identical career field.

- Specify accomplishments regarding activities that you note. Each bullet should be able to answer the question "So what?" It should be *quantifiable, specific*, and *relevant* to the opportunity. For example,
  - ▶ Don't say, "Deployed 176 personnel and over $30 million of equipment 500 miles."
    - So what? Did you also return with no losses? Maintain a 99 percent readiness rate throughout? If so, say so. Did your unit outperform others? What was your role in doing so? Quantify, specify, make relevant to the role to which you are applying.

- ▶ Do say, "Personally supervised the deployment of 176 personnel and over $30 million in equipment over 500 miles without loss while maintaining a 99 percent readiness rate, best among five peers in the organization."
- Translate any accomplishments that deal with death or lethality. Unless you are doing contractor work for the Department of Defense, you will likely not be using a weapon in your new role. Prior accomplishments with the use of those weapons are relevant only in the sense that you finished near the top of your peers in the performance of a critical skill. No one will hire you to kill anyone or because you might be good at it.
  - ▶ Don't say, "Raised army-wide standards for the anti-tank guided missile Stryker."
    - I'm sure that was a nice accomplishment in the military, but it means nothing in the civilian world as it is written.
    - Some improvements would involve:
      - ▶ Translating the applicability to the organization to which you might be applying. No one hires you because you know how to pull a trigger. You improved the performance standards for your basic issue equipment for the entire army.
      - ▶ Quantifying the relative nature of the task. Give the reader a sense of the scope of the effort.
      - ▶ Specifying your role in the outcome. Did you lead the effort? Did you directly enable it? Or were you just along for the ride?
  - ▶ Better: "Enabled improvement of enterprise-wide standards for the primary equipment in the organization."
- List only those professional affiliations that may be relevant to the intended audience. Enumerating a litany of

organizational memberships is not necessarily impressive; it may well take up valuable space on the page that could otherwise be devoted to listing your valuable quantifiable results.

- Understand how some military terms can potentially offend:
  - ► *Command*: In the civilian world, you will command no one (both in the organizational understanding of the term—as a noun—and in the directive nature of the term—as a verb). You will supervise. You will motivate. You will inspire. You will lead. You will *not* command.
  - ► *Second in Command (2IC)*: Beyond the similar issues with the word *command*, I would use *assistant manager* or *chief of staff*.
  - ► *–man* (as in "I was assigned to a 200-man organization"): Do not use this even if you were assigned to an organization that contained no members of the opposite sex. This will label you to a prospective employer as someone who can't get along with women, who represent roughly 50 percent of the US population and will surely be a prominent part of whatever organization you join. Use *person*. This advice applies to the opposite gender—and in role-reversal situations—as well.
  - ► *Spearheaded*: This comes across as a militaristic term and unnecessarily pigeonholes you as overly authoritative. Use *led*, *initiated*, etc.
  - ► See www.matthewjlouis.com for a helpful military-to-civilian thesaurus to translate additional terms.

Please take heed: This is not a game. This is not a temporary or arbitrary change of vocabulary. This is how the rest of the world communicates, writes, talks, and thinks. I realize this is different; this is a change. But success requires your adoption of this alternate way of thinking and communicating. You communicated this way before you entered the military, and you can do it again. Work on building a robust vocabulary for use in this new career. Your audience will attribute your intelligence level to your ability to do so. Make it a goal to learn a new word every day. Wordsmith.org allows you to register to receive a new word for free every day.[15]

Here are some grammatical reminders:

- Spell out numbers less than two-digits
    - ▶ For example, use one or four, not 1 or 4.
    - ▶ Conversely, use 12 or 155, not twelve or one hundred fifty-five unless those are the first words of a sentence.
- Do not use personal pronouns in your résumé.
- Only use a period at the end of a bullet if there are two or more sentences contained in the bullet. If a bullet contains only one sentence, do not use a period. Simple as it sounds, this will save you some space on the page.
- It is okay to use M or B as abbreviations for millions or billions.
    - ▶ For example, 50M personnel or $1.2B.

★ ★ ★

TROOPS IN THE TRENCHES

"I felt that many people looked at me like I was a zoo animal. Here I am, a relatively old guy, interviewing for a manager-level role. The assumption appeared to be that I was a total loser. And yet, I have worked in forty countries. I have a couple of graduate degrees. I regularly made decisions on the allocation of billions of dollars. It was exasperating."

FORMER ARMY COLONEL

I know, this can be frustrating. I've had lots of firsthand experience with this. I remember feeling as if seemingly no one understands the incredibly valuable things you've done the past five, twenty, thirty years. From your perspective, you've moved mountains. You've worked for the highest offices in the land. You've protected the backsides of the American people and secured their freedom. And yet none of it seems to matter.

Well, the reality is that it does matter. By and large, your prospective employers just don't have an appreciation for it. They don't understand what you've done; they don't speak your language. Moreover, they don't have the time to learn. So *you* have to be the one to go the extra mile and translate it for them. And that's a job in and of itself. You're in the middle of it, but the goal line is in sight.

Keep at it! Keep the faith! Those who can persevere—much as in the service—will succeed. Those who can't get their head around this or give up will be the ones who settle for suboptimal opportunities in career fields they do not prefer and soon end up leaving their initial job following active duty. For everyone's sake, this is what we need to prevent.

A WORD ON THE APPROPRIATE ROLE OF RECRUITING FIRMS (AKA HEADHUNTERS)

There are several businesses in the industry of helping veterans land positions outside of the military. They tend to have varying components to their businesses:

- *The Scope of Their Business*: Some work only with JMOs. Some work only with very experienced veterans or retirees. Others will take all comers.
- *Exclusivity Clauses*: Some may make you sign an agreement that restricts your job search to working with that organization.
- *Contingency Basis*: Most of these businesses don't get paid until you land a role at a potential employer. On its face, this provides an incentive to get you placed sooner rather than later in a role that may or may not be to your liking. (The alternative way in which headhunters get hired is on retainer or on a retained basis. In this approach, the employer pays the headhunter a fee up front

to find them their best candidate. This approach is usually preferred by job candidates, as the headhunter's incentives are more aligned with yours.) Regardless of the basis on which a headhunter is hired, you should not have to pay them anything for their services. The employer pays them.

- *Payment Terms*: The typical way in which these businesses get paid is having your prospective employer pay them a portion of your first year's salary. The incentive, in this case, may work in your favor. The recruiting business, like you, wants you to get a higher salary in your first year. Keep in mind, however, that the business has a profit incentive. While your initial pay may indeed be to your liking, it may be in a role that may or may not be to your liking.

- *Coaching and Preparation*: Most of these businesses will walk you through portions of this process. They will provide guides on how to dress. They will help you with your résumé preparation and skills translation. They will practice interviewing techniques. They will guide you on networking skills. They will even facilitate hiring conferences to get you in front of prospective employers.

What they have to offer is potentially helpful. But I urge you to consider the potential limitations. Ask yourself: Would they always be acting in your best interests? I offer the following few words of advice: To thine own self be true; you owe them nothing. And buyer beware; they are supposed to be working for you.

★　　★　　★

TROOPS IN THE TRENCHES

"I made the mistake of not vetting the headhunters that I used. They saw me as simply fitting an open role that they had available. I took the job because the CEO of the target company was a fellow Navy grad. But I ended up quitting the job after just three weeks. It was in no way a fit for me."

JON SANCHEZ, FORMER NAVY SEAL

For help in pulling together your résumé, your local military transition assistance office will normally have several resources or counselors to whom they can refer you. So start there. But you should seek additional perspectives and take advantage of a few resources outside of the TAP program. For starters, take advantage of military friends who have already made the transition to the civilian world (as you'll see in chapter 5, this is one reason to document your network before you transition). They are well positioned to understand—and translate—the language of both the military and civilian sides. Next, consider any number of not-for-profit veteran collaboratives (see the sidebar "Veteran Collaboratives") around the country who provide pro bono services to improve your résumé. If you are enrolled in or an alumnus of a college, their placement office or alumni organization is another good source of support. Consider using the resources provided by one of the nearly twenty-five hundred American Job Centers (AJCs) around the country.[16] They provide a robust set of resources, support, and training. Post 9/11–era veterans should take advantage of the AJCs' Gold Card Initiative,[17] which involves intensive assistance and six months of follow-up employment services, including:

- Job readiness assessments, including interviews and testing
- Creation of an individual development plan
- Career guidance
- Information on transfer of skills and occupational details
- Referral to job banks, job portals, and job openings
- Referral to employers and registered apprenticeship sponsors
- Referral to training opportunities
- Monthly follow-up by an assigned case manager for up to six months

If you feel you still need support beyond these options, think about the possibility of paying an expert in this area for their support. Search "military résumé writers" online and you'll find a plethora of options. You'll find experts operating on both an individual basis and as part of for-profit organizations focused on career management services. Since these services can range in cost from hundreds to thousands of dollars, you should screen these individuals for their depth of experience in helping military professionals transition to the civilian world. You don't want to work with a rookie résumé writer on this task. While this option represents money out of your pocket, it could be an investment well worth making if it produces the interviews you are seeking.

★ ★ ★

TROOPS IN THE TRENCHES

"Take your time with your résumé and find a number of experienced professionals that can review and provide feedback from their perspective."

MALISSA GALLINI, FORMER ARMY CAPTAIN

VETERAN COLLABORATIVES

Veteran collaboratives exist to bring veterans, agencies, organizations, and community members together on a local basis in an atmosphere of mutual support to systemically solve issues that each could not address alone. While they can certainly help with your résumé, they exist to do much more than résumé writing. Most of them offer support in areas such as employment, education, healthcare, housing, wellness, and family support. They exist in recognition of the fact that either (1) there is a lack of support resources in some communities or (2) there is an overabundance of support resources in some communities, leading to confusion, apathy, and unsought support. When you in-processed in the military, you likely did so through a military one-stop processing center that took care of all your needs: ID cards, benefits, housing, finance, transportation, travel, claims, etc. They did it all. You should think of these veteran collaboratives as your one-stop in-processing center for your new community. They should be some of the first resources you seek out in your local community. You would be wise to include among your geographic location preferences the existence of one of these veteran collaboratives. They can be incredibly helpful.

For example, Houston (home to 270,000+ veterans) contains hundreds of nonprofit organizations that have the word *veteran* in either their mission or vision statements. Try navigating all of those yourself and you would quickly get confused. So, Combined Arms was formed to act as your one-stop shop. If you're moving into that area, you should contact them well in advance of your move. They will help organize all the support you need from the best local agencies.

Some other examples from around the country include (see www.matthewjlouis.com for hyperlinks):

- Combined Arms in Houston, Texas
- The Tristate Veterans Community Alliance in Cincinnati, Ohio
- Mount Carmel Veterans Service Center in Colorado Springs, Colorado
- Military and Veterans Success Centers–East and West, Glendale, Arizona
- San Diego Military Family Collaborative
- Still Serving Veterans in Alabama
- Arizona Coalition for Military Families in Phoenix
- Los Angeles Veterans Collaborative
- Allies in Service in Dallas
- The Warrior Alliance in Atlanta
- Illinois Joining Forces in Chicago and Springfield, Illinois
- The Veterans Community Action Teams in Michigan
- Serving Together in the Washington DC area
- Greater Boston Veterans Collaborative (GBVC)
- AmericaServes affiliates in several regions of the United States: New York City; Upstate New York; Charlotte, North Carolina; Coastal North Carolina (Jacksonville); RDU/Fayetteville, North

Carolina; Lowcountry, South Carolina; Pittsburgh; and Greater
Puget Sound in Washington State
- America's Warrior Partnership affiliates in Pensacola, Florida;
Orange County, California; Charleston, South Carolina; Buffalo,
New York; Minneapolis, Minnesota; Greenville, South Carolina
- National Veterans Intermediary Partners
- United Way's Mission United
- Code of Support Foundation

Call the chamber of commerce of the community in which you plan
to settle to research the existence of a collaborative there. This one act
will pay many dividends. Take advantage of this for your family if not
yourself.

Once you have worked with any of these organizations and reviewed this with an objective, independent resource, you will then
be prepared to begin engaging with individuals who either could
hire you or know of individuals who could hire you. The first step
in approaching these individuals is the subject of our next chapter.

KEYS TO SUCCESS

★ Your personal strengths and skill sets acquired through time in
service are valuable. But no one will understand them and take
advantage of them and you if you think and speak as you do today.
Change is a requirement for almost everyone reading this book.

★ Do:
  ▶ Translate the first version of your résumé.
  ▶ Solicit an outside perspective, namely, someone in the civilian
world who can help you with your translation. There are many
sources for this:
    - Peers who have left the military and are now at work in the
civilian world

- Alumni organizations
- College placement offices
- Nonprofit veteran collaboratives

▶ Tailor your résumé to the specific needs of the hiring organization and to avoid getting screened out by applicant tracking systems. Use keywords.

★ Don't:

▶ Get frustrated with yourself. This is not easy, but it can and must be done.

▶ Be satisfied with the first version of your résumé. It will not be civilian-ready. Be open to the feedback that will help you get this right.

▶ Get confused. Every person whose help you seek may have a slightly different opinion on the optimal way to approach this. Some of this guidance may seem conflicting. They all mean well, but you will have to decide which advice is most applicable to your situation.

CHAPTER FIVE

DOCUMENT YOUR NETWORK

THIS CHAPTER MAY BE THE ONE THAT PAYS YOU THE MOST DIVIDENDS IN THE long run. For some, this little exercise may well end up being a large part of your value proposition. It is fairly simple, and it may seem like overkill, but trust me on this: It will significantly pay you back over the course of your career.

In this chapter, we will discuss:

- The purpose of networking
- Debunking some military myths about networking
- The network documentation process

The outcome of this step in the process should be a robust list of identified networking contacts—some known, some unknown—

whose ultimate engagement (as will be addressed in the next chapter) will produce the job offers you seek. Over the course of your engagements, you will find this chapter's activities are reciprocal with the following chapter. It will be important to continue to document your expanding network as you meet new people.

One of the simple realities of the civilian world is that a lot of what you can achieve depends on who you know and who those people know. This was documented by Stanford sociologist Mark Granovetter in a study of the strength of weak ties and popularized in Malcolm Gladwell's *The Tipping Point*.[1] What Granovetter found was that more people find jobs through acquaintances than friends because casual connections can plug them into networks and information to which they wouldn't otherwise have access. In a word, the process of connecting with these acquaintances to build relationships is called networking.

Networking is alive and well in the military. Think of the last duty station or role you were trying to procure for yourself and/or your family. I'll bet you reached out to those who were in administrative positions that controlled those assignments. I'll bet you reached out to unit leaders at those locations. I'll bet you reached out to peers you knew at that location. I'll bet you reached out to prior bosses who might have been influential in swaying that decision. That, my friends, is called networking, and it translates perfectly into the real world.

You will find this approach rapidly becomes the way in which things get accomplished during and after your transition. And so, to be prepared for your transition—but also to develop good habits that lead to a successful career—you must document your network.

★　　★　　★

TROOPS IN THE TRENCHES

"In the military, I tended to view with some suspicion individuals that spent a lot of time networking. I always wondered why they weren't spending more time focused on doing their jobs well instead of focusing on schmoozing for their next job. So the idea of networking initially had a fairly negative connotation for me. One of the biggest realizations for me during my transition to the private sector is that because there is no set path and no real guarantee of a next job, people network to build relationships and share opportunities. Once I got over that mental block, I discovered I really, really enjoy networking and meeting new people, learning about new career fields and paths, and sharing opportunities."

CHIP COLBERT, FORMER ARMY LIEUTENANT COLONEL

Now, you may have to overcome some negative perceptions about networking. During your time in the service, networking may have taken on some negative connotations (see Chip Colbert's Troops in the Trenches quote above). The true intent of networking is a positive, productive experience for the people involved. It is about building relationships. It involves creating new connections as well as cultivating and deepening existing ones. Relationship building happens constantly. Relationships grow and develop by engaging with others in various settings:

- Formal (job fairs, career conferences) or informal (weddings)
- Group or one-on-one
- Virtual or in person
- Planned or serendipitous (your seatmate on an airplane)

Networking is a two-way street. In an ideal state, it is intended to benefit both people involved in the relationship. To cite a previous example, a unit or a post leader ends up with a good leader in you; you end up with the unit or location or boss you desire. This dynamic is the same in the real world.

★ ★ ★

TROOPS IN THE TRENCHES

"The number-one piece of advice I would offer people transitioning is to learn to network. You have to get over being shy. If you're enlisted, don't be afraid to call officers. The old military rules about hierarchical relationships no longer apply."

JON SANCHEZ, FORMER NAVY SEAL

You will use networking initially to aid in your transition. Networking will help you identify or clarify the nature of potential employers. It will provide you with intelligence about specific opportunities you may be pursuing. It will help you find peer coaches or mentors who will support your transition. It will help you acquire relationships that will provide perspective on the life and career decisions you are about to ponder. Your network contacts will help you as much or more than you are about to help them.

As you further your career, networking takes on additional forms and provides even further benefits. It will help you acquire intelligence about opportunities you may be considering. It will help you solve problems with which you may be struggling. And it will help you help others in ways that will benefit both of you.

To take this holistic approach to networking, you should first document your network. This involves some detailed thinking about your existing and desired relationships and recording those details in a format that can be readily and easily updated over time.

The contacts on this list should involve two sets of people: friendlies and targets. First, include anyone who comes to mind when you ask: Who do I know, personally or professionally, who could aid in either my transition or future career? This could include family and friends, nonprofit veteran collaboratives, civic organizations, military peers and bosses, college alumni points of contact, or other social relationships. These individuals are your friendlies.

★ ★ ★

TROOPS IN THE TRENCHES

"Strategically, you should target actual people within the organization—not recruiters. Recruiters become desensitized to individual
stories. I found more success in avoiding recruiters. I would reach
out to the open position's colleagues or chain of command."

TRAVIS LONG, FORMER NAVY PETTY OFFICER

Some great resources for pulling this friendlies list together
and seeking a potential mentor for this process include alumni
networking websites, LinkedIn groups, and the many veteran
transition organizations around the country. Check out Veterati
or American Corporate Partners to identify a professional mentor. Most colleges (and some high schools) facilitate alumni development networking websites. The service academies have their
alumni organizations or one of many local/regional networking
sites (search the following phrase online: "service academy networking").[2] On LinkedIn, search for "veterans groups," and you
will find many options for engaging with peers who have either
already transitioned or are in the process of doing so. Some of
those veteran peers also have available jobs posted. Finally, as
mentioned in the prior chapter, there are an expanding number
of veteran collaboratives around the country that you should
seek out. They can be a great source of local contacts in your
targeted geographic area.

Next, include on the list anyone who comes to mind when you
ask: Who do I need to get to know to enable a successful transition
and future career? These could be hiring managers or other decision makers at companies that might be of interest to you. These
could also be fellow veterans who work at these companies. These
could be alumni groups, civic organizations, or professional societies. These individuals are your targets.

★ ★ ★

TROOPS IN THE TRENCHES

"The best part of my transition was meeting new people and having new learning experiences. I found myself learning something new every day. Meeting new people and understanding their perspectives helped in my attempts to build new relationships."

FORMER ARMY COLONEL

You may not yet have all the information you need for all your targets, despite the abundance of information online or on social media. In fact, you may only have the name of a prospective employer in mind, and you may not know anyone who works there. That's okay. We'll discuss that in the next chapter as one of the benefits of engaging with your documented network. One easy way to start, however, is to leverage your friendlies for some of that information. You could also easily identify other veterans who work at the prospective employer. LinkedIn is a great tool for this. You can search for profiles of people who both work at the employer and have served in some capacity in the military. For example, you might search for "Amazon" and "army" to identify an initial list of networking targets.

★ ★ ★

TROOPS IN THE TRENCHES

"You should triple the number of companies you think you'll need to target. Where you ultimately end up is entirely out of your control. But you should be focused in selecting your targets. Use a rifle, not a shotgun approach."

DOMINIC LANZILLOTTA, FORMER ARMY CAPTAIN

At this point, you might say, "That's great. But how do I go about identifying the best employers?" That's a good question, and perhaps the best place to start for identifying your networking target list. The good news is there is no lack of resources available today for the transitioning veteran to identify prospective employers.

The *Military Times* produces an annual list of best employers for veterans.[3] GI Jobs also produces an annual ranking of military-friendly employers and schools.[4] Finally, VetJobs is a veteran-friendly job board that lists jobs available for transitioning veterans.[5]

A helpful way to visualize and organize your network is portrayed in Figure 5-1.

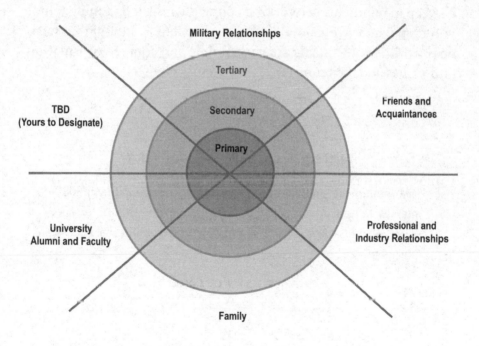

Figure 5-1. Network organization chart.[6]

Each slice of the chart represents a different aspect of your life. The center circle is for your first order and usually strongest relationships. These are people you know well. Moving away from the center, the relationships are less strong.

- *Primary*: Relationships that are deep and long-term (e.g., mentors and those who can be called upon when you need a problem solved). This group should certainly be considered friendlies.
- *Secondary*: Relationships that represent solid connections that are regularly maintained (e.g., colleagues and contacts). This group is part of the friendlies contact list as well.
- *Tertiary*: Relationships that are just being developed (e.g., acquaintances). These are friends of friends, and you may not know the person yet. This group tends to represent your targets.

Keep in mind, this networking contact list is a living thing. Once you complete it, you should regularly update it. In a global business world, professionals are very mobile and contact information and professional circumstances frequently change.

★   ★   ★

TROOPS IN THE TRENCHES

"My veteran peer network provided a bridge for me. They taught me how to network, how the world works, where to turn for answers, how to define my value, and how to talk about real issues intelligently."

FORMER ARMY COLONEL

A format that may work well for documentation purposes involves a simple spreadsheet (see Table 5-1 for an example; see www.matthewjlouis.com for a downloadable template). In it, you would document several things about the individual with whom you have the relationship:

- Name
- Organization
- Role in that organization
- Phone number
- Mobile number
- Email address
- Assistant (if the individual has one)
- Assistant's contact information
- Reference basis (the individual who may have connected you to this person)
- Date of last contact
- Notes from last contact

Contact Name	Business Name	Position/Role	Phone	Mobile	Email	Assistant

Assistant's Contact Info	Relationship/Reference	Date of Last Meeting	Notes from Last Meeting

Table 5-1. Sample contact list format.

You could also use this list to identify potential personal or professional references by using a color scheme to highlight specific individuals in the spreadsheet.

This approach is generic and would consistently apply to any career path. The nature of the contacts would obviously vary, depending on your chosen field of endeavor, but the process of identifying and documenting that network remains the same.

With your contact list now organized and in hand, we'll put together an action plan for engaging with your targets and review successful tactics for doing so in our next chapter.

KEYS TO SUCCESS

★ Don't skip this step.

★ Organize your networking contact list.

★ Review and refresh your networking contact list on a regular basis.

★ Leverage your list of friendlies for engaging with targets.

★ ★ ★

CHAPTER SIX

ENGAGE THE NETWORK

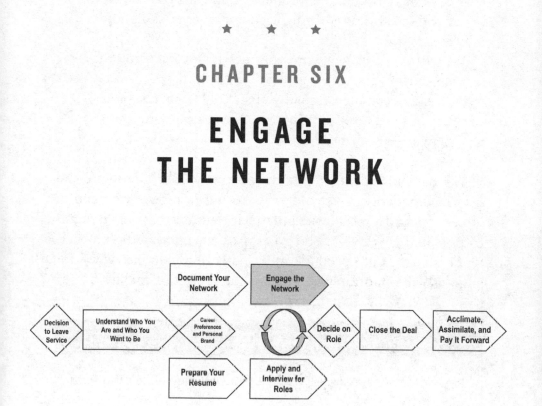

LET'S TAKE STOCK FOR A MOMENT. YOU'VE COMPLETED THE HARD WORK OF translating your strengths into a résumé that can be understood by the 99.5 percent of the population that hasn't served. You have identified a potential career path (or two) and a networking target list. And you have produced a personal brand statement (elevator speech) that spotlights who you are, what you've done, and what you want to do. Great work! With a bit more preparation, you will be prepared to engage in a professional conversation with those individuals in your networking target list. You may well find this step in the process to be the most productive and most important over the course of your career.

In this chapter, we will discuss:

- Creating an action plan for engaging with your targets
- Creating stories to highlight your strengths, skills, and experience
- Tactics for engaging with your newly documented network
- Avoiding common empathy mistakes in conversations
- Establishing a social media presence to support your network engagement

The outcome of this step in the process will be a growing and informed network, a list of stories to use in networking and in interviews, and a social media presence that reflects your strengths to potential employers. The process of engaging with your network is intended to produce and usually results in interviews for employment opportunities, which is the subject of chapter 8.

CAUTION

Two words of caution to those readers who may be looking for a shortcut:

1. Do not jump to this chapter and start your work here. Doing so will not enable the sustainable success we desire for all transitioning veterans, their families, and employers. Please do yourself, your family, and your future employer a favor and begin your work at the start of this book.
2. Follow the suggested approach. Networking has proven to be the most effective, reliable way to find a role that matches with your preferred career path. While there is nothing wrong with replying to want ads online or in your local paper, that approach has proven to be less effective. Promise to at least follow a parallel path with these approaches.

★   ★   ★

TROOPS IN THE TRENCHES

"Nurture the many connections you have made both inside and outside of military circles. The people you know and have worked with are the ones who will most likely put you on the path to your post-retirement position. When word gets out that you are transitioning, the people you helped and who have helped you along the way will reach out with opportunities."

DAVE RAYMOND, FORMER ARMY LIEUTENANT COLONEL

As in the military, any mission should begin with a plan. In this case, we need a plan for building relationships with targets in our network. A simple tool to facilitate this plan is Table 6-1, a relationship tracker. The tracker is intended to prompt you to identify specific action steps for engaging with individual contacts as well as what outcomes you expect from those interactions. These outcomes should identify your purpose for engaging with this person. In considering what would be appropriate to ask your target, consider their role and level within their organization. For example, if you need help with your résumé, it would not be appropriate to ask the chief human resources officer of a company in which you are interested, but it would be appropriate to ask a friend who works in your targeted career field.

•   •   •

★   ★   ★

TROOPS IN THE TRENCHES

"Don't discount the value of meeting strangers. I was at Starbucks one day and a total stranger sat by me and struck up a conversation. It turns out this stranger had spent time in the military, so we exchanged information. A year later, when I was looking for a new opportunity, he put me in touch with leaders in my target industry. One of those contacts resulted in my next job."

BRIAN HANKINSON, FORMER ARMY LIEUTENANT COLONEL

With that in mind, choose four or five relationships that you are ready to commit time to strengthening. Think about the specific actions you could take to develop those relationships and how that might help you. Consider questions such as:

- How does nurturing the relationship I have targeted help me to achieve my career and life objectives?
- Do those relationships allow me to meet others in the career field in which I'd like to be employed?
- Where do I have especially strong relationships? Can I leverage those relationships to build new ones?
- Where do I need additional contacts?

★   ★   ★

TROOPS IN THE TRENCHES

"Begin networking early. Research industries and don't be afraid to ask for help. Also, don't be afraid to cold-call companies. Tell them you are interested in their company, that you're just doing some research, and ask if there is anyone with whom they could connect you."

DAVE USLAN, FORMER AIR FORCE SENIOR MASTER SERGEANT

With these answers in mind, use the relationship tracker to put your action plan in place, to keep a record of your interactions with your network, and to keep track of meeting outcomes and action items for which you may be responsible. Remember to leverage family and friends in the process. They are vested individuals who want to see you succeed and may be able to provide access to others who can help. Conversely, your networking targets may have a need a friend or family member can address. Connecting other people helps to build *your* relationships, which is one of the main purposes of networking. The bottom line is this: Don't be afraid to ask for an introduction. Doing so is not considered a weakness.

Name	Date of Last Contact	Meeting Objectives	Meeting Outcomes	Next Steps and Action Items

Table 6-1. Relationship tracker.[1]

With your plan in hand, let's turn our attention to formally engaging our networking targets. Engaging targets will take place in any number of forums, from a simple phone call to a job fair or a career conference. It will involve your personal brand statement and will likely necessitate additional stories that will require you to recite the applicable strengths you have documented on your résumé.

In chapter 4, we created a résumé that translated your strengths into something a civilian hiring manager could understand. Before we start engaging with others about what is written on that page, however, we need to create some compelling stories regarding the bullet points on your résumé in anticipation of the questions you will likely receive in engaging with those networking contacts.

★   ★   ★

TROOPS IN THE TRENCHES

"Once you get into where you end up, some of the military stories you tell will be compelling to civilians. You can use your military experience as a corollary to bring home some lessons, so don't lose those anecdotes. People respect that. What you learned in the military and have spent years doing may have incredible value to civilians in industry."

MARK PREISSLER, FORMER NAVY LIEUTENANT COMMANDER

At a moment's notice, you must be able to recite a pertinent, applicable, easily understood story in response to a typical question you might receive in a networking situation: "How can I help or what can I do for you?" "Tell me about yourself and what you want to do." "Tell me about a time where you have demonstrated [pick a strength]." For most networking ice-breaking questions, your personal brand will suffice as a response. For more detailed questions, such as the last one above, you'll need to think through and practice your responses ahead of time. Composing such responses resembles telling a story. Stories can be used to provide greater detail about a specific activity or accomplishment, to illustrate a strength, to reinforce your point of view, or to simply give the interviewer a broader sense of who you are as a person, beyond the details of your résumé.

There is an art to telling stories, and there is a process to enable the art. A great story paints a mental and memorable picture and begins with listening and empathy. You need to be able to answer the following question: How can I make my story relevant, relating my experiences to something the other person knows and understands?

The first step in constructing your story is to identify the simple truth, the main point of your story. You should be able to distill this simple truth into one sentence.

For example: "I led a team conducting a counterdrug operation that the sponsoring organization's CEO recognized as one of the best he has ever seen."

The second step in constructing your story is to define the three elements of your story arc (think of the life cycle of an airplane flight):

- *Takeoff*: Begin with a specific time and place. Describe the main character (could be you) and her or his goal. Once we get the story off the ground with a good takeoff, we get to the flight itself. In our daily lives, we want our flights to be smooth and uneventful. But a story where everything is smooth and uneventful is probably a boring and unbelievable story. Problems and challenges are what make our stories interesting.
- *Turbulence*: Describe the conflict the main character (you) experiences on the journey. It is important the listener can identify with your challenge. Feel free to add drama, detail, and dialogue to bring it to life. Once we successfully navigate the turbulence, we need to bring our listener to the destination. They need to understand where the journey took them and why we decided to take them there.
- *Touchdown*: Resolve the conflict and convey a meaningful message on the moral of the story. Tell how obstacles were overcome and share lessons learned. Make the outcome relevant to the audience. Have a defined end point so the story has an appropriate wrap-up.[2]

For example:

- *Takeoff*: "A couple of years ago, I demonstrated initiative by volunteering my team for a dangerous counterdrug mission in California. Very few similarly sized organizations are selected for such an operation, and I wanted to prove that my team was up to the task."
- *Turbulence*: "While we trained extensively for the effort, we encountered a host of challenges once on-site. Besides operating in territory that was relatively unchartered, there were mountain lions, rattlesnakes, black bears, poison oak, and perhaps worst of all, a member of the wasp family called a meat bee, which, unlike regular bees, can sting and bite repeatedly without dying. Several patrols were disrupted, and I had to send more than a few of my team members to the hospital over the course of the operation."
- *Touchdown*: "In spite of these challenges, I led my team through it without any permanent injuries or losses of equipment. The operation uncovered several methamphetamine labs, and the sponsoring organization's CEO recognized our effort as one of the best he had ever seen. I take great pride in my ability to persevere in such circumstances."

That's it. But for many of us, storytelling is not easy. Like most skills, however, you can improve it with practice. Keep in mind that stories are not speeches; you do not need to memorize them. That's the great thing about sharing a personal story; you already know it because you lived it!

Stories can be a great aid in networking. While networking is not intended to be a formal interview, the stories you will compose will be applicable in both instances. Formally construct your answers to anticipated questions in the manner just described. Your verbiage in responding to questions should be like that used in translating the detail on your résumé. As before, avoid acronyms, military jargon, ranks, and other terminology that civilians may not understand. Responses should be no longer than a minute, followed by a question, asking the individual if there was anything about which you could elaborate. Have a number of these stories prepared to respond to opportunities that highlight your strengths.

★   ★   ★

TROOPS IN THE TRENCHES

"Be patient with people who don't have the same perspective and life experiences as you. You shouldn't expect that any of these people have seen combat or traveled the world as you have."

DAVID USLAN, FORMER AIR FORCE SENIOR MASTER SERGEANT

You will want to practice these responses repeatedly. Applying the military's crawl-walk-run approach, practice these responses with a friendly audience (spouse, roommate) in the crawl phase. In the walk phase, consider participating in speed networking sessions; these will garner you experience with relative strangers in a comparatively non-pressure situation. What is a speed networking session? You likely encounter speed networking opportunities all the time. Here are some examples:

- Job fairs with recruiters from different organizations and other job seekers with whom you can network
- Alumni gatherings where you can network with people who share a similar academic background (e.g., tailgating for an athletic event, reunion, etc.)
- Charity events for a cause you support (e.g., silent auction, golf outing, etc.)
- Children's school activities
- Social events with family and friends (e.g., cocktail party, wedding reception, etc.)

- Community athletic leagues (e.g., bowling, softball, etc.)

As you engage in such activities, don't do so passively. Approach them with a goal in mind. Depending on the situation or what point you may be at in your transition, those goals could take one of several forms:

- Develop your skills:
  - ▶ Practice a smooth and articulate introduction.
  - ▶ Hone your conversation and storytelling skills.
  - ▶ Work on describing your military experiences in ways that are relatable to others without a military background.
- Expand your knowledge:
  - ▶ Learn more about an industry.
  - ▶ Learn about a role or job function.
  - ▶ Learn about a company from someone who works or has worked there.
- Grow your network:
  - ▶ Make a connection with a person who could introduce you to someone in a target company.
  - ▶ Walk away with two new contacts with whom you will follow up.
  - ▶ Identify a potential job lead.

With that in mind, and now that we have some compelling stories to use with our target audiences, let's turn our attention to the process of engaging with them.

The first step is to conduct a final bit of preparation. It is a critical step and requires you to do some research. *Do not* head out to a job fair or career conference without knowing about the organization and, if possible, the individual with whom you will be speaking. Winging it will result in an unacceptable failure rate and result in an unwanted reputation. Some of the individuals you will be engaging with will be high-ranking, and you do not want to be seen as wasting their time. Moreover, effective preparation will separate you from the pack, most of whom will not take the time to sufficiently prepare. This is the time to execute on the phrase you should remember well from the military: Proper preparation prevents poor performance.

So, what does success look like?

At a minimum, successful research enables you to speak intelligently about the organization's and the target individual's backgrounds. You don't want to waste your or their time asking questions that could be easily resolved by doing an online search. Even better, successful research should enable you to ask intelligent questions whose answers help address expected outcomes in your relationship tracker. Optimally, it looks like telling the target individual something about themselves or their organization they may not know. That will definitely leave a positive impression. This sounds like a tall order, but it is truly not that difficult. Many of the organizations with which you will be engaging are sufficiently large that it would be impossible for an individual to know everything about their organization. The point is this: You need to do some homework.

We do this by executing on two parallel paths. The first path is doing your own research. The second path is engaging with your friendlies network to bone up on your target network. Call it your intelligence-gathering phase.

For the organization, check out their website and do an online search. Assuming they are a public company, read their latest annual report from their website or from the SEC's EDGAR database.[3] Check out online news stories within the past six to twelve months that include the organization. Set up Google alerts on the company for news events as they occur. See what other individuals are saying about the organization on the LinkedIn, Glassdoor, and Indeed websites. If you have a personal relationship with someone who works at the organization, ask them for insights into the organization—and perhaps the individual with whom you will be speaking. You will want to understand what the organization is like, how they have performed over the past few years, and what their opportunities for continued growth are. You will want them to describe the culture, career progression possibilities, and opportunities for growth and learning. You will want to understand how they support veterans like yourself who are transitioning from the service. How do they rank on best-of-employer lists? You will also want to keep your ear to the ground for potential red flags, such as high turnover rates or poor ratings by employers on surveys or websites. (Now is *not* the time to discuss compensation or benefits. That will be part of several follow-on conversations and is covered in chapter 9.)

For researching specific individuals, LinkedIn is a great place to start. Most professionals have established pages on LinkedIn, and this is something you will want to establish as well (more on that in a bit). Perhaps you have a friend, a former coworker, or a fellow alumnus who may work at the same organization. They may be able to tell you about the individual in question. You will want to know what to expect from your contact with the target. What is the person like? What kinds of questions should you expect? What idiosyncrasies does this person demonstrate? What should you say or not say to this individual?

Another easy way to gather information on organizations or targets is through alumni organizations. This could be from your high school or college experience. Some high schools and almost all colleges maintain some sort of alumni database with employment and contact information. Call them, explain your background and career search approach, and ask if they can provide you with some contacts at your target(s). Chances are, they can connect you with individuals with whom you have something in common (your school) who could educate you on your intended target.

Further, there are two more direct approaches you should investigate to attain firsthand knowledge of your targeted career field and organization. The first of these is called *informational interviewing*. It involves arranging an interview with someone who works either in your preferred career field and/or at the organization you are seeking to join. The point of conducting these interviews is to find out more about a target industry, company, career field, or role within an organization. It may also involve seeking advice about your career transition. It is most definitely *not* about hiring for a specific job. Accordingly, your interviewee should not be the hiring manager or someone with whom you would expect to be working if you were lucky enough to land a role at that organization.

★   ★   ★

TROOPS IN THE TRENCHES

"Seek a mentor and do as many informational interviews as possible. I learned more from my friends, classmates, and peer informational interviews than I did doing anything else. I'd also recommend networking early. You have to build a network and you have to do it well before getting out. Although I found my job through a career fair, I relied heavily on my network for guidance and potential opportunities."

KEVIN BERRY, FORMER ARMY COLONEL

Here's how it works: Email the interviewee, explain your background and career search approach, and ask if you could have thirty minutes of their time to discuss the dynamics of your preferred career field or the nature of their organization. Chances are, the interviewee will make the time to meet with you. Be as flexible as possible in meeting their schedule availability (be open to conducting this meeting remotely by phone) and, afterward, send them a personal, handwritten thank-you note demonstrating your appreciation for their time and consideration. If there were any action items you committed to during the session, you should follow through on them shortly after the meeting (ideally within twenty-four hours). This will take effort and diligence, but quick response times will make a positive impression on your targets.

★   ★   ★

TROOPS IN THE TRENCHES

"The best part of my transition was learning to network. I got to shadow people and learned what I would like and not like. I ended up connecting with financial services and couldn't have been more excited to start my new job. I found myself in the right place with the right people. Within a year, I was validated as a top performer in the organization. Any self-doubt I had about being successful in the business world went away."

JON SANCHEZ, FORMER NAVY SEAL

The second direct approach for researching your targeted career field or organization is *shadowing*. This is more involved than a simple informational interview. The duration could vary widely, from a few hours to perhaps even a day or longer. The intent is to immerse yourself in the career field or organization for a short period to better understand your fit within either/both. This approach could obviously be combined with informational interviewing. The approach for setting up a shadowing session is very much the same as informational interviewing. It is recommended, however, that you have a personal relationship with the individual you will be shadowing, as you will be requesting a commitment from them (in terms of time and attention) that is out of the ordinary. As with informational interviewing, show your appreciation for those you shadow in some manner immediately after the session. Promptly following through on action items is equally applicable here as well. These relatively simple post-meeting actions alone will help distinguish you from your peers.

Some questions you might consider asking your interviewee during these sessions include:

- How have you been successful?
- What challenges are you and the organization facing?
- What keeps you up at night?

- What do you like about this organization?
- What do you enjoy most about your job?

Finally, and somewhat akin to shadowing, you could also consider a volunteer or temporary role with the organization.[4] If you're having difficulty in making the transition, this could also be a way to gain some experience while filling a potential gap in your résumé. For temporary roles, you should research local temporary agencies before seeking those that might have opportunities.[5] See the Resources page of www.matthewjlouis.com for details on volunteer roles, potential internships, or temporary roles.

★ ★ ★

TROOPS IN THE TRENCHES

"Loosen up. Interviews are not superior officers asking questions. Interviews are discussions with possible employers. Open it up as a conversation. Don't be a fish out of water."

JON SANCHEZ, FORMER NAVY SEAL

All the interviews mentioned above are conversations. The point of these conversations is to have a two-way flow of information. You don't want to find yourself monopolizing the conversation. You seek great conversations with these audiences. So what makes a conversation great? Among other things:

- Both people involved in the conversation are actively engaged.
- Participation is equal; neither person dominates the discussion.
- The conversation is a win-win where both people gain something from it.
- The topic is something in which both people are interested.

Another way in which you must prepare is to put in place a proactive social media strategy. For better or for worse, having an online presence is now a necessary part of any career change. Whether you realize it or not, you already have a social media presence. Prospective employers will simply Google your name and read those search results. That's right. Like it or not, this is how you appear to the outside world. Now if you just choked on your drink, realizing that all that racy Facebook posting you've been doing is fair game in the job search, you have reason to be concerned. Here's the thing: You can proactively control what these prospective employers see, and you should take advantage of that opportunity. Here are a few steps you can—and should—take.

First, and applicable to all transitioning veterans, is to establish a professionally focused social media platform. While there are many platforms, I strongly suggest LinkedIn, the world's largest online professional network. People use LinkedIn to showcase their background and expertise, stay connected with people they know and find new connections, and research jobs, companies, and industries. LinkedIn can help you organize your network and assess gaps. Remember that secondary connections are important. It's not just about who *you* know but who *your connections* know. Companies often use LinkedIn for recruitment and business development. According to their "About Us" page (as of this writing in 2019), LinkedIn has more than 610 million members in over 200 countries and territories. That's a lot of potential professional connections!

★ ★ ★

TROOPS IN THE TRENCHES

"A great way to bolster your connections is through professional networking sites such as LinkedIn. LinkedIn provides free premium memberships to retiring service members. Work on your résumé, being careful to civilianize it with the help of professionals in the industry that you would like to work in. Once that is done, use it to fill out your LinkedIn profile to make it one-stop shopping for potential employers. Then spread the word that you are transitioning. Relationships are key!"

DAVE RAYMOND, FORMER ARMY LIEUTENANT COLONEL

By the way, veterans and their spouses can receive one year of free LinkedIn Premium service, which includes access to over ten thousand LinkedIn learning courses.[6] There is no charge for standard LinkedIn service.

As you set up your LinkedIn account and profile, I suggest you check out the following *leading practices* in doing so:

WRITE A POWERFUL HEADLINE

- Be concise and avoid filler words.
- Be authentic and consistent with your personal brand.
- Include keywords to improve the ability of recruiters to find you when searching.
- Use | or * to divide text to make your headline more readable.
- Avoid using your job title and company. This information is already listed in the experience section of your profile, and your headline should differentiate you from others who have similar titles and/or keywords.
- Do not use all-uppercase letters.
- Do not include a phone number, email address, or URL.

USE A PROFESSIONAL HEADSHOT

- Professional headshots . . .
  - ▶ Are taken at the workplace or a natural location (i.e., no staged or studio shots).

- ▶ Use depth of field to focus on the subject.
- ▶ Use interesting crops, focused around the face.
- ▶ Show natural emotion and an open, approachable body position.
- ▶ Use warm, natural light that fills the entire space to create brightness on the subject and surrounding elements.
- What to avoid:
  - ▶ Selfies
  - ▶ Low-quality images that are grainy or pixelated
  - ▶ Unusual angles or clichéd poses
  - ▶ Filters, black-and-white, or recoloring of the image
  - ▶ White background or taking the photo in front of a window where bright light will wash out the image

CRAFT AN INFORMATIVE SUMMARY

- Describe your background and expertise in an engaging narrative format (unlike a résumé).
- Don't be wordy but take advantage of the fact that this section has the highest character count in the LinkedIn profile template.
- Include who you are as a person (e.g., your interests outside of work).
- Use straightforward language.
- Include your goals.

OPTIMIZE YOUR PROFILE

- *Experience*: Ensure this section is complete, up-to-date, and honest. Do not attempt to stretch the truth. Remember the admonitions above in chapter 4 when we built your résumé.

- *Connections*: Use LinkedIn as a tool to build your network. Search for connections and reach out. Keep connections fresh by periodically sending a note to a person with whom you haven't spoken recently, not to ask for anything, just to reconnect.
- *Skills*: When a person endorses you for a particular skill, it appears in the skills section of your profile. For each skill, your profile also shows the total number of people who have endorsed you. If you feel the skills listed on your profile do not fully or accurately represent your capabilities, add or remove individual items from your list.
- *Groups*: Participating in select groups can lead to new connections and opportunities, but investigate a group before you join it. There are hundreds of thousands of groups on LinkedIn. If you think a particular group might be a good fit for you, click the "Information and Settings" icon next to the Join button and review the "about" data, including the group's demographic statistics.

• • •

Send Personalized Messages. When you use the Connect button, LinkedIn will prepopulate a message with simple, standard text. However, the system also provides an option to customize that text. In connecting with others, you should always personalize your message and clearly articulate why you are reaching out. For example, provide context by including a brief reminder (e.g., "I enjoyed meeting you at the Santa Cruz job fair today") or thank-you (e.g., "I appreciate the time you spent with me on Tuesday discussing your experiences in the telecommunications industry").

Next, you'll want to remove any unwanted content and the associated search results. To do this, you'll need to discover who controls the unwanted content, namely, the website owner (webmaster) at each of those sites. If the unwanted content is on a site you control, delete the content yourself. If the unwanted content resides on a site or page you don't control, you can do a couple of things. If the unwanted content is considered sensitive personal information, you can ask Google to remove it.[7] However, if you want to remove a photo, profile link, or web page from Google search results, your best option is to ask the webmaster to remove the information. Why? Even if Google deletes the site or image from its search results, the web page still exists and can be found through the URL to the site, social media sharing, or other search engines. The webmaster, on the other hand, can remove the page entirely.[8]

A third option for career military professionals is to register your own domain name and set up a simple website. There are several services that do this. Use the search term "register domain name" and peruse the results. This doesn't cost a lot of money, and it allows you to control the content others will see. How you ultimately organize your website is up to you, but at a minimum it should contain your bio or résumé with contact information.

In addition to a social media presence, I recommend a few additional items to ensure your personal brand is well represented in your communications and networking meetings. In no particular order, these include:

- Produce some business cards for yourself. To some this may sound like a terribly old-school way of communicating your contact information, but there are many in the business world who still use them. There are many outlets (FedEx stores, Office Depot, Staples, or their online competitors) that produce them inexpensively. You can also print them at home with the proper paper and printer. These cards should be simple, with your name, phone number, and email address. As with your résumé, avoid the use of military rank on your business card or the use of military references (e.g., ooorah, hotsteel, queenofbattle, etc.) in your email address.
- Format your signature block for email communications in applications such as Microsoft Outlook. For networking

targets who may lose your business card, this may be their only reference point for your contact information. As with your business cards, keep it simple. Include at least your name, phone number, and email address.

- Likewise, format your signature block for smartphone communications. Most phones will allow you to tailor your signature block in a similar manner to email programs.

With your research complete and your LinkedIn profile established, you're now clear to begin sharing your personal brand and well-constructed stories in networking conversations and formal interviews. Engaging your network will likely result in any number of opportunities to apply and/or interview for employment opportunities, the subject of our next two chapters.

KEYS TO SUCCESS

★ Have an action plan for engaging with your networking targets.

★ Schedule time on your calendar to hold yourself accountable to making planned networking appointments.

★ Use well-constructed and rehearsed stories to support your networking. Translate your terminology, much as you did when composing your résumé. You will use these same stories in the next chapter to respond to formal interview questions.

★ Research your networking targets before engaging with them.

★ Send appreciative thank-you notes when others spend time to help you in your research.

★ Diligently follow through on all action items emerging from your networking meetings.

★ Avoid monopolizing conversations. Remember that networking is a two-way street.

★ Have a proactive social media strategy. Google your name and fix those results.

★ Complete a LinkedIn profile. Take advantage of the free year of premium service provided to veterans.

★ Procure a set of business cards for use in networking.

★ Format your signature block on email and smartphone communications.

CHAPTER SEVEN

APPLY
FOR ROLES

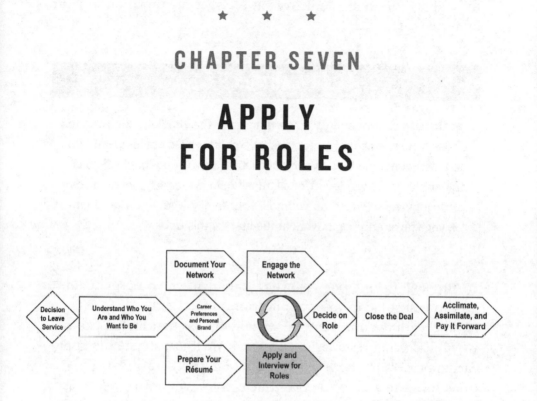

SO NETWORKING HAS LIKELY PRODUCED SOME POTENTIAL OPPORTUNITIES for which you might be interested in applying. Great! The process of doing so, however, has tripped up more than a few applicants. The seemingly administrative nature of the task may lull them into a sense of complacency. Don't let this happen to you. Now is not the time to let up by assuming unimportance. Diligence in the application stage is the only way to progress to the interview stage, where decisions regarding your fit for potential roles take place.

In this chapter, we will discuss:

- Differences between the federal and civilian application processes
- Applying for available roles

By the end of this chapter, you should be prepared to successfully apply for an available role at a target organization in your preferred career field.

CAUTION

At the risk of repeating the warning from the previous chapter, to those readers who may be looking for a shortcut: Do not jump straight to this chapter and begin your work. Doing so will not enable the sustainable success we desire for all transitioning veterans, their families, and employers. Please do yourself, your family, and your future employer a favor and begin work at the start of this book.

Although the interview is what you are after, you usually must go through some form of application process either before or in parallel with the interview. So we will discuss that first. As above, when discussing résumés in chapter 4, we'll investigate the application process for both federal roles and civilian roles. (Applications for state and local government roles will not be addressed, given their high degree of variability. However, see my website [www.matthewjlouis.com] for a list of veteran employment services websites for all states and territories.) After reviewing the application processes, we will dive into detail on interviews, the make-or-break part of the hiring process.

★

APPLICATIONS FOR FEDERAL ROLES

Before applying for federal roles, make sure you understand the required qualifications, knowledge, skills, and abilities to be eligible for specific pay levels. The Office of Personnel Management (OPM) offers some handy functional guides that provide precisely that for GS roles.[1]

There are also some important facts to understand about the federal hiring process:

- The federal government has a standard job application. Your résumé is your application.
- Hiring agencies use the job announcement to describe the job and list the required qualifications and responsibilities.
- After applying, the hiring agency uses the information in your résumé to verify if you have the required qualifications stated in the job announcement.
- Once the hiring agency has determined who is qualified, they may use other assessments, such as interviews or testing, to determine the best qualified applicants.

So how does the federal government hiring process work? See Figure 7-1 for a summary:

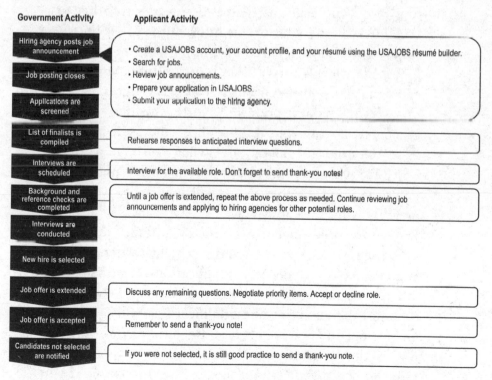

Figure 7-1. Federal government hiring process.

Let's walk through the steps of the hiring process from the standpoint of the applicant. In order, USAJOBS recommends you do the following:[2]

1. Create a USAJOBS account and your résumé (covered in chapter 4). You will need to create an account and complete your profile to apply to any job on USAJOBS. With a USAJOBS account and profile you can:
   - Save the jobs you're interested in.
   - Save and automate job searches.
   - Upload résumés or create one using their résumé builder.
   - Upload and save required documents.
   - Apply to any job announcement on USAJOBS.

2. Search for jobs. Once you create your account, you can begin searching for available jobs. In doing so, it's best to sign into your account before doing a search because USAJOBS can use your profile information to produce job search results more tailored to your profile. You can search for jobs in various ways (basic, advanced, or map search), and you can use different filters (such as geographic location, desired salary, preferred work schedule, or hiring agency) to narrow your results. Those filters effectively act as search criteria for you, and when you save a search, USAJOBS will automatically look for jobs that match what you're looking for and can email you daily, weekly, or monthly with those jobs.

3. Review job announcements. Once you find a job you're interested in, review the announcement to determine if you're eligible and meet the qualifications. Read the entire job announcement before starting your application; for each job there are specific qualifications you must meet and include in your application. Read the "Who May Apply" section to determine if you're eligible to apply for the position. Read the "Qualifications" section to see if you

meet the qualifications of the position. If you have questions about the job, contact the agency representative listed at the bottom of the announcement.

4. Prepare your application in USAJOBS. Read the "How to Apply" section of the job announcement before starting your application. USAJOBS will walk you through a five-step process to prepare your application, including attaching a résumé and other required documents. During the process you can review, edit, delete, and update your information. The site will automatically save your progress as you go, so you won't lose any changes. If the agency does not accept uploaded résumés or documents, you will skip this step during the USAJOBS application process. You may be asked to upload a résumé when you enter the agency application system. Federal experience includes positions you have held as a civilian employee paid by an agency of the federal government. The pay plan, series, and grade fields refer to executive branch competitive positions and are not mandatory fields. If your experience does not fit, simply leave those fields blank. Note: *Active duty military experience or experience working for a private contractor of the US government does not qualify as a federal position for this purpose.*

5. Submit your application to the hiring agency. Once your application is ready, you'll be transferred from USAJOBS to the agency application system. You may need to complete additional agency-required steps such as:
   - Providing more personal information
   - Providing more documentation
   - Answering eligibility questions
   - Completing an occupational questionnaire

   After you submit your application, go back to your USAJOBS account and make sure the hiring agency received your application. You can see status updates in the "Application" section of your account. Be patient. It may take a few hours after you complete your application for the agency to update your application status. You may also receive an email confirmation from the agency application system, but not all agencies send confirmations.

6. The hiring agency reviews your application. Once the job announcement is closed, the hiring agency will review your application to make sure you're eligible and meet the qualifications for the position. The hiring agency will place applicants into quality categories:
   * Minimum qualified
   * Highest qualified

   The hiring agency may update your application status to "Reviewed," but not all agencies provide this status. After all applications are reviewed, the hiring agency will send the highest-qualified applicants to the hiring official; these applicants will see a "Referred" status in their application status. Applicants not being considered will see a "Not Referred" status.

7. Interview for the available role. The hiring official will review applications and select the applicants to interview based on the hiring agency's policy. Hiring officials can interview applicants using:
   * A panel
   * In-person
   * Video
   * Phone

   The hiring agency will contact applicants directly to schedule interviews. Tips for conducting the interview itself are featured in the section below.

   Note: The "Work Experience" portion of the résumé and the interview tend to be the two main determinants of your qualifications for the job opportunity in the eyes of the hiring agency.[3]

8. Candidate selection. After interviewing applicants, the hiring agency will select a candidate and contact them to start

the job offer process. The hiring agency will notify applicants who were not selected by updating their application
status to "Not Selected."

9. Job offer. The hiring agency will extend a tentative job
offer contingent upon the applicant's passing a background
investigation. The job offer is only final when the background investigation and any additional security checks
are successfully completed. Once the job offer is accepted
by the candidate, the hiring agency will contact the candidate directly to set up a start date.

★

APPLICATIONS FOR CIVILIAN ROLES

In contrast to the federal application process, the civilian application process is not necessarily a requirement for securing a role,
and it is not consistently structured from organization to organization. In fact, I suggest you adopt a strategy that *avoids* the formal application process at an organization. Apply the strategies
recommended in chapter 6: Utilize friendly relationships to connect with targeted relationships and relate your value proposition.
If you simply go through an organization's application process,
you will run into a process that is designed to screen you out at
every step, which I will describe below.

Regardless of which strategy you take, you will ultimately have
to interact with some portions of the application process. In comparison to the federal model, the civilian corollary is so much more
variable as to almost not represent a process whatsoever. That does
not make the process unimportant; it is just that the process varies
significantly from company to company. You will note the process
contains any number of screens that could act as potential hazards.
There is good reason for this. The cost of employee turnover is
very significant and has gradually increased over time. As a result,

companies are taking strides to minimize it. One way in which employers minimize the cost of employee turnover is to ensure new employees are a good fit with the organization and will remain with the company for the foreseeable future. The general approach to hiring, then, tends to contain the following elements:

- *Completion of a Formal Application of Some Sort*: Most applications are online these days, but some may still be found in a hard-copy format. Consider any application both a permanent record and a tool with which an employer can eliminate you. Attention to detail on its completion is critical. You will never secure an interview if you don't show up on the application as someone the employer wants to hire. Even though you may be submitting a résumé along with the application, you should assume the application itself may stand alone as its own document.
  - ▶ Here is some advice for approaching a hard-copy version of a job application:[4]
    - When retrieving the form from the employer, dress as you would if you were being interviewed. There is an outside chance you could be interviewed on the spot.
    - Either take two copies of the form or make a copy of the form you procure. Use the first to draft your responses. Use the second to produce an error-free document to submit.
    - Type your responses if you can. If you must write your responses by hand, write neatly.
    - Attach your résumé to the application form.
    - Sign and date the application.
  - ▶ This advice applies to all job application formats:[5]
    - Read the instructions carefully and follow them completely. Consider this your first test.
    - If you can't follow instructions, there will likely be no interview.

- Use black ink to complete or print the form. This will enable clear copies of the original document and present a more professional appearance.
- Answer each question. If one truly does not apply, then respond with "not applicable."
- Complete all sections of the application, which may require some additional research. Take the time and do it right.
- Include *all* former employers, even if you were fired.
- Translate specific military terms into terms civilians can understand.
- Be as specific as possible about the details of your skills and qualifications, which may include interests or hobbies relevant to the role.
- Avoid abbreviations.
- Handle sensitive questions with tact. Some examples:
  - ▶ Salary: Say "Negotiable" or "Will discuss in the interview" or "Commensurate with the skills and responsibilities of the role." Worst case, respond with a reasonable range based on your research.
  - ▶ Reason for leaving previous job: Say "Seeking a career in [insert name] industry." Keep it positive.
  - ▶ Location: Although you may have geographic preferences, you want to emphasize your flexibility. Say "open" or, worst case, a region of the country.
  - ▶ Criminal charges: You should be open and honest on all details. Whatever you state here should be corroborated by the background check the employer will certainly do (see below).

- Double-check for correct grammar, punctuation, and spelling. Have a trusted advisor proofread the application.
- *Background, Employment, Reference, and/or Credit Checks*: Prospective employers may conduct one or more of these checks either prior to or following a formal job offer. Regardless, the point of doing them is always the same: to validate the information you have shared on your application or résumé—or during an interview—and should they not match, act as a screening tool. Armed with the following information, you will be able to turn these potential screening devices into yet another opportunity to shine. Here is some detail on each and how to prepare for them:
  - ▶ *Background Checks*: The range of items from your application and résumé that an employee might check could range from nothing to everything. You should assume the employer will check *all* details and follow up with *all* provided references. The optimal way to avoid issues here is to be truthful. That said, you needn't necessarily provide exquisite levels of detail if it is not called for. For example:
    - Use years (versus months and years) to reflect the duration of time in a role to avoid the appearance of an employment gap (if there is one).
    - Emphasize skill sets acquired through any means possible if skills applied in your most recent roles don't seem to directly translate to the open position to which you are applying. Hobbies, volunteering work, or pro bono efforts are all legitimate ways to demonstrate experience in a given skill set.
  - ▶ *Employment eligibility form (Form I-9)*. This is a standard government form that all US employers must complete on all employees. According to the US

Citizenship and Immigration Services, "Form I-9 is used for verifying the identity and employment authorization of individuals hired for employment in the United States. All US employers must ensure proper completion of Form I-9 for everyone they hire for employment in the United States. . . . On the form, an employee must attest to his or her employment authorization. The employee must also present his or her employer with acceptable documents evidencing identity and employment authorization."[6] If the form cannot be truthfully completed, you cannot be employed in the United States.

▶ *Reference Checks*: Prospective employers conduct reference checks to verify your performance and authenticity as a candidate. Prospective employers may or may not request these. Unless they do, there is no reason to volunteer them. As stated in the résumé section, please don't state "references available upon request" on your résumé. Reference checks tend to be a more standard part of the federal hiring process than the civilian counterpart, and they may or may not be conducted as part of the above background checks. When employers request a list of your personal or professional references and follow up with them, there is little limit to what they might ask. Although the policies of former employers prevent them from sharing many details beyond your last position and salary, most individuals, when asked, will end up sharing more than that. To perform optimally in this area, you might consider several actions:

- Pull together a list of only those individuals from your professional background to act as a reference who are familiar with your career accomplishments to date and will consistently sing your praises. Avoid listing personal references unless they are specifically requested.

- Proactively reach out to those individuals whose names you plan on supplying to your prospective employer. Ask them for permission to use them as a professional reference. Make them aware of the call they might receive and the questions they might be asked. Feel free to ask them to highlight specific experiences or skill sets you are trying to emphasize with the employer.

- Only supply your prospective employer the names of those professional references you have listed above and from whom you have secured approval. Only supply the number of references the employer requests, not more, not less. Doing otherwise demonstrates you don't know how to follow instructions. Provide this list on a page with the following line as a header: "Professional References for [Enter Your Name]." List the names and contact information of each reference with a space in between each. If supplying the list in hard-copy format, use the identical paper and font size/type/color as your résumé.

- If you are concerned about a reference (a former supervisor, perhaps) potentially providing a less-than-optimal review, you can hire a professional reference checker to proactively verify your hypothesis before providing that individual's name to the employer. If this cannot be avoided (perhaps you had to provide the prospective employer the name of a previous supervisor on the employment application), you should proactively call that individual yourself and ask for their cooperation with this process.

- Upon completion of the reference checks, send a thank-you note to your references to express your gratitude.

  ▶ *Credit Checks*: Credit checks enable employers to learn about your financial background and your personal ability to manage money. Running a credit check will enable your prospective employer to confirm much about you: your name(s), previous addresses, and debts you have incurred over time. These debts could include credit card debt, mortgage debt, car loan debt, and any student or other types of loans. Moreover, the employer would learn about your payment history on all the above debts, including information on any late payments or loan defaults. The best way to address any potential negativity associated with this report is to run a credit report on yourself right now (multiple outlets allow a free report to be pulled annually) and proactively address any potential negative or inaccurate information contained in the report. You should do this little exercise on an annual basis to maintain a clean report.

- *A Talent Assessment and/or Drug Test of Some Sort*: Many employers conduct talent (or skills or personality) assessments on potential employees. For similar reasons noted above (avoiding turnover), employers want to ensure a best fit for prospective talent. These tests are usually conducted online either before or after personal interviews. And you may or may not learn how you performed on the test. For the best outcome, answer the questions honestly and don't try to game the test. Regarding drug testing, these days most companies perform them as a matter of course and, in some industries, may be required by law to do so. Coming from the military, you are likely aware of the nature of drug testing and likely participated in the administration of various drug tests to those in your charge. Suffice it to say there are many kinds of tests available to employers, and passing whichever one they choose to administer is typically a condition of employment.

- *Any Number of Interviews, Conducted in One of Many Formats*: There are several types of interviews, and they tend to follow a rather predictable pattern, but one that has much variability in format. The typical sequence you might experience is an initial screening interview, followed by one or more formal interviews and perhaps one or more informal interviews. Although screening interviews tend to be done over the phone or via Skype, and formal and informal interviews tend to be in person, there can be much variability in an employer's approach, depending on its industry or cultural norms. For example, some companies prefer to do panel interviews, where you are interviewed by multiple people simultaneously. Those interviewing for management consulting roles should expect case studies to be part of their interviews. Interviews with Silicon Valley employers may be less formal than interviews with investment banking companies. Regardless of the interview type or format, their purpose is the same: to ensure you are a best fit for the organization and vice versa. What does *fit* mean exactly? The best definition I've found describes *fit* as (1) your ability to perform the role for which you are applying, (2) the level of interest you express in desiring to attain the role, and (3) the degree to which you can build and maintain rapport with those within the prospective organization.[7] The next chapter goes into much further detail on this topic and provides some advice for acing your interviews.
- *A Formal Job Offer and, If Accepted, an Onboarding Process of Some Sort*: Job offers normally have two steps. The first step is typically a phone call or email to let you know that an offer will be forthcoming. The second is the

actual offer in either email or hard-copy form. It will usually contain information such as your role, starting salary, and start date. Upon consideration, you may decide to accept or decline the offer. If you accept the offer, there will be several forms to complete, which will include at a minimum your I-9 form and tax-withholding paperwork for federal (your W-4 form), state, and locality, if applicable. Each organization has its own process and may include initial enrollment in all applicable benefits. We will go into further detail on these topics in the next two chapters.

APPLICANT TRACKING SYSTEMS

As introduced in chapter 4, applicant tracking systems (ATS) exist to help employers, not you. You should not view them as your friend. Part of their purpose is to screen out candidates. Your best strategy for dealing with ATS systems is to avoid them entirely. You can do so by networking your way into an interview for a role based on your established relationships. This is further evidence of the value you will realize from engaging with the network, as discussed in the previous chapter.

★   ★   ★

TROOPS IN THE TRENCHES

"You have to understand that people hire people—not systems. Talk to people in the company, not some online application system. It doesn't matter how talented you are; application systems will reject your résumé."

TRAVIS LONG, FORMER NAVY PETTY OFFICER

So that's the application process. You probably noticed lots of caveats for the civilian version of the process. That's because the reality is that no two companies are alike when it comes to their application process. Interviews, while they certainly have some variability in their content and format, tend to take on a slightly more consistent feel. As the most important part of the application process, interviews require a detailed review so you can be optimally prepared.

And that's the subject of our next chapter.

KEYS TO SUCCESS

★ Treat the application as if it were the only qualifying factor in the hiring manager's decision-making process.

★ For civilian roles, avoid the standard application process if possible by leveraging your network to secure potential interviewing opportunities.

★ ★ ★

CHAPTER EIGHT

INTERVIEW FOR ROLES

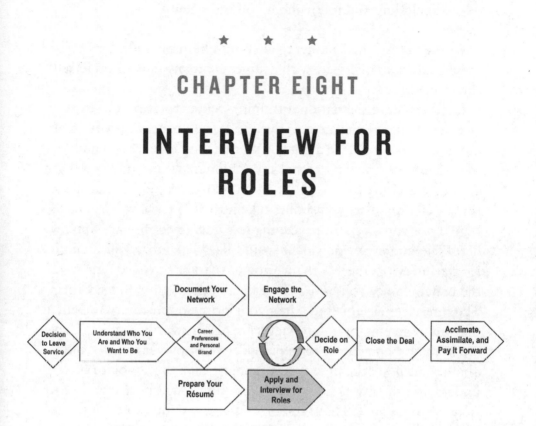

BY NOW, YOU'VE PUT IN A LOT WORK NETWORKING AND SUBMITTING APPLICA-
tions to secure a formal interview with a prospective employer.
Trust me when I tell you it will be time well spent. Now it is show-
time. We won't go live instantaneously, however. We will take a
crawl-walk-run approach to this, much as we did with any task in
the military. If you ever did a live-fire exercise, went to a gunnery,
or deployed to a combat training center, those missions were not
accomplished without a lot of preparation. Same thing here. Interviews can be make-or-break experiences for your candidacy for an
opportunity, so we must be fully prepared.

In this chapter, we will discuss:

- Preparing for, rehearsing, and conducting interviews

• Concluding and following up on interviews

By the end of this chapter, you should be prepared to success-fully conduct an interview with a target company in your preferred career field.

Interviews are the national training center rotation or sea ser-vice deployment equivalent of the application process. If you treat it as such, you will have a much better chance at success. Think of the amount of time and preparation, blood, sweat, and tears that go into preparing for a rotation at a combat training center. That is the exact mind-set you should take into an interview. The adage "the more you sweat in peace, the less you bleed in war" applies here. The interview equivalent would be, "The more you prepare for the interview, the less chance you have to be screened out—and the better chance you have to receive an offer." Why do I say this? The interview is game time. It is your prime opportunity to shine in front of an employer. Interviews are also a two-way street. They are both an opportunity for a prospective employer to learn more about your potential fit in their organization and for you to better understand the inverse. Just as the employer will be asking ques-tions of you, you will have opportunities to ask questions of them. It is the culmination of all your work to date and will likely be the primary deciding factor by the company whether to bring you on and by you as to whether you feel the employer is a good fit. So let's break it down.

Interview Preparation: I'll repeat a phrase you've surely heard in the military: Proper preparation prevents poor performance. It cer-tainly applies here. You will want to undertake several activities before you step in front of a prospective employer.

Document: First, ensure that you've catalogued all your experi-ences to date, along with related accomplishments and lessons learned. You've already done some of this in producing your ré-sumé. But this is a more thorough review of your past, coupled with the same critical mind-set an interviewer would take. This collection of evidence will provide the raw materials that, when combined with your research of the organization and its individuals, will lead to excellent answers to interview questions. In *101 Great Answers to the Toughest Interview Questions*, Ron Fry described a research approach that I suggest you adopt and build upon.[1] For every professional, academic, or volunteer role you have assumed, document the following:

- Name and contact information of the organization
- Name and contact information of supervisors and peers (these would act as potential references)
- Time frame and duration of role
- Hours worked and compensation realized
- Duties and responsibilities of your role
- Personal strengths and transferable skills utilized in the role
- Quantifiable results driven by your personal actions
- Awards, recognition, honors, accomplishments realized
- Training, certification, degrees, or licenses accumulated during the role
- Failures experienced or challenges overcome, along with lessons learned

For those of you with more time in service, this list will be voluminous. That's perfect. At this stage, the more raw materials you have, the better.

Research: You must do your homework on the organization, the individuals who might be interviewing you, and the requirements of the job. You should strive to walk into your interview knowing as much as you can about all of them. Your work from earlier steps in the process to (1) decide on a career path in chapter 2 and (2) engage with your network in chapter 6 will greatly enable this task. Researching your objective may be new to you, but if you liken it to intelligence preparation of the battlefield, you will better understand why we do it.

Let's start with the target organization. Some basic information you want to understand and suggestions about where you might find that information are featured in Table 8-1:

NEEDED INFORMATION	RATIONALE	SOURCE OF INFORMATION
FOR GOVERNMENT AGENCIES		
Agency background	Understand agency history; its purpose; its legislative or executive authority; its programs and activities; and information, addresses, and phone numbers to find information on contracts and grants, employment, and publications.	Agency website or US Government Manual[2]
FOR ALL NON-GOVERNMENT ORGANIZATION TYPES		
Recent news	Understand what may be late-breaking, hot-button issues with which the organization may be dealing.	Set up a Google alert to deliver regular updates on the organization to your email address.
Third-party analysis	Understand what industry experts outside the organization are saying about the organization's current performance and plans.	Google the company's name but also check out websites such as D&B Hoovers or Dun & Bradstreet. These are both subscription services, and most libraries have licenses to them.
Occupational trends	Understand projections for the duties, education, training, and pay associated with specific occupations.	Bureau of Labor Statistics' Occupational Outlook Handbook[3]
Insider insights	Understand how individuals who have worked at the organization view the organization, salary ranges, and benefits package for your target role.	Best source for accurate facts is your personal network. Accounts provided on websites mentioned here are not corroborated: Glassdoor, Indeed, Vault, and Salary Expert. Remember to factor cost-of-living adjustments into any salary estimate.

Table 8-1. Types of business research.

NEEDED INFORMATION	RATIONALE	SOURCE OF INFORMATION
FOR PUBLIC COMPANIES		
Annual Report	Provides senior management's point of view on organizational performance, strategic plans, financial results, and competitive dynamics within the industry.	Company website or the SEC's EDGAR database. On the EDGAR site, 10-K reports are the official filing of the organization's annual report with the SEC; 10-Q reports are their quarterly equivalent. Seek the latest 10-K filing and the 10-Q reports filed since then.
FOR PRIVATE COMPANIES		
As much information as possible	Private companies are more difficult to research than public companies because they do not report to the SEC.	Company website or Library of Congress and the additional resources that they suggest
FOR NONPROFIT ORGANIZATIONS		
Form 990, organizational history, purpose, performance, and plans	Understand organizational mission and purpose, financial performance and stability, and plans.	Organization's website or one of several additional resources: The National Center for Charitable Statistics, GuideStar, or Charity Navigator

Table 8-1. Types of business research (*continued*).

Another site worth checking out is the library at Stanford University's Graduate School of Business, which has collated many free websites, generally organized by subject, for researching businesses.[4] In fact, most libraries remain great sources of information and likely have licenses to some of the subscription services noted above. If you're looking to avoid costs, take advantage of what libraries have to offer.

FEDERAL RESEARCH

Other than LinkedIn, there are a couple of subscription services that will provide detailed contact information and background on both individuals and agencies. You might check out LegiStorm or CQ Roll Call.

One of the more elusive things I suggest you research is the organization's culture. An organization's culture represents the shared beliefs that drive behavior within the organization. It manifests itself in the way things get done on a regular basis within the organization: how work gets done, who gets rewarded, what gets prioritized, etc. The culture of an organization, and your ability to successfully interact with it, may well determine your tenure at the organization. It is not something you will be able to overcome, so you should understand if you will be able to live with it. TheBalance.com provides some insight into what you should be asking your network about in order to better understand the culture of your target organization.[5] Career websites can also be helpful in suggesting additional details to research as well as acting as a source for that additional information. TheMuse.com and Glassdoor offer some options.[6]

Next, you'll want to research the individual(s) who will be interviewing you. When the prospective employer calls to schedule the interview, you should ask for the names of the individuals with whom you'll be interviewing. LinkedIn is a great resource for initial research, as is Google. Also, always remember to engage with your personal network; they or their friends may have some intelligence that could prove beneficial.

★   ★   ★

TROOPS IN THE TRENCHES

"I went in for what I thought was a networking opportunity. The target turned the discussion into an interview on the spot. I hadn't done my research to understand who this person was and how his background might influence the conversation. Suffice it to say, it did not go well. But I learned I needed to be prepared for all meetings, even those I might perceive to be inconsequential."

FORMER ARMY COLONEL

A final bit of research I'd recommend is to effectively reverse engineer the upcoming interview. You would do this by thoroughly researching the job description. In reading the description, make a list of the personal strengths or transferable skills required to succeed in this role. Once that list is compiled, you can easily come up with several questions regarding each of those skill requirements. For example, if one of the required skills is team leadership, you would generate a few questions designed to test whether you are proficient at that skill. One of those questions might be, "Tell me about a time where you demonstrated team leadership." You would then generate a list of answers to those questions and rehearse the answers as noted below.

Rehearse: Once you've done your homework, you will want to rehearse your answers to the interview questions you should expect. To get a sense of specific questions—beyond those identified above—check out what recent interviewees may have posted on Glassdoor.com for interviews with your target company (see the "Interviews" or "Company Overview" pages). If your target is in consulting, accounting, banking, or law, the Vault.com might be a good resource as well (see the "Employee Review" portion of the "Research Companies" page for your target). In general, you should be prepared to handle any number of situational or behavioral questions. If you are considering professional services, you should expect case studies to be part of the interview. If you are unfamiliar with case studies, you will absolutely want to prepare for them. Use the online search phrase "case interview guides" and you will find several, with some free versions offered by colleges and some fee-based.

For a list of specific questions, there are many online. TheMuse.com and TheBalance.com provide good samples.[7] I also have several additional resources on my website (www.matthew-jlouis.com). While I was going through my transition, my wife quizzed me nightly on questions from several of these resources. You might consider a similar tactic. Regardless of the sources you ultimately research, I would add the following points of emphasis:

- By and large, you didn't have to interview for positions in the military. You were assigned them. This is likely new to you, and it will take much practice to be successful. Commit to being a success.
- Rehearse responses to all the questions you deem applicable with a civilian outside of the military, preferably one who is familiar with the industry of your target organization (this is another area where your network can pay big dividends).
- Time your answers to last between thirty and ninety seconds. There are always exceptions, but try not to say too much or too little. Also, in sequencing the content of your response, put the most important, most relevant, or most impressive information up front. This is especially true when interviewing with senior leaders, who tend to have short attention spans.
- An easy method to remember for formulating your responses to most résumé-based questions is the STAR method, which stands for situation, task, action, and result. Those four words should frame your responses and help tell a story. For example, in response to a "Tell me about a time when . . ." question, you would respond with:
    - *Situation*: Spend less than twenty-five seconds teeing up the basic facts of the case, providing the necessary context for the issue you will describe resolving.
    - *Task*: Spend less than twenty-five seconds describing the issue or problem posed by the situation.
    - *Action*: Spend less than twenty-five seconds describing the action you (not the team) took in dealing with the issue or problem.

- ► *Result(s)*: Spend less than twenty-five seconds detailing the quantifiable outcomes of your specific actions.
- As with writing résumés, translate all military terminology into verbiage the 99.5 percent of the population who hasn't served can understand. This will be frustrating but can be overcome with practice.
  - ► Use "I" instead of "we."
  - ► Avoid military acronyms.
  - ► Avoid military sayings, call signs, or courtesies; for example, roger, over, out, check, yes/no ma'am/sir, too easy.
  - ► Absolutely no cursing or acronyms that refer to cursing. You know the ones (CF, NFW, AFU, etc.).
  - ► Use a twelve-hour clock to refer to time, not a twenty-four-hour clock.
- Use declarative sentences without qualifiers that leverage the strengths exercises from earlier in the book. Emphasize how what you did in the military aligns with those strengths.
- Expect questions about how your military experience would apply in the target organization. Again, interviewers will likely have little appreciation for this. You will have to educate them in language they can understand. In helping them, you will be helping yourself.
- Be prepared to explain why you are leaving the military and looking for a career at the target organization. Leverage the value proposition and elevator speech we developed in chapter 3.
- Be prepared to speak to the failures you have experienced. Veterans don't tend to dwell on failures or weaknesses, but it will be important to the prospective employer that you know yourself well enough to identify them and that you have acted to understand root causes and address them through some plan of continuous improvement or remediation.

★ ★ ★

TROOPS IN THE TRENCHES

"From my perspective, career fairs provided invaluable opportunities to establish contact and have a conversation with potential employers. These interactions served as a key step in the research process for targeting companies."

DAN HODNE, FORMER ARMY COLONEL

A great way to combine both research and rehearsal is to attend job fairs or career conferences. We discussed these as networking options in chapter 6, but they serve an additional purpose here. Both are great opportunities to gain firsthand knowledge about target organizations or career fields. At these events, you are surrounded by hiring representatives from each attending organization, as well as any number of peers undergoing the same career transition as you. This is a prime opportunity to both practice your interviewing skills, gain some market intelligence about your preferred career field(s), and to further expand your personal network. Some job fairs or career conferences targeted at veterans include:

- VA for Vets hiring events
  - ▶ Includes Hiring Our Heroes and DAV events
- Recruit Military veteran job fairs
- VetJobs career fairs
- Service Academy Career Conferences

In addition to preparing answers for any number of questions from your prospective employer, you will want to come prepared with your own list of questions for the employer. Don't forget: An interview is also your opportunity to query the employer on items you need to understand to make an informed decision about which organization to join. Target your questions around your primary decision-making criteria. Your opportunity to ask these questions typically comes at the end of the interview. The questions you ask should be based on all the information you've gleaned to date and during the interview itself. Assume that you will have time to ask no more than three questions, so don't waste your time asking about things that you can find online. Review some of the interview-related resources on my website (www.matthewjlouis .com), which offer additional thoughts on the matter.

In addition to those questions, you might inquire about the kinds of resources or support groups available for veterans within the organization. How active are they? How many employees are involved? At what level in the organization are these resources sponsored? To the extent that these kinds of resources exist, they will help smooth your transition and improve the likelihood that you will remain with this chosen employer for a considerable time.

Wardrobe: The next bit of preparation you'll need is to get your wardrobe in order. Chances are you have a closet full of military garb and very few civilian business clothes. This will need to change. You'll still want to maintain a basic set of uniforms for wear during reserve duty or various retirement-related ceremonies, but by and large you will now be able to downsize the amount of gear in your closet. You will replace this with a basic set of civilian business dress. The amount and type of dress you ultimately accumulate will depend on your chosen place of employment (some employers dress more casually than others), but you will need some essentials during the interviewing phase.

★ ★ ★

TROOPS IN THE TRENCHES

"Update your wardrobe. It's easy to get lost in the cultural gulf that is the military. Whether it was three years or thirty, it is such an isolating place. It is such an insular culture. We joke about the time

machine effect, with people dressing in styles that were popular
when they entered the service, even decades later. I think this is
magnified for senior NCOs or senior officers who were even more
immersed in the culture."

PERRY JEFFERIES, FORMER ARMY FIRST SERGEANT

———————

Remember the finding from chapter 3 that the visual aspects of communication account for 55 percent of the impact a communication opportunity has on an audience? Your personal appearance has an awful lot to do with the visual aspects of your communication. This is very important. As the saying goes, you never get a second chance to make a first impression.

While this will likely require an outlay of some amount of cash, you need not go high on the hog. If you have some secondhand clothes you could tailor to fit nicely, so much the better. Most of you, however, will be looking at a retail store of some sort, where an experienced salesperson will help guide you. How much to budget for these purchases will vary, but I advise investing in the highest level of quality of goods you can afford. After all, if you're not willing to invest in yourself, why should anyone else?

So let's talk basics, not fashion, just the basics. Standard old-school, conservative business dress wins the day in almost all instances. Save your higher-order fashion sense for some time in the future. Your appearance should be professional and understated. You want the interviewer to remember what you said, not how you looked. Also, as a rule, your dress for interviewing at any organization should be one level above whatever that organization's dress code is. If their dress is normally casual, you would dress in business casual garb. If their dress is business casual, you would dress in business formal garb. If you're not clear on what the organization's dress code is, call the HR department or leverage your personal network. There are several guides to the basic-issue items you will want to procure if they don't already exist in your closet.[8] You'll also find a list on my website (www .matthewjlouis.com).

Grooming: Coming from the military, it is easy to get stereo-typed as a "high-speed, low-drag super trooper" if you come into the interview with a fresh high-and-tight haircut. That may not carry the day in a civilian environment. The overriding rule, again, is to assume a professional, understated civilian appearance. The length of your hair should resemble what it looks like the day before you would normally get your haircut. Also, while you might be proud of your tattoos, piercings, and other forms of body art, an interview is not the place to show them off. Keep such things under wraps. Your nails should be trimmed and neat or polished in subtle hues that don't distract. Avoid too much cologne or per-fume. Makeup should be simple; avoid bright colors or a heavy application.

Travel and Day of Interview: If you must travel for the inter-view, I recommend arriving the night before. This effectively guar-antees you will be present on the day of the interview, allows you to reconnoiter the location of the interview, and enables you to get a good night's rest prior to the interview—all of which are impor-tant. If the company provides a host for your visit, this tactic will enable you to have dinner with this individual and ask some last-minute questions. The more intelligence you have about the organization before engaging with a hiring manager, the better. (Note this dinner engagement may require an additional set of clothing beyond what you have packed for the interview. Treat the dinner dress as a step below the interview dress requirement; that is, if the interview requires formal business dress, assume the din-ner dress is business casual. When in doubt, ask.) Before you turn in for the night, iron your suit, shirt/blouse, and tie/scarf so you don't need to bother with it in the morning.

On the day of the interview, you'll want to burn off some excess energy with a morning run or some other form of exercise. This gets the blood flowing and prepares the brain for optimal engage-ment. Have a balanced breakfast and depart in time to arrive at least ten minutes early of your appointed time. Be kind and courteous and connect with all of those with whom you interact at the company. Sometimes even the receptionist is asked to weigh in on your manners and behavior while you are waiting for the interview.

Interview Conduct: Any military mission you've undertaken likely involved some amount of reconnaissance. Knowing what to expect when you enter a room to be interviewed is invaluable. Knowledge is power. So let's review the mechanics of conducting the various interview types and formats in which they take place—and what you can do to prepare for them.

Screening Interview: As mentioned above, the first interview is normally a screening interview that might take place over the phone or Skype. They are normally conducted by HR or some screening entity other than the hiring manager to ensure you meet the basic qualifications of the role to which you are applying. Beyond that, the main purpose of the screening interview is to do just that: screen you out of competing for the role. They ask basic questions during these screening interviews. Some are more administrative ("What is your current compensation?"). Some are more behavioral ("Tell me about a time when you demonstrated [some required skill]"). Some are situational ("What would you do if confronted with [some scenario]?"). Your simple goal in passing the screening interview is to secure a formal in-person interview with the hiring manager. Here are some tips for passing this first interview:

- To the extent you can, schedule the interview at a time when you can focus exclusively on the interview. If you get surprised by an on-the-spot call from an employer, ask if you can schedule the conversation at a more convenient time. But do so in the very near future; you don't want the opportunity to slip away. If that's not possible, make the best of it by applying the following tips.
- Prepare for and treat the screening interview no differently than you would a formal interview, even if it is

over Skype. This includes your dress, your posture, and your attitude.

- Find a private setting in which to conduct the interview that is free of distractions. Turn off your phones and shut down any distracting apps on your computer. Put a Do Not Disturb sign outside your door.

- Test your Skype app, if that is how the interview will be conducted. Clear the background in the room of any distracting or potentially offensive materials. Rehearse your responses over Skype with a trusted friend so you get used to looking at the interviewer and not your own reflection.

- Have a pen, a sharpened pencil (in case the pen runs out of ink), and paper at the ready. Some interviews may require you to have a calculator or a computer at your disposal, especially if you are interviewing for a technical role. Take notes as needed and refer to them later when writing your thank-you note.

- Have a copy of your résumé and application handy in case specific questions are asked about portions of them.

- Take some time to break the ice with small talk at the beginning of the interview. With your military background, you may be tempted to cut to the chase and dive right in. Presumably, you will have done your research, so take the opportunity to highlight something that impressed you about the individual or something you may have in common. Worst case, engage in pleasantries, share a silly anecdote, or talk about the weather—something to show you have a personality and break a potential stereotype that some people have about military personnel. Always avoid politics, religion, and sex.

- When questions are asked, listen for what the interviewer is seeking and provide only that information. Don't answer any unasked questions. If asked to tell the interviewer about your last job, highlight those job requirements that you successfully performed using your transferable skills and highlight quantifiable achievements you personally enabled. Do not go on to describe any elements of the job you found unappealing or are inapplicable to the job for which you are interviewing.

- In your answers, feel free to use an item that is music to anyone's ears: the interviewer's name. Take your cue from how they have introduced themselves. If the interviewer says, "Hi! My name is Shirley." Then you should call her Shirley. If the interviewer introduces himself as "Mr. Jones," then call him "Mr. Jones." Don't resort to the military habit of addressing everyone as "sir" or "ma'am." People in the real world have names; use them. They love to hear them. It's an old sales tactic, and it works.

- If you have difficulty hearing or need clarity, repeat the question to ensure you heard it properly.

- Answer the interviewer's questions as an opportunity to highlight your strengths, the same ones we highlighted earlier. Pick from a list of your experiences or stories that speak to your strong suits. Your answers should exude your passion for the opportunity in play and your interest in fulfilling that role in this prospective organization.

- Keep all your answers positive, even those about your weaknesses. Do not criticize former bosses, peers, or organizations; that criticism will ultimately reflect poorly on you. In discussing weaknesses, I suggest two tactics:
  1. Identify something that could be a desirable characteristic, such as being a workaholic.
  2. Identify something in your past that you have learned from and resolved.

- In either case, point out what you are doing to improve yourself and learn from past mistakes.

- Avoid becoming an air hog by keeping your answers between thirty and ninety seconds. If you are interrupted or asked for clarity in the middle of your answer, roll with it. If your answer is met with silence, ask the interviewer if they would like additional detail or clarification.

- Ask your own questions, one of which should be about scheduling a follow-up conversation with the hiring manager. You should not raise the subject of compensation, but you should expect a question about it. Even though your salary is publicly available information, employers will still ask what it is.
- Take notes on any action items (e.g., providing a list of references) to which you committed during the interview and follow up on them immediately.
- Once the interview is over, thank all representatives on the line for their time, reinforce your interest in the organization and the role, and speak to your eagerness in proceeding with the formal interviewing process.
- Send thank-you notes to your interviewers immediately after the interview. These can be either handwritten or typed. The note should thank the interviewer for their time, reference some of the interaction during the interview (especially how your strengths match their needs), and reinforce your passion for the work and your interest in working for this organization. As with résumés and cover letters, make sure you do a spelling and grammar check. See my website (www.matthewjlouis .com) for a sample.

Formal Interviews: Formal interviews are normally conducted in person and on-site at the potential employer's office by the hiring manager, his or her peers, and your potential peers. Several of these formal interviews may take place either in sequence throughout the course of a day or all at once in a panel interview. The number of interviews tends to correspond with the level of the role; the more senior the role, the more interviews tend to be conducted. This makes sense. From the prospective employer's standpoint, senior roles tend to cost them more; so these hires are riskier. Thus, they want to be certain the individuals filling these roles are a good fit for the organization. The same can be said of the length of the interviews. Most will be between thirty and sixty minutes in duration, but the higher the role in the organization, the longer the interviews may run.

Whereas the purpose of the screening interview is to screen you out, the purpose of formal interviews is to ensure you are a good fit for the organization. You should also view them as an opportunity to determine whether the organization is a good fit for you. Remember to come prepared with your own set of questions for the company.

Regardless of the number of interviews you have, these interviewers are the people you really need to impress. To do so, you will want to be thoroughly diligent in your preparation in all the items we covered above, even more so than in the screening interview since you would have accumulated some additional intelligence about the organization by this time. The types of questions you should expect will run the gamut and go beyond those asked of you in the screening interview. You should expect some open-ended questions ("Tell me about yourself"). You should expect some behavioral or situational questions. You may also meet with some companies that like puzzle questions ("How many golf balls could you fit into a Goodyear blimp?"). And most professional services organizations will include case studies (where you are provided a scenario and asked to provide a method to approach the scenario and a recommendation resulting from your method application). Lastly, there is a group of questions I call inappropriate, if not illegal ("What is your sexual orientation?"), that you still should be prepared to answer tactfully. The purpose of formal interview questions is to learn more about you, your work habits, and your personal tendencies. They are also designed to see how you think. Sometimes the solution you provide is less important than the rationale or method you use to arrive at that answer.

FORMAL FEDERAL INTERVIEWS

Federal interviews are different from their civilian counterparts in a few respects. You should:

- Bring a copy of your DD-214.
- Bring a prepared list of references (not a bad idea for civilians either).
- Bring a portfolio of completed work samples or products to demonstrate your expertise (not a bad idea for civilians either).
- Be aware that the interviewer may be joined by a human resources representative to ensure fairness.

Here are some tips for excelling in your formal interview:

- Assume you are being observed in all ways and mannerisms from the time you step onto the organization's property until the time you depart. Show respect for everyone with whom you come into contact. You never know who you're going to meet and who those people might know. That's not intended to make you paranoid; it's to encourage professional business behavior always and avoid scenarios that would screen you out of an opportunity. Look at it this way: Only good things can happen by applying this advice. Bad things could happen if you don't.

★   ★   ★

TROOPS IN THE TRENCHES

"I was at the store getting fitted for my new suit, and I struck up a conversation with the tailor. She was curious about what I'd be doing with the new suit. I told her about my pending interview, and it turned out she knew some people at the company. Upon further discussion about my potential opportunity, it turned out the hiring manager was her brother. It just goes to show: You should treat everyone with respect. You never know where your next opportunity is going to come from."

SCOTT WILLIAMS, FORMER ARMY LIEUTENANT COLONEL

- Bring a copy of your tailored résumé with you for each interview you expect to have. If you have interviews scheduled over the course of a day with five people, bring five copies of your résumé. While you don't want the résumé to be the entire basis of the conversation, you want to ensure the interviewer has seen it. In today's busy world, there is a chance the interviewer may not have looked it over. Keep that in mind when responding to questions. Don't hesitate to highlight some of the major accomplishments you've documented on your résumé.

- Bring a leather folio with you with copies of your résumé, a pad of paper, a pen and pencil, copies of your business card, and (for federal interviews) copies of your DD-214 and samples of your work products.

- Turn off your phones, any watch alarms, or anything else that has the potential to distract or interrupt the interview.

- It should go without saying, but smoking or chewing gum are verboten.

- If, while waiting, you are offered something to drink, make it water. Keep it simple. You'll already be nervous. You don't need sugar or caffeine to exacerbate the situation.

- Greet the interviewer with a firm handshake, a smile, and direct eye contact. Exude the confidence you should have, given all your preparation.

- Sit in the chair to which you are directed or, if given a choice, sit in the chair directly across from the interviewer. Maintain eye contact and good posture—no slouching or crossed arms or legs, but not at the position of attention either. Aim for something in between those extremes.

- As with screening interviews, take some time to break the ice. Since formal interviews tend to be a bit more structured, you will likely have more time to prepare; so your knowledge of the interviewer and the organization should be deeper as a result. Here are a couple of tactics to use:

- ► Leverage your research to make a point to compliment the individual on something they or the organization may have recently accomplished.
- ► If you are in the interviewer's office, look around. What pictures or awards do you see that might indicate their interests? Golf? Hunting? Fishing? Family? The military?
  - Highlight something you may have in common. A small attempt to make a personal connection normally helps start the conversation off on the right foot.
  - The key is to get them to talk about themselves. This will provide some insight about their perspective and will help you in answering their questions.
- If you have yet to secure the name and contact information of your interviewer, exchange business cards with them so you can follow up after the interview.
- Answer questions in much the same way as during screening interviews. Remember to take notes on relevant items and to ask your own questions toward the end of the interview.
- Be open and honest. Don't exaggerate or fabricate facts. If you don't possess a specific trait the employer is seeking, admit it—if you are directly asked about it. But immediately follow up your answer with two things:
  - ► What strengths or skill sets you possess that would easily compensate for that missing item.
  - ► What plan you have in place to pick up that required trait.
- Be prepared to be asked for multiple examples on behavioral questions. Don't be surprised that your initial answer to one of those "Tell me about a time when . . ." questions is followed with, "That's great. Could you share another example with me?" Another interview tactic sounds like this: "You have two or three minutes to

provide as many examples as you can about. . . . Ready, go." A good practice is to have at least two or three stories rehearsed and at the ready for most formal behavioral questions.

★ ★ ★

TROOPS IN THE TRENCHES

"When interviewing, have specific, detailed examples ready for being innovative, developing leaders, making tough decisions, and delivering results. Employers today want to see how you will impact their company and if you have the grit to overcome obstacles."

FORMER ARMY CAPTAIN

- For case interviews:
  - ► Take notes as the detailed information of the case is relayed to you. Upon digesting the case, ask the interviewer for whatever additional information you think you will need. You may be surprised what they are willing to offer.
  - ► Be diligent in applying a decision-support framework that works best for the case in consideration. For example:
    - The four p's (price, product, promotion, place) is a classic approach to dissecting a marketing case.
    - Porter's five forces model is a classic approach to dissecting an industry analysis case.
    - SWOT (strengths, weaknesses, opportunities, threats) analysis is a basic analytical framework to strategy cases.
  - ► With any remaining time, rehearse your presentation. Incorporate visual aids where possible. Take

advantage of whiteboards or projectors if they are available.

- For panel interviews:
    - ► Although one person asks a question, direct your answers to the entire group. Make eye contact with everyone on the panel in relating your responses.
    - ► To the extent you can in responding to questions later in the interview, refer to earlier questions asked by different people on the panel and your responses to them. Doing so will demonstrate your ability to connect data points and synthesize information from multiple sources.
- Beware the puzzle question. These questions are designed to see how you think and how you approach problems or scenarios. For example, "How would you measure the strength of an egg?" Google, Microsoft, and other tech companies have been known to use these, but they are not alone. You should approach such questions by taking a moment to gather your thoughts, ask clarifying questions, and voice over your thinking about how you would approach the issue. In this example, you would want to define what is meant by strength. The thickness of the egg's shell? The rigidity of the shell? Is it the amount of force the shell could withstand before cracking? With that clarity, you would then be able to provide a logical answer to the question.
- Beware the inappropriate question. Understand there may be some interviewers who have not been trained in all the HR policies of the organization or may have a lack of understanding about the military. They may simply be curious and not realize they should not ask about some items. For example, if you get a question about your marriage status, your type of discharge from the military, your political/religious/sexual preferences, your disability rating, or other types of HIPPA-protected information, remain calm. Repeat the question to make sure you heard

it correctly. That alone may trigger a realization it should not have been asked. If the interviewer is still oblivious, ask how this relates to the position for which you are applying. Chances are, it doesn't, and the question can be avoided. If the interviewer persists, consider the interviewer may be using it as a screening tool. In which case, you might answer with something along the lines of, "I'm not sure that the specifics matter, but I can assure you this item will have no bearing on my ability to perform successfully in this role."

★   ★   ★

TROOPS IN THE TRENCHES

"Be prepared to interview the interviewer. Know what questions you want to ask. Ask about the corporate culture and leadership styles that work in the organization. Focus less on you."

FORMER ARMY COLONEL

- Make the most of what little time you will have to ask some questions of your own. As discussed in the interview preparation section, focus them on true unknowns that relate directly to your decision criteria. Remember that the questions you ask tell the interviewer a lot about the research you have done and what your intelligence level is. Consider including among your questions:
  - ► How much travel is required.
  - ► How the variable component of compensation is structured.
  - ► How the annual performance rating process works.
  - ► How the organization's business plans will influence the role for which you are interviewing in both the short term and the long term.

  ▶ Most important, when you can expect to hear back
     from them. This will indicate to you when it is okay
     to follow up with them.
- At the end of the interview, close with confidence. Thank
  the interviewers for their time and, assuming this is true,
  state something to the effect, "I've thoroughly enjoyed
  our conversation. It's confirmed my belief—based on all
  my networking and research—that this organization is
  the best fit for me. I would welcome and accept this
  opportunity if you were to offer me the role."
- Send thank-you notes, as above.
- If costs are incurred to travel to the site of the interview,
  the prospective employer will normally cover or
  reimburse you. But keep your receipts to document the
  amounts that require reimbursement.

Informal Interviews: While these tend to be conducted outside
of the office, you should view them as no less important than formal interviews. In fact, for more senior roles, prospective employers may view these as more important than formal interviews.
Senior roles and sales roles tend to involve relationship-building as
a required skill, and informal interviews tend to be a better setting
for observing your ability to perform that skill. As with formal
interviews, the purpose of informal interviews is to ensure your fit
with the organization. But the focus is on more of the soft skills
used in building human relationships.
  Tips for excelling during the informal interview include:

- Bring a pen and some three-by-five cards for taking notes.
  The military teaches that a good solider or sailor always
  carries pen and paper, and that is a lesson you should
  carry over into the civilian world.
- Do what you can ahead of time to have a bead on the
  organization's culture, especially concerning how
  individuals in the organization are expected to act in
  social settings. It will pay big dividends for some of the

decisions you'll need to make in the following situations. Leverage sites such as Glassdoor.com and your personal network.

- Within limits (e.g., you wouldn't jump off a bridge if they did), the order of the day is, when in Rome, do as the Romans do. If there is a question about how to act or what to do, or if you haven't been able to uncover any intelligence about the organization's culture, that is the safest route.

- For meal settings:
    ▶ Research the menu ahead of time so you can spend time focusing on the interviewer and questions, not the menu.
    ▶ Order foods that you can chew and swallow quickly (e.g., a salad). Realize that you will be the one doing most of the talking, so don't make your interviewer wait twenty seconds for responses to questions while you are working on the last bite of your burger.
    ▶ If you are asked first what kind of drink you would like, go with water, tea, or soda—basically anything nonalcoholic. If your host is asked first and alcohol is involved, there are two schools of thought: (1) Since the outcome of the interview is so important to you and your family, you should abstain from alcohol entirely and state that as your reason for declining and ordering something else, or (2) you should order a similar beverage. For example, if the interviewer orders a bottle of wine, have a glass while complimenting them on their choice. My advice, however, would be to follow the former school of thought. But if your organization's cultural research steers you toward the latter approach, be sure to limit your intake to no more than one drink. And make sure you are drinking lots of water. Your ability to control yourself in this manner could very well be a test.

▶ Mind your manners. The military provided you with some basic training in this regard. But you are no longer in the military, and you may need a refresher. If so, you might check the latest edition of *Emily Post's Etiquette*.[9]

• Be on guard for either (1) bad actors or (2) slippery-slope interview tactics that could be a test. For example, if a suggestion is made to attend an illicit or adult-themed club, do what you can to redirect the conversation back to business topics. If the interviewer persists, call it an evening and move on. Maintain your standards, just like in the military. You don't want to associate with professionals who find this kind of behavior acceptable. Moreover, you may not want to associate with organizations that use such interviewing tactics. We would all like to think otherwise, but these people do exist and these kinds of things do happen. But that is not how you want to be known or remembered. Don't fall for it.

• Approach questions as noted above in the screening interview and formal interview sections.

• As above, be prepared with your own set of questions.

• As above, follow up with thank-you notes.

Follow-Up Process: Once the interviews are complete, take some time to conduct a personal after-action review. Document what went well, what went wrong, why, and a plan to reinforce success and address root causes. Use the template in Figure 8-1 to record your insights and follow-up plan:

Organization:	
Date:	

(continues)

Figure 8-1. Interview after-action report.

Primary Interviewer:	
Interviewer Contact Information:	
What went well?	
Why did it go well?	
Plan to reinforce success	
What did not go well?	
Why did it not go well?	
Plan to address root causes	
Action Items:	
Follow-Up Date:	

Figure 8-1. Interview after-action report (*continued*).

As mentioned in the detailed interview guidance, send personal thank-you notes to the interviewer. If you had multiple interviews, send the note to the primary interviewer or, if you couldn't decipher who the primary interviewer was, send notes to all who interviewed you. Do this within twenty-four hours of the interview.

★   ★   ★

TROOPS IN THE TRENCHES

"Be relentless. Be persistent. Send follow-up emails. Hiring managers understand your situation, so don't be afraid. Take your personal pride out of the equation. Be humble and willing to accept help, personal connections, and useful resources."

DOMINIC LANZILLOTTA, FORMER ARMY CAPTAIN

An organizational representative will eventually contact you with their decision. This could happen by phone, mail, or email. While you are awaiting a response, you are best served by continuing to pursue additional opportunities. As the saying goes, do not put all your eggs in one basket. If the agreed-upon follow-up date has passed without an update, call the interviewer or the HR representative for an update. In doing so, again emphasize your interest in and passion for the role and the organization. Eventually you will get a response from the organization.

While I hope all your responses are positive, there is the possibility your efforts may not meet with success. That's okay. This is normal and expected. This is a process of selling yourself, and as any sales professional will confirm, you can expect ten rejections for every acceptance. While the process we've indicated will significantly improve your chances, some resilience and persistence will be required before the day is eventually won. I urge you to take the opportunity to learn from all these experiences. In the army, we would say, "Embrace the suck."

★   ★   ★

TROOPS IN THE TRENCHES

"The most difficult part of my transition was the early rejections. You think you're good. You think, 'Who wouldn't want to hire me?' You start to doubt yourself. But you have to ignore that. You have to realize that it's not you; it's your technique. And once you fix your technique, things will become exponentially easier."

TRAVIS LONG, FORMER NAVY PETTY OFFICER

When you receive a rejection letter or call, engage the company representative in discussion. In a positive tone, reinforce your interest in and passion for the role and the organization and ask why you were not selected. Give the individual a chance to respond, without interrupting. Digest the response, and you will have some options depending on your conclusions:

CONCLUSION	POSSIBLE ACTIONS
This role has been allocated, but there are others available like it in the organization.	• Thank them for their feedback and ask for the opportunity to interview for related roles.
The role has been allocated, and there are no others available.	• Thank them for their feedback, as it will benefit your ongoing job search. • Advise them you would like to stay in touch should similar roles become available in the future.
The role has not been allocated, but the organization felt that you were not a best fit for it.	• Thank them for their valuable feedback. • Attempt to clarify the elements that, had they been demonstrated, would have won you the role. • Assure the company representative that you possess those elements perceived not to have been demonstrated. • Ask for the opportunity to reinterview for the role.

Do not engage in a tit-for-tat discussion, attempting to debunk the very valuable feedback the company representative provided. Accept and learn from their observations and perceptions; they will help you in your next set of interviews. Your incorporation of their feedback will continuously improve your approach and eventually enable you to meet with success. And when that success comes—write another thank-you note!

With some patience, persistence, and perhaps a bit of luck, the above approach should eventually net you one or more opportunities. If you only have one offer, keep plugging away. Options beget power and room for negotiation. Your next challenge will be to decide which option is best for you and your family and how to finalize that offer to your satisfaction. Chapter 9 addresses what you will need to consider in making those decisions and recommends some tactics for closing the deal.

Nice work! We're getting there.

KEYS TO SUCCESS

★ Practice, practice, practice your interviewing skills and verbalizing the translation of your military terminology.

★ Take advantage of job fairs and career conferences to research target organizations and rehearse your interviewing skills. Be focused in your approach.

★ Thoroughly research the culture of your prospective employer. Culture eats strategy for lunch and will have a heavy hand in determining the extent to which you will enjoy working there.

★ Prepare, prepare, prepare for your interviews. Research the employer, rehearse answers to questions, and dress for success.

★ For your interviews, *show up*! Be on time, be positive, be present, be respectful.

★ Be prepared to answer not only a host of questions but also to ask your own insightful questions. The latter may tell the employer more about you than your answers to the former.

★ Avoid answering the compensation question in a finite manner during initial interviews. While it is best to address it after you have an offer on the table, you should answer any premature inquiry by responding with a salary range based on your best intelligence from your research.

★ Persistence pays off. Don't let rejection get the best of you. Everyone goes through this. See yourself through to the eventual offer(s).

★ After your interviews, *follow up*! Write thank-you notes and demonstrate passion for and interest in the opportunity.

CHAPTER NINE

CLOSE THE DEAL

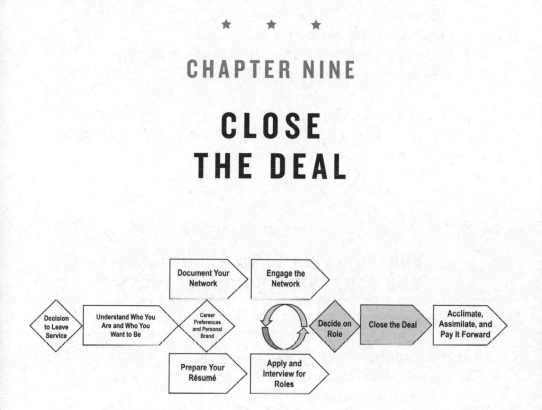

IF THIS CHAPTER PARALLELS YOUR PROGRESS, THIS SHOULD BE A HAPPY TIME for you. Congratulations are in order. After much work and lots of rejection, you likely have a job offer or two in hand. Well done! That's good news. But to solidify that progress, we still have much more work to do. This may be one of the few times in your career where you have the upper hand in negotiating with your prospective employer. You need to take advantage of this fleeting moment. So let's dive right in.

In this chapter we're going to touch on several topics that will help you successfully plan for, conduct, and finalize the negotiation of your job offer(s):

- Understanding your financial needs and compensation differences
- Negotiating and finalizing your job offer
- Understanding what veteran support networks might exist at the prospective employer

By the end of this chapter, you should be prepared to finalize discussions with your prospective employer regarding your job offer to your and your family's satisfaction.

★

UNDERSTANDING FINANCIAL NEEDS AND COMPENSATION DIFFERENCES

As Stephen Covey advocates in *The Seven Habits of Highly Effective People*, we should "begin with the end in mind." Nowhere is that more apropos than in understanding your financial needs. Without that understanding, you have no basis for judging whether your offers are satisfactory.

Let's conduct a few exercises to determine what your financial needs will be, both heading out of the service or into retirement and beyond. You will find these exercises on my website (www.matthewjlouis.com). Please, please, please conduct these exercises before proceeding with the negotiation detail below. The first exercise will involve identifying your savings requirements upon retiring at age sixty-five. The second exercise takes that figure and backs into the required annual salary you will need upon leaving the service to realize that savings goal. An embedded analysis in the second exercise will identify the different ways your compensation will be treated by the tax authorities once you are outside of the military, and it is not the same as you have come to expect during your years in the service. You may be in for a surprise! Populate the table below with your answers to these first two exercises. A third and final exercise will compare the benefit components of your military compensation with their civilian equivalents. Combined, these exercises will be fodder for what we choose to negotiate with the prospective employer in the next section.

Your savings requirement upon retirement:	$
Your required annual salary to meet that retirement savings requirement:	$

ANNUAL BUDGET

An annual budget is a simple way to keep track of your household income and spending on a month-to-month basis to ensure the amount you spend does not exceed your income. It is one of the most basic, most critical, and yet most overlooked financial management tools available to you. It requires some work to maintain, but the work is not significant if you update the budget on a regular (e.g., monthly) basis. The level of detail at which you want to track is up to you, but I suggest the following as a minimum:

CATEGORY	JAN	FEB	MAR	APR	MAY	JUN	JUL	AUG	SEP	OCT	NOV	DEC	TOTAL
INCOME													
SALARY													
GIFTS													
INTEREST, DIVIDENDS, ETC.													
INCOME SUBTOTAL													
EXPENSES													
SAVINGS (529 PLAN, IRAS, ETC.)													
AUTOMOTIVE													
CHARITY													

(continues)

CATEGORY	JAN	FEB	MAR	APR	MAY	JUN	JUL	AUG	SEP	OCT	NOV	DEC	TOTAL
CHILDCARE/DAY CARE													
CLOTHING													
DINING													
EDUCATION													
ENTERTAINMENT													
GROCERIES													
GROOMING													
HOME REPAIR/IMPROVEMENT													
INSURANCE													
MEDICAL EXPENSES													
MORTGAGE/RENT													
RECREATION													
SUBSCRIPTIONS													
TAXES													
UTILITIES													
VACATION													
EXPENSES SUBTOTAL													
BALANCE													

The idea is to maintain a positive monthly balance and certainly a positive yearly balance. You would adjust what you spend on one or more of your expense categories if that threatens to not be the case. There are many software programs available to help with (and semi-automate) this tracking and maintenance task, but you can manage the task just as well using spreadsheets. Microsoft Excel offers several budget templates that you might use. Go to File, New, and enter "annual budget" in the search field. This will produce several templates from which to choose. Whichever you choose is fine if you take advantage of it and apply it to your household cash flow on a regular basis.

Upon completion of the final exercise, answer the following question: How does your prospective employer's compensation package stack up to your needs? Complete Table 9-1 to help in answering this question. Doing so will help prepare you for the negotiation of your compensation package. In the first column, identify the desired benefit. In the second column, identify whether the desired benefit is a requirement or simply a nice-to-have addition. In the third column, identify whether the prospective employer's compensation package addresses the desired benefit. The fourth column should capture what you will do with the information in the first three columns. You might:

- Ask a clarifying question of the employer.
- Negotiate its inclusion (more on that below).
- Determine if the unaddressed benefit could be addressed by some combination of the above post-military benefits.

BENEFIT	MUST-HAVE OR NICE-TO HAVE?	INCLUDED IN COMPENSATION PACKAGE?	ACTION STEP

Table 9-1. Compensation package negotiation planning tool.

The above analyses make a couple of basic points:

- You should understand your retirement needs and corresponding annual net income requirements.
- You should understand that compensation is treated differently outside the military, and should thus judge the

contents of any civilian compensation package in
equivalent terms.

To those, I would add a third: You should realize your military
compensation and benefits package is actually quite generous, and
your expectations for the same upon departing the military should
be adjusted accordingly. "The Eleventh Quadrennial Review of
Military Compensation" found that average compensation for the
enlisted force corresponded to the 90th percentile of wages for
civilians from comparable comparison groups, and the average
compensation from the officer force corresponded to the 83rd percentile of wages for civilians from comparable comparison groups.[1]
This is due to some military compensation policy changes adopted
shortly after the millennium and a corresponding civilian economy
that saw no real growth in wages during the same time period. So
while the current economic scenario could certainly change course
in the coming years, the current reality is you may realize a lower
salary immediately upon departing the service.

★   ★   ★

TROOPS IN THE TRENCHES

"You can't expect to get the same salary initially. In fact, expect a
salary dip. O-5s and O-6s should prepare to have a lower level of
responsibility. You have to understand you have the ability to manage people, not business. You have to first learn the basics of business. Come in and nail your initial role, prove that you can learn and
take a can-do attitude. Volunteer to lead things that demonstrate
your ability to influence. Once people recognize that, you can go on
to much bigger roles—and there is no promotion board!"

SCOTT WILLIAMS, FORMER ARMY LIEUTENANT COLONEL

I suspect these exercises may have left your head spinning. Well, there's good news. The Consumer Financial Protection Bureau can provide a financial coach to help you with some of these topics.[2]

Now, back to the task at hand. Regardless of what you glean from the above exercises, none of them helps you understand how much you are truly *worth*. This concept of relative worth may be new to you. In the military, the existence and monetary value of all your benefits was widely known and understood. In most cases, and by law, almost every benefit available to you in the military is public information. You can calculate your salary based on military pay tables down to the penny. You know your SGLI rates in detail. You know the value of your GI Bill benefits. These are facts, and they are publicly known. Now contrast those known knowns with most civilian benefits. The value of nearly every one is highly variable and subject to debate.

In contrast to life in the military, your value as an employee in the civilian world will be judged by your prospective employer. That estimated value is reflected in the entirety of the compensation package they offer you, and it may or may not square with your thoughts or research on the subject. Now is your opportunity to address any potential disparities. So let's discuss how to optimize the compensation package by negotiating your job offer.

★

NEGOTIATING AND FINALIZING YOUR JOB OFFER

You should feel very satisfied about the offer(s) you currently have in play, for they are the product of your significant work to date. I urge you to view them, however, as invitations to negotiate. You should take advantage of the fact this is perhaps the one and only time in your job search where you retain some negotiating leverage with your prospective employer. Consider that every incremental dollar you can secure in salary or benefits accrues to you as an annuity (a recurring annual payment, not the contractual financial product). This is a powerful financial tool, like the power of compound interest, which will have a profoundly positive impact on your accumulated compensation over the ensuing years. If you're concerned an attempt to negotiate will be off-putting to the prospective employer, don't worry. It is rare that an initial offer of employment is final in either the federal or commercial workplaces.

You should recognize that, as it relates to job offers, this negotiation skill may be new to you. When was the last time you negotiated your salary and benefits with an employer? It has probably been some time, if at all. So let's break it down. For the sake of our discussion, let's define negotiation as an interactive process of discussions with the goal of influencing the behavior of others to reach a mutually satisfactory agreement. There are several ways to approach this task. In *Getting to Yes: Negotiating Agreement Without Giving In*, Roger Fisher and William Ury advocate for a principled negotiation method of four points:[3]

- "People: Separate the people from the problem." People's behavior is driven by their perceptions. How the other party perceives the problem may be very different from you. Take the time to put yourself in the other person's shoes and view the issue from their perspective. For example, if you are a military retiree, an employer may perceive you to be an expensive hire.
- "Interests: Focus on interests, not positions." An employer's initial job offer is their going-in position based on issues and the underlying interests at the organization. For example, an organizational issue could well be pay band limits, and one of their primary interests may be to save costs or limit spending on labor.
- "Options: Invent multiple options looking for mutual gains before deciding what to do." Continuing our example, and understanding the underlying interest, we could come up with an alternative that cuts back on benefits the employer might see as costly while maintaining our desired salary. (After all, with our veteran benefits, we may be able to

cover some of those employer-provided benefits on our own.) This gets the employer what they want (cost savings) while maintaining what we want (a market-rate salary).

- "Criteria: Insist that the result be based on some objective standard." Using our example, the cost of the benefit(s) and the market-rate salary figure would be our objective standards.

You'll recognize this approach reflects a win-win mentality, that is, both parties gain through its outcome. This is the sort of approach for which you should strive. It forms the basis for an enduring relationship. Any alternatives to this approach (either win-lose, lose-win, or lose-lose) results in one or both parties losing something through its outcome and, resultantly, lacking the basis for an enduring relationship. At this point in your potential career with a prospective employer, that's not the right kind of foot on which you want to get started.

Because of that, we should have the best of intentions in approaching these discussions. However, we should also approach them with the understanding they could very well end up without an agreement, which is perfectly fine. But we need to do a bit of preparation to understand the point at which we should walk away from the discussion. That walk-away point is what is known as a BATNA (best alternative to a negotiated agreement). The more and better BATNAs you have, the greater negotiating leverage you have. Think about it: How would you feel negotiating for a higher salary if you had two other job offers with higher salaries in your hip pocket? How would you feel if you had no other offers? Here's the point: Options beget power. So try to go into the negotiation with some options in mind. How do we create these BATNAs? Fisher and Ury in *Getting to Yes* suggest, "Generating possible BATNAs requires three distinct operations: (1) inventing a list of actions you might conceivably take if no agreement is reached; (2) improving some of the more promising ideas and converting them into practical alternatives; and (3) selecting, tentatively, the one alternative that seems best."[4]

BATNAs are just the start of our homework, however. We have a bit more planning to do before negotiating with a prospective employer. We need to think through in more detail our approach to the discussion with the prospective employer and to think through theirs as well. For those purposes, we should identify the following items from both the prospective employer's standpoint (aka, the other party) as well as ours:

- *Goals*: What is our goal? What is the other party's goal? How can we make that a shared goal?
- *Power*: Who has what power in the discussion? Sources of power could include knowledge, confidence, commitment, aspiration, deadlines, etc.
- *Issues and Interests*: What are our key issues and interests? What are the other party's? Are any of those held in common? Are there any where agreement might be difficult?
- *Possible Options, Including Trade-offs*: What would we be willing to give up to get what we want? What would the organization be willing to give up to get what they want?
- *Objective Criteria*: How will we measure success? How will the other party measure success?
- *Strategy*: What is the logic or rationale we will use to influence the other party to accept our solution? What logic or rationale do we expect the other party to use to influence us to accept their solution?
- *Tactics*: What persuasion principles can we use to influence the other party? What persuasion principles will the other party use to influence us? How would we counter them?
- *Initial Position*: Based on all the above, how would we state our initial position? Based on what we know, how would we expect the organization to state their position? How would we counter it?
- *Information*: What else do we need to know or verify before we meet with the other party? What information

do we expect the other party to attempt to extract from us? What information will we not divulge?

To help in planning your negotiations, see the planning worksheet in Figure 9-1. Taking the time to populate this worksheet prior to your negotiations should reward you with positive outcomes that build bridges, which is exactly what we want starting a new job outside of the military.

PLANNING ITEM	OUR POSITION	OTHER PARTY'S POSITION
Goals		
Power		
BATNAs		
Issues and Interests		
Possible Options		
Objective Criteria		
Strategy		
Tactics		
Initial Position		
Information		

Figure 9-1. Negotiation planning worksheet.

Assuming you are following our approach, you have already done some of this work. Your research from chapters 7 and 8 should have provided some idea of the salary range and benefits package you might expect from a prospective employer. The above savings and salary exercises will provide you with a sense of your required remuneration. And the military-to-civilian benefit comparison will provide you with an idea of compensation package components that might be possible to negotiate.

With your planning complete, it is now time to rehearse. As we did with interviews, make sure you take time to rehearse your approach to the negotiation, preferably with a civilian knowledgeable about the organization or industry. Practice responding to various scenarios or contingencies you expect to come up in the conversation with the employer. The more you practice, the more confident you will be during the discussion. When you are ready, it's time to make that call.

The process of engaging with a prospective employer is relatively straightforward, assuming you have done all the planning noted above and you are prepared to think on your feet. This discussion will normally take place with the point of contact that the organization appointed on the email or snail mail offer you received. You should think of structuring the conversation in the following manner:

- *Opening*: Regardless of your stance regarding the offer, open the conversation with gratitude. The prospective employer has extended a lifeline to you. Regardless of the condition of that lifeline, you should be grateful for it. After expressing that emotion, you can set the table for the rest of the conversation. It might go something like this: "Mr./Ms. Smith, I want to thank you so much for the opportunity to work for Corporation X. I learned a lot through the interviewing process, and I look forward to adding value as a [insert role]. Before I accept that role, however, there are a few things I was hoping to discuss with you. Getting clarity around these items will enable me to focus entirely on the job at hand."

★   ★   ★

TROOPS IN THE TRENCHES

"The military does a great job moving you from place to place. But don't expect the same in the civilian world. There are no checklists. There is no time off on both ends. The logistics are simply not handled for you in the same way."

SCOTT WILLIAMS, FORMER ARMY LIEUTENANT COLONEL

- *Body*: This where the details of your planning worksheet above will come into play. Your conclusions from that exercise will drive your approach here. I'll illustrate just one approach from my own experience. My prospective employer held most of the power in the negotiation, although I knew I had some leverage based on a recruiting campaign that led to my offer. My goal was to secure the offer while improving some of its terms. I knew the base salary was within an acceptable range, but I was looking for improvements in the following areas: signing bonus, relocation allowance, and initial level. I was prepared with options around the relocation allowance and initial-hire level. I figured there was more flexibility in the signing bonus than the relocation allowance. And while I knew the reasons behind their offer, I knew I could succeed at the next higher level. Here is how I handled each:
  - ► The employer would not allow for a relocation allowance, but I effectively secured as much by increasing the amount of my signing bonus to cover it.
  - ► The employer would not budge on the hiring level. But I secured an agreement that if I successfully completed (defined as receiving the highest rating) all my assignments in my first year, I would be promoted to the next level the following year. This

was no sweat off the employer's back but held a big upside for me. This tactic, as it successfully played out, had the impact of doubling my year-end bonus (a bump for performance coupled with the increased salary associated with the increased pay band).

- *Closing*: Close the conversation as you began it: with gratitude. Add a sense of eagerness about starting work and adding value. If you are willing, accept the role on the spot and complete the process at the end of this chapter. Otherwise, commit to providing a final decision by a specific date (within the next forty-eight to seventy-two hours). Don't leave the employer hanging. Something like this would be appropriate:

  ► For accepting on the spot: "Mr./Ms. Smith, thank you once again for taking the time to clarify these points. With this improved understanding, I look forward to beginning work as [insert role] and adding value to this fine enterprise. If you would please provide an updated offer reflecting this clarity, I will sign it immediately and begin work on [date]. Again, thank you so much for this opportunity!"

  ► For committing to provide a timely response: "Mr./ Ms. Smith, thank you once again for taking the time to clarify these points. With this improved understanding, I can now make a fair assessment of my career options. If you would please provide an updated offer reflecting this clarity, I promise to get back to you on my decision within the next forty-eight hours. Again, thank you so much for the opportunity to work for this fine organization!"

★

UNDERSTANDING VETERAN SUPPORT NETWORKS AT THE PROSPECTIVE EMPLOYER

Imagine a scenario where you follow the entire process laid out in this book, do all the self-discovery and due diligence, land your dream job, and show up to work the first day only to find that you are the only veteran at the organization. That would result in a lonely existence that would likely end in a stunted transition. Like it or not, landing the job is only the start of your transition. There will be many years spent adjusting to life outside the military. An important way to shorten that time frame is to ensure the presence of veteran peers at the prospective organization. Better yet is a scenario where the prospective organization has gone to lengths to proactively organize those veteran peers into a support group or network. Even more encouraging is an organization that has for-mal transition support and retention practices in place and actively supports veteran-related causes in the community.

★   ★   ★

TROOPS IN THE TRENCHES

"Search for a mentor. It's probably the stupidest thing I didn't do. Most vets change jobs one or two times after leaving the service. You may well work in areas not related at all to what you did in the military. You don't know what you don't know. There are so many unwritten rules. Ask someone to tell them to you."

PERRY JEFFERIES, FORMER ARMY FIRST SERGEANT

———————————

Peer support groups can be helpful in several ways. For starters, it is helpful to know that others are going through or have gone through the same transition experience. Typically, they will be able to offer tips for dealing with life at the new organization or with life in general as a civilian. Because some of them have likely been at the organization for some time, they will have their own networks established with which they can connect you. (Yes, networking very much continues as a way of life in your new world.) At times, you will undoubtedly run into questions or have doubts, and it is most helpful to have a group of individuals that you can trust in approaching them with those questions or doubts and be able to ask for help. Finally, peer support groups can be the source of one of the most important tools in enabling your successful transition: securing a mentor.

★   ★   ★

TROOPS IN THE TRENCHES

"Seek out separate mentors for different things. Have a transition mentor, a personal mentor, a professional mentor. And make sure you have support from both your immediate and extended families."

DAVID USLAN, FORMER AIR FORCE SENIOR MASTER SERGEANT

Mere presence, however, does not necessarily indicate efficacy. As you conduct your due diligence on the prospective employer, you will want to probe with several questions in this area:

- How long has the group been established?
- How prevalent is the group's existence in all its geographic locations? (For example, does it exist in only two of ten offices or eight of ten?)
- How active is the group? What sorts of activities does the group regularly do?
- Is the group sponsored by executive-level professionals in the organization? How involved are those sponsors?
- How does the group measure success and how has it performed vis-à-vis those metrics?

- What kinds of career success have group members realized within the organization?
- Does the organization support veteran-related causes outside of the group? For example:
  - ▶ The White House's Hire Our Heroes initiative
  - ▶ Involvement in the Warrior Games
  - ▶ Support of a local veteran collaborative
  - ▶ Support of the local VA

The answers to such questions will be good indicators of the relative health of the support groups in existence and, in turn, should act as a potentially significant criterium by which you will make your ultimate job selection.

Well, that was a lot of planning. With all that effort complete, we still need to decide. Should we accept the offer or not? Or better yet, which offer should we accept?

Remember our prioritization matrix from earlier in the book that we used to determine a career path? We can use the same construct here if you are trying to decide between multiple offers. See the sidebar "Prioritization Matrix."

PRIORITIZATION MATRIX

If you are debating multiple employment options, try this to narrow your choices:

- Make a list of the criteria by which you would judge the employment options, ranking the criteria on a 1–5 scale (1-less important, 5-most important).
- List your employment options on the horizontal axis and score them using the following scale (1-not a good fit, 3-good fit, 9-best fit) with input from your family.
- Multiply the criteria rankings by the score of each career field option and sum those products. This will produce an emotionless direction for you. In theory, the highest-scored option will best

match the relative importance of your stated criteria. In Table 9-2, Employer B is the clear winner.

Sample Criteria	Ranking	Employer Options			
		Employer A	Employer B	Employer C	Employer D
Career Field Match	5	3	9	9	1
Leadership Potential	3	3	3	1	3
Compensation	4	9	9	3	9
Travel Requirements	2	1	3	9	1
Culture Match	5	3	9	1	3
Benefits Package	4	9	9	3	9
Etc.					
	Outcome	113	177	95	103

Table 9-2. Sample prioritization matrix.

Once you have finalized your decision, you will need to inform your employer. For the offer you accept, you want to call the individual who offered you the role, accept it with enthusiasm by once again reaffirming your passion for the role and a desire to get started, thank them again for the offer, and confirm your start date and any other details that need to be settled. Once you've hung up the phone, draft a final thank-you note.

★   ★   ★

TROOPS IN THE TRENCHES

"Be appreciative. The patriotic swell in the country is pretty big right now. Realize there was a time when it didn't exist. Don't spoil it! You owe that to future generations of veterans. Understand that you represent a whole different class of people. Do what you were taught in the military—be accountable, be respectful."

JON SANCHEZ, FORMER NAVY SEAL

For the offers you decline, you will likewise want to speak in person with the individual who offered you the position, thank them for the offer, and state the reason(s) for your declining. Keep it upbeat, wish them well, perhaps even provide a referral, and leave the discussion on a high note. A nice personal touch would involve a personal note thanking them for their consideration. You never want to burn bridges, for you may find yourself needing to work with these same individuals at some point in the future.

The final step in our process, but perhaps the longest part of your transition, will be your onboarding and acclimation at your eventual employer. That is the subject of the final two chapters.

KEYS TO SUCCESS

★ Begin with the end in mind I: Determine your financial retirement goals.

★ Begin with the end in mind II: Determine your annual cash flow requirements and maintain an annual budget.

★ Understand that military and civilian compensation packages are very different. Conduct any comparison on an equivalent basis.

★ Don't expect to earn a greater compensation package immediately upon departing the service.

★ Don't be afraid to ask for needed benefits in light of a prospective employer's compensation package offer. Don't assume it would be offered if you were eligible.

★ Take advantage of all veterans benefits for which you are eligible within the time they are available to you. Include your family in these decisions.

★ Even if you don't plan on using it in the short term, you should still enroll in the VA healthcare program. You only have to enroll once. You never know when you might need it, and you can't take advantage of it if you don't enroll.

★ Successful negotiations follow a win-win approach and consider the issues from both sides. Always take the high road.

★ Don't burn bridges.

★ Send thank-you notes!

★ ★ ★

CHAPTER TEN

ACCLIMATE TO YOUR NEW CULTURE

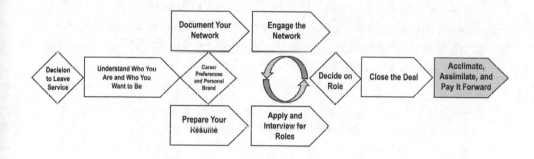

SO YOU'RE HIRED! JOB WELL DONE! YOU MAY BE SWIMMING IN A SEA OF GOOD feelings right now. The image of actress Sally Fields comes to mind in accepting her second Oscar: "You like me! You like me!" Enjoy the feeling. But get ready for the last phase of your transition. I have news for you: Your work is not done. Trust me on this. For some of you, this last phase may seem relatively insignificant. For others, it may be one of the more troublesome periods since leaving the military. For all, it will involve some amount of adjustment over a time that could well stretch into several years. With all the work you've done, it may be hard to believe, but this final step of the process—acclimating, assimilating, and contributing to your new environment—is precisely where many transition efforts fail. Recall the turnover statistics from the introduction. A little foresight and planning in this regard can help immensely in avoiding becoming one of those statistics. The good news is that the end is in sight, and you are on your way.

In this chapter, we will discuss ways to recognize the nature of your new station in life that will eventually lead to your adaptation to it:

- Recognizing and acclimating to your new culture.
- Finding new meaning in your work.

The outcome of this chapter will be an understanding of the multiple dimensions of your new work environment and how your role plays a part in adding value to your new organization.

By beginning with the end in mind, let's first define what success looks like. As annotated in Figure 10-1, the Tristate Veterans Community Alliance has defined a hierarchy of behaviors known as the Four Cs, whose realization closely aligns with what one would deem to be a successful transition. As the pyramid indicates, they tend to occur in successive order and build upon one another. Achievement of one does not necessarily depend on the other, but I discourage any overt attempts to leapfrog the natural progression to claim a premature victory. Just because you may be giving back to the broader community in some way does not necessarily indicate a successful transition. Let's define these terms, and you'll get a sense of what I'm talking about.

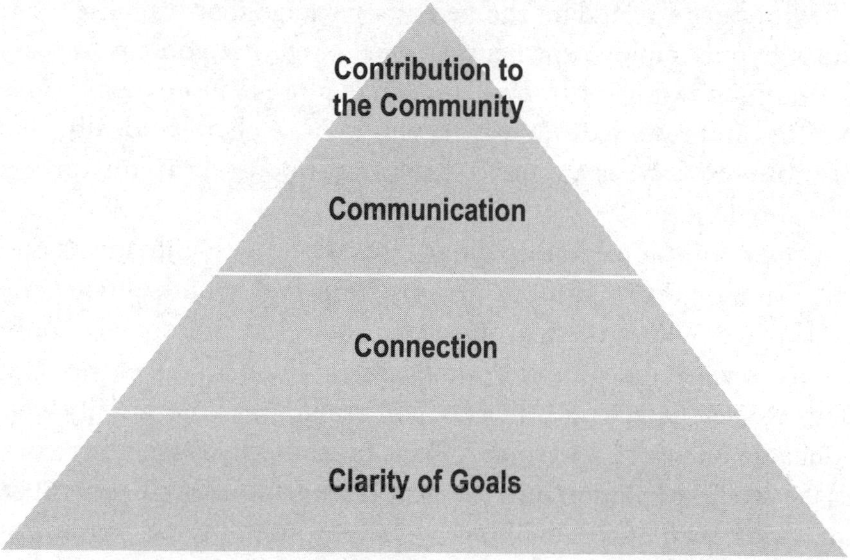

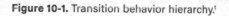

Figure 10-1. Transition behavior hierarchy.[1]

Clarity of Goals refers to having a clear understanding of your personal and professional goals for the next twelve months. In onboarding at your new employer, you want to discuss your performance goals with your supervisor soon after your arrival. And at home you will want to discuss your family's needs and prioritize those in accordance with your annual budget.

Connection means having an awareness of all the benefits and resources available to you as both an employee and a veteran and taking proactive steps to link those benefits and resources to your defined goals. In settling into your new community after relocating, you should connect with local support groups, such as veteran collaboratives, American Job Centers, the VA, or any of several veteran support groups, such as Team Red, White & Blue, the American Legion, Veterans of Foreign Wars, the Military Officer Association of America, and the Non Commissioned Officer Association. Collectively, they will inform you of any number of local resources and benefits of which you might avail yourself. Also, as part of your onboarding process at your new employer, you should take the time to validate the benefits package that was discussed during your employment negotiations. Now that you have access to an organization's intranet, you can explore in more detail those benefits and resources for which you may be eligible. Ideally, one of those resources is an internal veteran support or affinity group you should join.

Communication entails regular discussions with individuals and veteran support or affinity groups both inside and outside the workplace. Within these groups, you should identify one or more mentors who understand your background. These mentors can help connect you with other civilian employees who are likewise educated on your background. Over time, this increasing network eases your assimilation into the new organization. See Figure 10-2 for a portrayal of this evolution. The purpose of the communication should initially be focused on helping you meet your

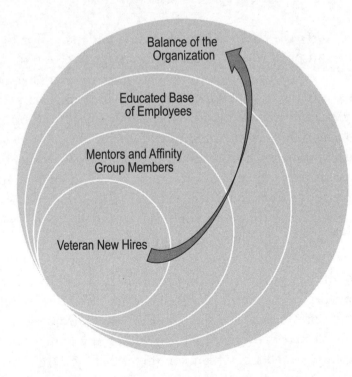

Figure 10-2. Ideal networking assimilation process.

above-stated goals. Over time, and as you gradually assimilate into the organization, the purpose of the communication will evolve to include two-way information sharing, with you contributing guidance and lessons learned to other newly transitioning veterans.

*   *   *

TROOPS IN THE TRENCHES

"Part of the difficulty in transition is there isn't the immediacy and importance on either decisions or results that there is the military. Actions you take don't have the effect they did in the military. You can't always make the difference at work or in daily life you did before. I think that's why veterans volunteer and get involved with organizations; it's that search for meaning and results."

PERRY JEFFERIES, FORMER ARMY FIRST SERGEANT

Contribution to the Community is the apex of the transition behavioral hierarchy. Doing so in a meaningful way occurs only after you have accumulated sufficient lessons from your experience and are willing, if not compelled, to volunteer them in a way that makes a positive difference in the transitioning veteran community. This can occur both inside and outside the work environment and can take the form of one-to-one mentorship or group leadership. The important point is that, by relating your experience in advising others, you are indicating you have come to terms with your new organization's culture and have likely acclimated to it.

If that's success, how do we get there?

We start with goals. While there will obviously be variability in goals from person to person, everyone can use the worksheet in Figure 10-3 to document their own list.

GOALS	NEXT SIX MONTHS	NEXT TWELVE MONTHS
Personal	1 2 3 Etc.	1 2 3 Etc.
Professional	1 2 3 Etc.	1 2 3 Etc.

Figure 10-3. Goals worksheet.

I encourage you to include among your goals the main strategies discussed in this and the next chapter:

- Recognizing and acclimating to your new organization's culture
- Finding new meaning in your work
- Securing onboarding resources
- Joining support networks
- Refining your personal approach and work style
- Passing on your lessons learned
- Contributing to the veteran network

In realizing these goals, you will naturally progress through the veteran transition behavior hierarchy: connecting, communicating, and contributing to the community. We will focus on each in turn.

★

ACCLIMATING TO YOUR NEW CULTURE AND FINDING NEW MEANING IN YOUR WORK

Before you can acclimate to your new organization's culture, you must first recognize what it is and how it differs from the military environment you just left. The basis for this is understanding how the values and beliefs of the military compare with that of your new employer. Values form the basis for behavior, and culture is formed by the collective behaviors of the organization. I've summarized the core values of the individual services in Table 10-1.[2] List your new organization's values and compare them to the military values list.

MILITARY VALUES	NEW ORGANIZATION'S VALUES
• Honor and integrity • Commitment, loyalty, and duty • Courage • Leadership by example • Selfless service • Respect • Excellence • Discipline	• • • • • • • •

Table 10-1. Comparison of military values to new organization.

Depending on the type of civilian organization you've joined, you're likely to find both similarities and differences. These similarities and differences will drive behaviors, which collectively form the basis for the new organization's culture.

Table 10-2 highlights the typical cultural dimensions of military and civilian organizations. Compare how the behaviors of military organizations differ from civilian ones. You'll note there are a range of behaviors, just as there are a range of organizations, and just like the above values, they offer both similarities to and differences with the behaviors of the military. Which of these representative behaviors do you observe in your new organization? What other differences have you observed? Use the empty rows at the bottom of the table to populate your thoughts. How does this compare with your new organization? Populate the last column with your thoughts and observations.

CULTURAL DIMENSION	MILITARY ORGS.	LARGER CORPORATE CIVILIAN ORGS.	SMALLER ENTREPRENEURIAL CIVILIAN ORGS.	YOUR NEW ORG.
Purpose	Mission	Money	Money	
Leadership Basis	Team	Individual	Team	
Organizational Structure	Hierarchy	Matrix	Hierarchy	
Power Basis	Formal	Personal	Personal	
Onboarding Process	Structured, thorough	Unstructured, limited	Minimal	
Training Administration	In-person, classroom environment, provided automatically	Self-service, virtual, provided upon request	Minimal	
Compensation and Benefits	Public	Private	Private	
Recognition and Rewards	Public	Private	Public or Private	
Rank/Level in Organization	Publicly known	Privately known	Privately known	
Personal Initiative	Muted	Expected	Encouraged	
Rules of Engagement, Standard Operating Procedures	Spoken, written	Unspoken, unwritten	Undocumented	
Work Intensity Duration	Shorter bursts, sprints	Longer-term, marathon	Combination	
Time in Grade/Role	Shorter	Longer	Shorter	
Talent Models	One	One or more	One or more	
Receptiveness to Change	Accepting	Less Accepting	Accepting	

Table 10-2. Typical military and civilian cultural dimension worksheet.

CULTURAL DIMENSION	MILITARY ORGS.	LARGER CORPORATE CIVILIAN ORGS.	SMALLER ENTREPRENEURIAL CIVILIAN ORGS.	YOUR NEW ORG.
Thrives On	Chaos	Order	Chaos	
Frequency of Feedback	More Frequent	Less Frequent	More or Less Frequent	
Requesting Help	Not Encouraged	Encouraged	Encouraged	
Lifestyle Choices	Few, if any	Many	Many	
After-Work Interaction	Much	Less	Some	
Employee Category	Just-cause	At-will or Just-cause (unions)	At-will	
Governing Law	UCMJ, Oath of Office, Enlistment Contract	Constitutional law, employment agreement	Constitutional law, employment agreement	

Table 10-2. Typical military and civilian cultural dimension worksheet (*continued*).

In populating this table, you will have drafted a definition of your new organization's culture. Now let's focus on the differences and ponder why they exist. Understanding and accepting the reasons for these differences will have a huge impact on your ability to accept your new organization's culture and fully assimilate into the new organization.

Purpose: One of the biggest differences with which you need to come to terms is your organization's purpose and your role in furthering that purpose. You are coming from an organization whose mission was as patriotic as it comes (defending the free world) and where your role involved contributing to a cause that was greater than yourself. Finding motivation was easy when your service is geared toward your team, your unit, and your country every day. Chances are, this mission gave your life deep meaning and personal satisfaction during your time in service. You were measured on your annual efficiency report for your ability to display the military values noted above, and you took great pride in your performance in doing so. Now, things have likely changed. Unless you've joined a nonprofit or continued work in the public sector, your new organization's purpose is quite different.

Assuming you've joined an organization in the private sector, their reasons for existing include solving problems, addressing customer needs, and in the process, making money. At a personal level, you will find motivations run the gamut from altruistic to utterly selfish and may include the accumulation of power or recognition. Statistics tell us you may have difficulty finding purpose and motivation in supporting what may seem to be a mission so different from the military. One study found 64 percent of veterans say they felt a greater sense of meaning and purpose in the military than they did in their current job.[3] A separate study found that active duty service members have higher rates of well-being than all American workers, and employed veterans fare worse than the general workforce.[4] So how does one avoid becoming a statistic?

You do so by finding new meaning in your work. You do so by redefining your mission to align with the new organization's product or service. Studies tell us veterans want to do work that allows them to promote global health, grow spiritually, protect the environment, save lives, develop deep camaraderie, improve the lot of humankind, and provide social services.[5] You must look past the core reason for a business' existence (making money) and tie your personal value to what the organization does or enables. For example, I work in professional services. I serve clients who have significant business challenges that require an outside perspective to help resolve them. In doing so, I'm not only helping improve their lot in life, I'm helping improve the lot of all *their* customers as well. For me, service is still the basis of my work (albeit for different purposes and in different capacities than when I was in the military), and I thrive on that. Service is still what gets me out of bed in the morning, just as it did when I was in the military. You will need to come to a similar realization to find your new normal.

Leadership Basis: One result of living the selfless service value in the military is that the team or the unit always took precedence. It was the basis for getting things done. Even if you had a significant individual accomplishment in support of the team, the ingrained servant-leadership character trait had you posing that accomplishment as part of the greater team effort. Moreover, much of the basis for your annual evaluation report had to do with the performance of your team or your unit. You would brag to others about what your team or unit accomplished, not yourself. In doing so, the first word you used was *we* and never *I*.

This approach changes somewhat in the civilian world. From the hiring organization's standpoint, they see you as an individual talent with specific strengths and skills. They are hiring you, not your team. In doing so, they want to hear about specific efforts that you—not your team—took to enable success; those are the transferable strengths and skills they desire. This is in part why the résumé creation exercise, and certainly interview preparation, may have been difficult. For perhaps the first time you are forced to speak on a singular (I) rather than a plural (we) basis.

In many corporate organizations, this focus on the individual continues beyond your hire date. You may find that personal evaluations and rewards tend to have more to do with your own efforts than that of the team. Internal promotion boards and evaluation review boards will focus on your individual contributions and your individual potential, just as in the original hiring process. The effect of this is seen in broader society on most social media outlets, where the focus is almost entirely on individuals. Identifying what percentage of posts highlight the efforts of the team versus an individual would prove my point.

Do not be mistaken, however, and do not lose heart. Your team-based focus remains exactly what these organizations need to bring people together and enable organizational goals. At your new organization, you will almost certainly find yourself part of a team composed of individuals who, in some instances, are not used to working as a team. This is where the skills you learned in the military directly translate and will enable you to shine. Just don't expect your team members to always prioritize the team's efforts over their own.

To enable your long-term success in this new environment, you will need to make an ongoing adjustment at evaluation or promotion time. Just as you did in documenting and annunciating your accomplishments in leaving the military, you will need to characterize your team's accomplishments in the form of what you personally enabled. Here is a tactic that can help: Create a folder in your email software program for personal plaudits. Whenever someone sends you a complimentary or thankful message for something you or your team enabled, store that message in this folder. Come evaluation or promotion time, collate those messages into a cohesive document that will inevitably and charitably speak to your individual contributions. This is an easy way to get used to selling yourself.

Organizational Structure: Military units are hierarchical structures. They are purposely designed to enable the exercise of authority and direction necessary for propagating missions and tasks. It's why they call them *commands*. As an example, a team leader reports to a squad leader, who reports to a platoon leader, who reports to a company commander, and so on. As a veteran, you implicitly understand how such organizations work and how directives are given and to whom you are accountable for your actions. In such organizations, that accountability chain tends to be singular: You are accountable to a single individual.

In the civilian world, you might find yourself in a similarly structured organization, but chances are you won't. Most organizations are structured in the form of a matrix (see Figure 10-4) where the accountability chain has multiple dimensions. In such organizations, you would likely be receiving direction from, and thus be accountable to, multiple individuals simultaneously. At first, this may seem confusing, but a review of the benefits of this structure may prove its worth.

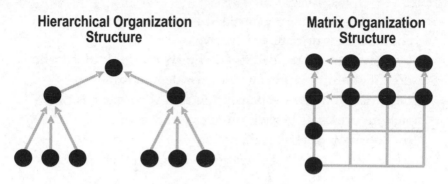

Figure 10-4. Hierarchical and matrix organization structures.[6]

A matrix structure tends to be looser and allows for more flexibility and responsiveness. It tends to promote collaboration, information flow, and knowledge sharing. Employees tend to be grouped by talents or clustered by projects. They may work on different projects simultaneously while communicating with multiple peers and reporting to multiple decision makers. Because you are exposed to multiple individuals in positions of authority, another benefit of a matrix structure is it allows for more career development and professional growth options. Lateral moves, which are more widely available, are viewed as advancement within the organization.

To succeed, however, it is critical that the multiple dimensions of the matrix be integrated in some way. As a leader in that matrix, part of your responsibility will involve ensuring that integration. You should position yourself as a champion of collaboration, coordination, information flow, and knowledge sharing. Doing this successfully will likely require you to leave your level (or job title) at the door; your rank has no place here. You may well be working with, if not reporting to, people who are junior to you. Get over it. Leverage your teaming skills and get to work. Realize that the collective viewpoints of the team will help reduce ambiguity as well as result in a more well-rounded solution.

Power Basis: John R. P. French Jr. and Bertram Raven defined six different bases of power:[7]

- Reward power: the perceived ability to give positive consequences or remove negative ones
- Coercive power: the perceived ability to punish those who do not conform with your ideas or demands
- Legitimate power: the perception that someone has the right to prescribe behavior due to election or appointment to a position of responsibility
- Referent power: the association with others who possess power
- Expert power: having distinctive knowledge, expertise, abilities, or skills
- Informational power: based on controlling the information needed by others to reach an important goal

The military is viewed as primarily leveraging legitimate power, reward power, and coercive power. Let's call this a *formal* power structure or basis. This makes total sense and is consistent with the military's command-and-control environment. Imagine if a combat leader had to take valuable time to explain the rationale for every order. By contrast, civilian organizations tend to leverage referent power, expert power, and informational power. Collectively, let's call this a *personal* power basis.

This difference will have broad implications for how you lead in your new civilian world. As a rule, you will no longer be *directing* or *commanding* anyone. You will, however, be *coaching*, *guiding*, *mentoring*, and *inspiring* others. It's still leadership; it just occurs in different ways. Effective leaders in the civilian world motivate others to achieve significant results by leveraging personal power. You need to learn to adapt your leadership style to this new way of thinking. We will cover more on this topic in the next chapter.

Onboarding Process and Training Administration: When you entered the military, you went through some sort of basic training experience that taught you from the ground up how to be a professional soldier, sailor, airman, or marine. That basic training experience was then augmented by a series of courses specific to your military occupational specialty that taught you your eventual military craft in a crawl-walk-run succession of learning steps. The process for getting you there was structured, formal, and automatically programmed and provided.

★ ★ ★

TROOPS IN THE TRENCHES

"The hardest thing for me to learn are what I call 'big boy' rules. Upon transitioning into a new organization, you have to figure some things out for yourself. There is not a lot of hand-holding. You don't get as much training up front as you would in the military. Most of my learning has been due to on-the-job training. It's been a bit overwhelming."

DOMINIC LANZILLOTTA, FORMER ARMY CAPTAIN

Do not expect the same upon landing at your civilian employer. As an experienced hire, your employer will be anxious to leverage your strengths and skill sets honed during your years in the military. And so formal onboarding or training may be slow in coming. Moreover, with the digitization of most curricula, whatever reference material the employer would use in those courses may well be available on your organization's intranet. To set expectations upon arrival at your new employer, ask when or if you will receive such training. If it is available online, take advantage of as much of that material as you can as soon as it's feasible. Take advantage of as many self-development opportunities as you can. And make sure you augment this academic material with the real-world lessons learned from your new peers and teammates. This is a great opportunity to begin to broaden your new internal network.

Compensation and Benefits: Remember when you had an upcoming promotion? If you were like me, one of the first things you wanted to understand was how much more you were going to get paid in both salary and benefits. The research needed to find those answers was quickly accomplished, as all military pay and benefits tables are public knowledge and easily accessible online. As a result, everyone knows how much everyone else is making. While you might have complained about wanting to make even more, discussions regarding compensation had little to do with guessing what the person next to you was making.

Not so in the civilian world. Compensation is a subject that borders on the taboo. Human resource departments treat most compensation and benefit details as personally identifiable information and thus something not to be shared with others. As a result, what you make is your business alone, and what others make is theirs. It is not appropriate to discuss in detail the figures in your or others' compensation and benefits package. And so you may need to adjust your personal behavior in approaching this topic. In your new world, you need to limit discussion regarding it to your immediate supervisor and/or the human resources department.

Recognition, Rewards, and Rank: In the military, you wore a uniform. On that uniform was your rank insignia, individual and unit medals or badges won, a unit patch, and other particulars that would relate in a very public manner your role, your organization, and your accomplishments. As a military member, you were able to garner a thorough understanding of a fellow service member's history and capabilities without ever uttering a single word. Moreover, you probably took great pride in wearing that uniform. Part of that pride sprang from the very public way many of those badges, awards, and rank were conferred. Typically, large public ceremonies were held for award presentations, promotions, or changes in command.

Well, you have changed uniforms. Your new uniform, whether it is formal or casual dress, has no such publicly visible signs of your past accomplishments or your level in the organization. Upon meeting an individual, you will be unable to instantaneously understand their background or their role in the organization. You will need to work much harder to understand their background, and this will require a deeper level of communication with people than you might have been used to in the military. Accordingly, you should avoid making assumptions about anyone based on physical appearance alone. To paraphrase Stephen Covey, you should seek first to understand the other person before asking them to understand you. Take the time to get to know people before you open your mouth. You may initially find this frustrating, but as stated above, this is yet another great opportunity to broaden your new internal network.

Beyond the physical display of awards and rank, your new organization also likely has few public ceremonies to recognize individual accomplishments, such as a promotion or an accomplishment of some type (there are exceptions, of course). Moreover, those awards tend to be slower in coming and of a different nature (monetary) than in the military. This should not prevent you, however, from implementing such an approach within the sphere of your influence. As long as you take a consistent, fair, and equitable approach to making such recognition public, it will go a long way toward motivating the people under your charge, much as it did in the military.

Time in Grade and Talent Models: The time frame you spent within a rank in the military was fairly well defined. While it becomes somewhat variable at the upper ranks, you had a general sense of when you should expect your next promotion. Early in your career, you rose through the ranks relatively quickly and likely rapidly progressed in the scope and scale of your leadership responsibilities. At the tail end of their careers, career military professionals who have served more than twenty years were cognizant of mandatory retirement dates applicable to specific ranks.

In joining your new civilian employer, since you are an experienced hire, you will tend to be joining at levels beyond entry level. Just as in the military, the time spent in those roles tends to be somewhat variable, even more variable than the military. However, unlike the military and by law, there is no mandatory retirement (although there are permissible exceptions).[8] And so you may expect to spend longer time frames than you are used to within your assigned roles. To reduce this ambiguity, you should get clarity on the organization's career path for your talent model and use this as your guidepost. Doing so will enable you to proactively manage your career.

Another aspect to understand is the different nature of some civilian talent models. Human resource professionals would describe the typical talent model used in the military as "up or out." If you didn't realize a promotion within the standard time frames, there were removal dates by rank within which you needed to depart the service. The good news is that some civilian organizations provide alternatives to this up-or-out model. Some organizations maintain talent models that allow for specialization or long-term focus on some aspect of the business. These models enable a steadier employment scenario but also tend to realize fewer monetary benefits than their up-or-out peers. In some organizations, you can move from one talent model to another over the course of your career, which provides for greater flexibility in your long-term career growth.

And so, you should seek clarity with your prospective employer regarding these opportunities and expectations. Arriving at work on your first day with your eyes wide open will prevent possible frustration with these cultural aspects.

Personal Initiative: In the military, service members follow orders. And those orders are the result of a very formal military decision-making process (MDMP).[9] That process and the orders it produced had the beneficial impact of removing ambiguity for those charged with executing them. Up to that point, detailed thinking was not required by those executing orders. That would always change, of course, as scenarios unfolded, and much thinking was required to decide on proper adjustments in course.

The way in which civilian organizations arrive at decisions does not tend to resemble the formality of the MDMP. The civilian decision-making process, to the extent it exists, tends to rely on the thinking, judgment, and problem-solving skills of individuals. As a leader in the organization, you will be regularly called upon to use your personal judgment in making decisions based on incomplete or inconclusive information. Dealing with this ambiguity may be new and unsettling. Time and experience are the surefire ways to eventually get you comfortable with doing so. In the interim, don't be afraid to use an abbreviated version of the MDMP to at least help you think through your possible courses of action.

Standard Operating Procedures: The military has a manual or a procedure for seemingly everything, from how to maintain your individual weapon to how to conduct large-scale unit movements. If there was an opportunity to screw something up, the powers that be tended to put a documented process in place to prevent future failures. These documents, which were published in the form of manuals or directives, were broadly distributed and widely available. Moreover, it was expected that service members had them readily available as a reference in performing the operation called for in the manual. When lives were on the line, this precision in clarity was a requirement.

Access to the same level of detailed instruction tends to vary in the civilian world. Larger organizations, or those governed by the Department of Labor, the Equal Employment Opportunity Commission (EEOC), or the Occupational Safety and Health Administration (OSHA), maintain required documentation. Also, organizations that require employees to maintain industry-recognized certifications will maintain needed documentation. However, while most organizations likely have a significant set of policies established that govern behavior, they are likely not published in a hard-copy format or physically present where they may be applied—the standard to which you may be accustomed. Moreover, most civilian organizations don't have lives at stake in what they do; so the thoroughness in their policies and procedures may lack what you experienced in the military. The result is that you may be left with less than perfect guidance. You will likely experience ambiguity in performing tasks, and you will need to develop a comfort level with that ambiguity to succeed.

Managing ambiguity is a competency that involves being adaptive and flexible as conditions change. This includes:

- Shifting gears or changing course quickly and easily when priorities change
- Making decisions with incomplete information

- Moving among multiple tasks without having to finish each one
- Maintaining a positive attitude when faced with uncertainty
- Viewing the situation inquisitively and seeing it as an opportunity to grow

A related aspect is the use of lessons learned from past performances of a task to inform future efforts. The military has this down to a science, and several civilian academics have noted as much. It would be rare to find a civilian organization, however, with the same infrastructure that exists in organizations such as the Center for Army Lessons Learned (CALL). Regular and formally conducted after-action reviews (AARs) are likewise a rarity in the civilian world. What civilian organizations tend to have in place, however, are documented approaches or methodologies to some of their more critical tasks. Where they exist, these methods are likely posted electronically and periodically updated to incorporate the latest thinking on performing a given task. While beneficial, the ultimate impact does not equate to the military's best-in-class approach to this matter. To whatever extent possible, you should leverage your military experience in conducting AARs and documenting lessons learned. This is a value-added element that many civilian organizations overlook.

Work Intensity Duration: Military activities can be very intense, both physically and mentally, but most tend to be relatively short (measured in days or weeks) in duration. Also, as noted above, these activities tend to have little ambiguity associated with them— at least at the outset.

This is somewhat in contrast to what you will likely experience in your civilian organization. Activities in civilian organizations will almost certainly not be as physically intense as most military activities, but you may find them to be more strenuous on a mental level. Furthermore, you may find them lasting longer (measured in months and years) than their military counterparts. Given their duration, and together with their more ambiguous nature, you may feel mental exhaustion setting in at some point.

Remember to give yourself a break and make sure you build regular exercise into your daily routine. There was a reason the military emphasized physical fitness. Not only did it help keep you healthy, it helped relieve stress. It works the same way in the civilian world, so take advantage of it.[10]

A related topic has to do with appropriately managing your time. You may find yourself having to juggle more responsibilities in the civilian world than you were used to in the military. But not all those responsibilities are equally important. When you run into such challenges in prioritizing your efforts, the Eisenhower Matrix could be a useful tool to consider. Although the Eisenhower Presidential Library cannot confirm this direct quote, our thirty-fourth president was known to say, "What is important is seldom urgent and what is urgent is seldom important."[11] The application of this concept takes the form of the two-by-two matrix reflected in Table 10-3. Upon review, you would obviously want to prioritize activities you would categorize in the upper-right quadrant.

	Urgent	Not Urgent
Important	Crises Pressing problems Deadline-driven projects Paying the mortgage **Must-Do Activity; Schedule It**	Prevention; Getting exercise Relationship building New opportunities Business development; Saving $ **Value-Added Activity; Do It Now**
Not Important	Interruptions Answering the phone **Non-Value-Added Activity; Delegate It**	Trivia Most social media **Non-Value-Added Activity; Do It Later**

Table 10-3. Eisenhower Matrix.

Receptiveness to Change: While the military has all its processes documented, they paradoxically don't always follow them. Historically, this has been the lament of many of our enemy's military leaders. Our military doesn't always follow the script. This is due to a cultural dynamic that encourages autonomy and flexibility when encountering the enemy. All operations orders (OPORDS) contain a commander's intent, which provides guidance to the organization about the end state. Some OPORDS contain contingency plans, but most state a basic plan, assume you can't plan for everything, and depend upon service members to adapt to and overcome any situation they eventually encounter. The cumulative result of this dynamic is a military that is prepared to adapt to, if not thrive on, change.

Civilian organizations sometimes portray a different dynamic. The larger an organization gets, the more set in its ways it tends to become. According to the *Harvard Business Review* article "Why Big Companies Can't Innovate," the measure of success for mature public companies is profit, and the optimal means to ensuring profit is operational efficiency.[12] This focus on operational efficiency tends to preclude the flexibility needed to respond to changes in the environment and innovate accordingly. Smaller, newer organizations, however, are designed to bring innovation to market. Their reward system is based on how they match a solution to the market's demands. So the behavior they demonstrate is much more akin to what you experienced in the military.

In sum, if you join a smaller or start-up company, you'll be in familiar company—at least as it relates to this cultural aspect. At larger, more mature companies, you won't be able to alter these deep-rooted behaviors, but you can always attempt to control the elements within your sphere of influence. Train your team members to react to situations that don't match the script. Make recommendations to your supervisor to address scenarios you encounter that run contrary to what that supervisor expected. Do what you can to help the organization succeed despite cultural aspects that may limit its ability to do so.

Lifestyle Choices: In the military, you were told when to wake up, what to wear, what to eat, where to live, how to walk, how to talk, what equipment to use, what your salary was, and what healthcare you had, among other things. You didn't have a lot of input on these things until later in your career. The upside to that lack of freedom was fewer things to worry about.

Upon entering the civilian world, you suddenly have tremendous freedom regarding nearly all these things. For some, that may seem long overdue and most welcome, but for others, those things may pose an exhausting problem set that you must actively manage every day. Gather as much information as you can upon arrival at your new employer to set expectations regarding these topics and establish what boundaries may exist. Also, engage with your veteran peers at the organization and solicit any lessons learned they might offer on these topics. Time, patience, and practice will be your watchwords until these things, like uniforms and formations in the military, become daily habits.

Frequency of Feedback: Formal feedback in the military normally occurs on at least a quarterly basis in the form of documented counseling forms. Informal feedback occurs on a much more regular basis, especially during field problems with AARs. Service members quickly become accustomed to receiving course corrections from helpful observers. And in the absence of this, they tend to proactively seek it out.

Feedback at civilian organizations occurs far less frequently, and you may need to seek it out. Do not be surprised to find the only formal evaluation you receive is conducted annually. If you work in an organization where projects form the basis for much of the work, you may be luckier in receiving formal evaluations on each project. Informal feedback tends to be willingly provided if you seek it out. The trick is to set expectations early with your supervisor regarding your feedback frequency needs, and then follow through on whatever is agreed to. Don't allow yourself to silently drown without feedback. When you get it, do something positive with it. Ask questions if you don't understand it; strive to remain open-minded and make the most of it.

Requesting Help: For better or for worse, military culture is such that it does not encourage individuals to seek help. Conformity rules the day. From the very beginning of basic training, sticking out from the group was usually not a good thing; it was usually the basis for a correction or adjustment of some sort—and those were never pleasant. Veterans tend to take this attitude with them when they transition to the civilian world. They tend to believe that seeking help is a form of weakness. But their persistence in this belief can lead to unnecessary delays or floundering on assigned tasks.

In contrast, larger, more mature civilian organizations value operational efficiency. They want to see any questions or issues addressed and resolved pronto. To them, time is money, and any inefficiencies caused by unaddressed questions or confusion in the employee ranks risks incremental profits. And so individuals are encouraged to seek help and ask questions when they encounter challenges they can't immediately address.

Thus, transitioning veterans should not hesitate to ask questions, but they should listen carefully and learn from the answers provided. If the same person asks the same question repeatedly during several performances of the same task, this is an indicator the individual is struggling with picking up the signal and may indicate other, more challenging issues that will require attention.

After-Work Interaction: The military was not just a job, it was a way of life. Camaraderie didn't stop at the end of the workday. Driven by the mutual availability of on-post/base facilities and housing, you and your families tended to live, work, and play together around the clock. When you weren't deployed, days at work were often followed by interunit sports competitions, social calls at the all-unit clubs, friendly games of golf, or other community events in the housing areas. You ran into each other at the on-post/base PX/BX, Class VI, or Commissary. You watched movies together at the on-post/base theater. In more trying times, it was a short drive to the on-post/base health clinic or hospital to support one another. Net, you were part of a mutually supportive community for nearly every need or want.

The social fabric of your civilian workplace will include less of this. Civilian professionals interact less so once the workday is complete. This is truer in larger, more mature public companies than smaller, private entrepreneurial companies. After work and as a rule, they will go home to their families in their communities and partake in separate social activities. While there will tend to be some support for company-sponsored activities outside of work, those instances tend to be an exception. This is another consequence of the greater freedom you will realize upon departing the military. While this may be somewhat disheartening to you, there is something you can do about it. People aren't necessarily opposed to getting together and interacting outside of work, but you will need to be proactive in making that a reality. After some time at your new workplace, feel free to engage others on the possibility of interacting outside of work. Doing so can act both as a great networking tactic as well as a means to build camaraderie within your new team.

Another consequence of this change is that your family becomes much less connected to who you are working with and what you are doing on a regular basis. Organizations are not used to including extended family members in most activities inside or outside of the workplace. Recognize that your family will be disappointed by this lack of connectivity in the new community to which you relocate and at your new workplace. To try to fill this gap, you will need to work harder at providing them with the information you receive at work on benefits, pay, schedules, or anything else that might concern them. They will not procure that information any other way. You can also ask if you can include your family in any onboarding activities, but don't be surprised if that request is denied. Also, encourage your family to build new connections in the community to which you relocated. Doing so will help ease their transition and partly replace the loss of their former military contemporaries.

Employee Category: From a legal standpoint, there are two categories of employees: just-cause employees and at-will employees. As the name implies, just-cause employees can only be terminated from their employment for a good reason and are usually entitled to some form of independent review of the employer's decision to terminate them. At-will employees can be terminated for any reason or no reason at all.[13] Federal employees are one of the largest groups of just-cause employees. The others are state and local employees and union members. Most civilian employees are at-will.

In joining your new organization, you should recognize you may be experiencing the terms of at-will employment for the first time. You should understand the implications of this new and different category. Unless you join a union, you can no longer be terminated for only just cause. Whereas the military had due process and reviews before formal termination took place, civilian employers can mostly avoid it. That may sound brutal and unforgiving, but that is your new reality. The flip side of at-will and another part of your new reality is your ability to depart your employer at any time. While not necessarily a good practice, it is an option with your new existence.

★ ★ ★

TROOPS IN THE TRENCHES

"As an employee of a university in an at-will state, I had to realize that, no matter how good a job you do, you could be let go on someone's whim or even for a budget decision made many levels removed. It brought a certain anxiety."

PERRY JEFFERIES, FORMER ARMY FIRST SERGEANT

Governing Law: Military behavior is governed by the Uniform Code of Military Justice (UCMJ), a separate—and some would say stricter—system of laws than standard constitutional law that governs civilian activity. Violations of the UCMJ tend to be met with swift repercussions, such as jail, fines, letters of reprimand, or other than honorable discharges from the military. These things, especially less than honorable discharges, leave a permanent stain on your record, negatively impacting your ability to thrive in the civilian world.

As noted above, by joining your new organization, you will likely be employed on an at-will basis and told to sign an employment agreement of some sort to ensure compliance with organizational policies, rules, and regulations. If you violate these agreements, the basic remedy for most civilian organizations involves the employment-at-will doctrine and dismissal. Compared to jail time and less-than-honorable discharges, this may not seem terribly impactful, but there are long-term implications.

Whether you were fired or you initiated your departure from an employer, the outcome is the same: another job hunt and the need to justify a job change on your résumé. Further, as employers tend to look askance at job hoppers, the long-term implication of such transgressions is a negative impact on your career earnings and a corresponding inability to build wealth.

The obvious lesson here is to abide by all laws, policies, rules, and regulations. With the increased freedom a civilian role enables comes increased responsibility. You owe it to your family and yourself to live up to that responsibility—or suffer the consequences.

• • •

This exercise of recognizing and acclimating to your new culture is necessary to enable a successful transition. Failure to adapt to your culture will result in failure to thrive in that culture. It can lead to feelings of isolation, frustration, and helplessness. Failure to thrive in the organization invariably leads to turnover and additional false starts. Let's not let that happen. While this isn't easy, it must be done. Embrace this experience and learn from it. Here are a few tips to help you through this cultural acclimation process:

- Accept that challenges are normal.
  - ► Accept that challenges and uncertainty are a normal part of the cultural adaptation process. Recognize what's happening, and don't be too hard on yourself.
  - ► Transitioning veterans often feel isolated, worried that no one will understand how they are feeling. However, the challenges and frustrations associated with adopting a new culture are common and faced

by many experienced hires, regardless of military background.

- Remember that everyone is different.
    - ► People are unique. The impact of culture change is experienced differently based on many factors—everything from your personality to having previous life experiences that required similar adjustments.
    - ► Many transitioning veterans say they feel lost and scared and then ashamed and embarrassed because they feel that way. But everyone is different; it's unrealistic to assume that just because you're tough, this experience will be easy for you.
- Focus on the positives.
    - ► Make a list of the positives. What are all the good things about your transition?
    - ► Mindfully focus on these positives when you find yourself dwelling on the challenges.
- Keep things in perspective.
    - ► Find ways to keep things in perspective. Use humor to cope. Be able to laugh with yourself and others over your mistakes.
    - ► Be active. Don't sit around feeling sorry for yourself. Exercise, read a book, listen to music—whatever works for you.
- Ask questions.
    - ► Ask questions and ask for help. Ask about anything that seems strange, difficult, or confusing. There are no foolish questions—only fools who stop asking what they need to know.
    - ► Knowledge is power. Ask and you shall receive. Chances are you're not the only one thinking of asking that question, but you should try to be the only one willing to.
- Broaden your network.
    - ► Be careful not to spend all your time with other veterans. When you do, don't let it turn into a gripe

session that will slow down cultural adaptation. Build a broader network. Find commonalities with non-veteran colleagues. You may have experienced things in the military that few civilians can relate to, and that can feel isolating. So build new experiences together.

- Stay connected with friends and family.
  - ► Keep in touch with loved ones. When you connect with them, don't dwell on the challenges of your transition but focus on your accomplishments and new experiences. Sharing the positives will be reinforcing.
  - ► Remember that your immediate family is going through this transition with you and act as a form of mutual support.
- Accept that transition takes time.
  - ► Accept that transition is a process, not an event. It typically follows a U-shaped curve, starting with a honeymoon phase, where your excitement is high, followed by culture shock and a general sense of unease, and moving up through adjustment and mastery as you become comfortable in your new environment.
  - ► Many transitioning veterans lament, "I've been here for months and still feel totally lost." However, there's no standard time frame for cultural adaptation. Be patient and accept that the process will happen gradually.
- Be open-minded.
  - ► Recognize that the military and your organization have different ways of doing things, not necessarily better or worse ways of doing things.
  - ► Make no assumptions and accept that you have a lot to learn.
- Don't fight it.
  - ► Learn to work with the new culture, not against it. Stop trying to change the new culture or making constant comparisons to the military.

▶ Figure out how to leverage the strengths of your new organization's culture for your own success and happiness.

With this in mind, let's turn our thoughts in the final chapter to fully embracing our new surroundings and assimilating to our new normal.

KEYS TO SUCCESS

★ Be patient—with yourself, with your family, with your new workplace.

★ Followership is a requirement for leadership. Seek first to understand before seeking to be understood.

★ ★ ★

CHAPTER ELEVEN

ASSIMILATE
AND PAY IT FORWARD

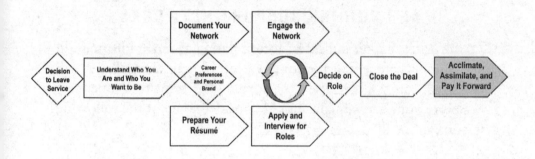

RECOGNIZING YOUR NEW ORGANIZATION'S CULTURE IS ONE THING. ACTUALLY embracing it and fully adopting it as your own is quite another. Yet that is the key to happiness in your new role, tenure at your new organization, and your corresponding ability to build wealth and enable your family's happiness. Recall the transition behavior hierarchy from the last chapter. You shouldn't consider yourself fully transitioned until you are willing to volunteer your lessons learned from this experience to make a positive difference in the transitioning veteran community. In the words of Yogi Berra, "It ain't over till it's over."[1]

In this chapter, we will discuss strategies for fully embracing your new normal:

- Seeking onboarding resources and support networks.
- Refining your approach and style as needed.
- Passing on your lessons learned and contributing to the veteran network.

The outcome of this chapter will be a successful transition and your corresponding ability to help others along the same path based on your experiences on this journey.

★

SECURING ONBOARDING RESOURCES AND JOINING SUPPORT NETWORKS

As the prior chapter indicates, accumulating as much information as you can before and upon arrival at your new employer will better educate you and serve to shorten your transition timeline.

Before your arrival, you should consider some of the following lessons learned:[2]

- Revisit the research you did in chapter 6 in preparation for your interviews, but with an eye toward your new role and team.
- If your prior research did not address the following items, ask HR or your new boss about:
    - ▶ Your new division or team, what it does, and how it supports the organization's goals.
    - ▶ Your role on the team and what customers you will serve.
    - ▶ The employee performance evaluation process.
    - ▶ Organizational reward or recognition systems.
    - ▶ Your talent model and potential career path.
    - ▶ A glossary of terms used in the organization.
    - ▶ The existence of veteran support networks.

  ► The process for being assigned a mentor.
  ► The ability for your family to participate in any
    formal onboarding sessions.
- Confirm your start date, time, location, dress code, and to
  whom you will be reporting.
- Research any team members with whom you will expect
  to interact on LinkedIn.
- Complete any remaining contingencies, such as a physical
  exam or drug test.
- Try to clear your plate of any major activities outside of
  work so you can focus on the important task of
  acclimating to your new environment.

Upon arrival, you will want to follow through on the following
activities:

- Address any of the above items that are not yet resolved.
- Arrive early on the day you are scheduled to report, stay
  late, and ask lots of questions. Willingly engage with
  others and keep all interactions upbeat and positive.
- Accumulate and digest any information shared by
  HR or your new supervisor. Make sure you and your
  family have a crystal-clear understanding of the benefits
  package and the procedures for taking advantage of
  them.
- Involve your family in as much of the onboarding process
  as your organization will allow. Make sure all their
  questions get addressed.
- Voraciously consume any intelligence regarding your new
  role. This first role in your new organization sets a
  precedent and solidifies a reputation, and you want it to
  be a good one. Get ahead and stay ahead.
- Commit to a professional reading program. There is
  much to learn about your new world. Use the best ideas
  to continually improve your organization. My website

(www.matthewjlouis.com) contains additional resources that could be added to your reading list.

- Establish expectations with your new supervisor regarding:
  - ▶ Your work schedule.
  - ▶ Your specific responsibilities and the metrics to which you will be accountable.
  - ▶ The nature of your reporting channels, assuming a matrix organization in which there may be multiple.
  - ▶ The schedule of formal and informal feedback discussions to which you both will commit.
  - ▶ The availability of and ability to participate in needed training courses.
  - ▶ The availability of and expected use of methodologies or standard operating procedures in the performance of tasks.
  - ▶ His or her communication preferences. Do they prefer email, phone calls, or one-on-one meetings? Do they require lots of detail or only a summary? How frequently do they require all the above?
- Share your frustrations with your family, veteran peers, and mentors. Worst case, maintain a personal journal to vent those frustrations.
- Avoid office politics and any discussions involving religion, sex, politics, or other hot-button topics.
- Identify yourself as a veteran and join at least one support network, preferably one within your workplace. Through this network, secure a mentor who can act as a senior leader advocate within your new organization.
- Secure a buddy or sponsor who can help show you the ropes regarding day-to-day procedures and expected behaviors in your new job.

★   ★   ★

TROOPS IN THE TRENCHES

"The best part of my transition was meeting fellow veterans who helped me make the transition. One of the concerns I had was thinking there was a lack of camaraderie in the civilian sector. However, my experience was just the opposite. I developed strong professional and personal relationships with fellow vets that continue today. I think that having a strong network is key to a successful transition."

FORMER ARMY CAPTAIN

Joining a veteran support network or affinity group may be one of the more important things you do in smoothing your transition. Why? In addition to what was noted in the previous chapter, these groups enable three factors, noted by Sebastian Junger in *Tribe: On Homecoming and Belonging*, that affect a veteran's transition back into civilian life and are not well enabled by society. First, these groups act as a cohesive and egalitarian tribal society, which helps mitigate the effects of any trauma. Modern societies are the exact opposite: hierarchical and alienating. Second, the groups don't see you as a victim. You're not excused from fully functioning in society. Finally, and most important, "Veterans need to feel that they're just as necessary and productive back in society as they were on the battlefield."[3] These societies provide the social resilience that society lacks. Moreover, as H. A. Lyons observed, "When people are actively engaged in a cause their lives have more purpose . . . with a resulting improvement in mental health." He added, "People will feel better psychologically if they have more involvement with their community."[4] These veteran affinity groups enable that engagement with a cause and involvement with a community.

Ideally a group like this exists at your employer. Ask an HR professional at your new workplace to guide you. If not, there are plenty of these groups available outside of your workplace. Here are a few to consider:

- Team Red, White & Blue
- Rallypoint
- Mission Continues
- Travis Manion Foundation

★

REFINING YOUR PERSONAL APPROACH AND WORK STYLE

COMMUNICATING WITH OTHERS

The military way of communicating reflects several positive characteristics: It is decisive, concise, direct, and respectful of authority. These characteristics are valued in the military, where regular application has a direct impact on successful mission accomplishment in an environment where lives are at stake. This approach works well in a military culture that has the dynamics that were highlighted in the previous chapter. The brevity of terms like roger and wilco in response to orders has the impact of communicating a lot of information. Those four syllables tell the other party (1) you understand what was communicated, (2) you are going to comply with the order and follow through on its execution, and (3) you have no questions about the order's intent or the process by which it should be executed.

Unfortunately, things are rarely as clear-cut in the civilian world and require an adjusted approach. As we've defined above, the dynamics of your new civilian culture will be quite different. Recipients of a request (civilians rarely give orders) will want to understand the rationale for it as well as thorough guidance for its successful implementation and delivery. Four syllables may not suffice. Those communication characteristics that benefited you so well in the military may be interpreted quite differently in the civilian world, as noted in Table 11-1. These perceptions don't serve you well, and so you will need to adjust the way in which you communicate with others.

MILITARY COMMUNICATION CHARACTERISTIC	CIVILIAN PERCEPTION
Decisive	Noncollaborative
Concise	Abrupt
Direct	Aggressive
Respectful of authority	Lacking confidence

Table 11-1. Civilian perception of military communication characteristics.[5]

If you are going to be the one responsible for making the generic request mentioned above, you need to understand your audience.

- What do they know about the subject?
- What are their personality types?
- What are their levels in the organization?
- What communication preferences do they have (email, phone calls, face-to-face)?
- How does this request relate to their current work?
- How soon do they need to react to your request?
- What do you want them to do with your request?
- What motivates them to fulfill your request?

When you understand these things, you can then craft the request. Now, that may seem exhausting compared to the communication style you're used to, but there is much more thinking required to successfully communicate in a civilian environment. But this is your new task and responsibility. Doing it successfully will take some time and practice. Typical communication challenges that veterans experience when attempting to communicate with their new civilian colleagues include:

- Asking for guidance and support when needed.
- Declining requests when overloaded or pulled in multiple directions.
- Speaking up and sharing ideas or perspective.
- Working collaboratively with others at varying levels.
- Working effectively on a virtual team.
- Addressing senior colleagues informally.
- Giving and receiving feedback.
- Avoiding profanity or rough language.

You must address these challenges or risk negatively impacting your performance or job satisfaction. In adjusting your approach to meet these challenges, you should ponder a way of thinking and behaving that recognizes the audience's experience and perspective, and then tailor your style accordingly. It's a way that bears the hallmarks of servant leadership and being of service to others. It's a way that reflects seeking first to understand the recipient of the information before transmitting the information. This approach should be characterized by:

- Being open and honest.
- Questioning with purpose.
- Actively listening.
- Bringing a point of view.
- Being proactive.
- Being responsive.
- Building relationships.

Let's take emails, for instance. Email is a ubiquitous form of business communication. If you don't already, you can expect to receive dozens of emails daily in your new role. As with verbal communication, veterans tend to struggle with the tone of written communication, such as emails. In crafting them, you should strive to compose messages with a reader-centric perspective and a professional and approachable tone. See Figure 11-1 for an example.

Email A	Email B
Mary – Have an issue. Could use your help. Customer has goods STUCK IN LOCKUP. When could you help us with this? Need it soon. v/r, - John	Mary, Thanks for facilitating today's session! You highlighted a few elements in the supply chain about which I wasn't aware. One of those has to do with a current customer of mine, who is struggling with the repatriation of goods encumbered by tariff and customs clearance issues. Would you be willing to meet with me to help our team prepare for a meeting with our customer on this topic? I can flex our schedules to meet your availability. Just let me know what you might be able to accommodate. Thanks so much for the consideration! All good wishes, John

Figure 11-1 Differing tones of sample email communication.

Compare Email A to Email B. What differences do you notice? What attitudes do they convey? If you were Mary, to which would you be more receptive? Are you beginning to get the picture? Tone is important. It impacts people's perceptions and carries a lot of weight. It connotes emotion, which is far more vivid and longer lasting than the words on the page. Remember, you are new and will need to build relationships with many individuals (especially in a matrix structure). These people have no history with you or context about your background. You will need to go the extra mile to communicate in a manner that appeals to them, so they don't misinterpret your written word.

Another aspect of email communication is knowing whether to send one at all. The military started each operation with a safety briefing. Consider this your email safety briefing. Applying these ground rules will save you some heartache and frustration and may preserve some of those new relationships that you are trying to build. When should you *not* send an email?

- When you are angry or if there is a conflict.
- If an immediate response is needed.
- If the risk of misinterpretation is high, especially in the case of jokes or attempts at humor.
- When sharing confidential or sensitive information.
- When sharing bad news.
- When explicit understanding is essential.

Consider the briefing or presentation style you've been taught in the military as well. Military style guides narrow the types of briefings you might possibly give and provide strict guidance for the content of each type of brief as well as the physical and verbal aspects of presentations. Presentations made in most civilian business settings typically don't resemble such formality. You'll no longer be confined to a podium or have to stand at the position of attention. You'll no longer have to use a specified pointing device or PowerPoint presentation templates. You'll no longer need to conclude your presentations with, "This concludes my brief. Are there any questions?" Every civilian organization has its own style when it comes to presentations. Few of them, however, document this in a formal style guide. You'll need to lean on your peers and mentors to better understand and adopt their style as your own.

Providing feedback is another area where your communication approach will need to change in the civilian world. Like the military, most civilian organizations have formal feedback processes, but sharing that feedback tends to take place in a different way. Feedback can be very powerful and can significantly impact the performance and job satisfaction of your team when well communicated. Well-delivered feedback tends to have the following characteristics:

- It is focused on specific behavior (not the person) and includes examples, describing them without judgment.
- It is actionable and can immediately be put into practice.
- It is timely, provided as closely as possible to the timing of the behavior.
- It is balanced in that it includes recognition of good performance along with redirection on the behaviors in question.
- It is empathetic, delivered in a safe environment that respects the person's perspective and feelings.

To provide feedback effectively, you will need to take the time to prepare it, even if it is somewhat in the moment. The following framework might help with your preparation. Although similar to the after-action-review process you might be used to, it goes a little further in focusing on next steps. It is called the EARN model:[6]

- Event
    ▸ What was the situation?
    ▸ When did it happen?
    ▸ Where did it occur?
- Action
    ▸ What was the observed behavior?
    ▸ What specifically was said or done?
- Result
    ▸ What was the impact or the consequence?
    ▸ Who was affected?
- Next Steps
    ▸ What behaviors should be continued or changed?
    ▸ By when should the behaviors change?
    ▸ How will you measure success?

Another communication topic with which you will need to become comfortable is asking questions, multiple types of questions at that. Questioning in a military environment wasn't exactly encouraged. Doing so might have been considered challenging authority or admitting a weakness. Questioning in the civilian world is precisely the opposite: The smartest people ask the best questions.

To do this well, you should be strategic and purposeful in asking the right kinds of questions in the right circumstances. Major types of questions include the following:

- Close-ended or open-ended
  - ▸ Close-ended questions invite a short, focused response. They answer specifics such as who, what, where, when, yes, or no.
  - ▸ Open-ended questions answer how or why. They are aimed at discovery and lead to additional information.
- Factual or evaluative
  - ▸ Factual questions are focused on facts, details, and concepts. They are common in military culture.
  - ▸ Evaluative questions query feelings and ideals. They are important for relationship building.
- Mirror
  - ▸ Mirror questions use or paraphrase the speaker's words with a questioning inflection. They can be used to confirm understanding.
  - ▸ Example: "The customer has concerns about the project plan?"
- Leading
  - ▸ Leading questions offer a desired answer, usually subtly, to point the respondent in a specific direction.
  - ▸ Example: "Did you have a good day at school?" instead of "How was school today?"
- Probing
  - ▸ Probing (or nudging) questions prompt the respondent to elaborate or explain.
  - ▸ Example: "Can you tell me more?" or "What makes you say that?"

Using these types of questions at different points in your new civilian role will make you a better communicator and contribute to your relationship-building skills.

Successful communication involves building relationships and being both more responsive and proactive than you might have been in the past. Part of proactively building relationships and being responsive requires thinking and behaving in a way that recognizes the other party's perspective, which includes understanding that party's work style and communication preferences. A system designed by Deloitte to enable this understanding is called Business Chemistry®.[7] It identifies four primary work styles that define how others prefer to communicate and collaborate on shared objectives (see the sidebar "Business Chemistry® Work Styles"). Most people's behavior and thinking corresponds with one or two of these work styles.

BUSINESS CHEMISTRY® WORK STYLES

- **Pioneers** value possibilities, and they spark energy and imagination on their teams. They believe risks are worth taking and that it's fine to go with your gut. Their focus is big-picture. They're drawn to bold new ideas and creative approaches.
- **Guardians** value stability, and they bring order and rigor. They're pragmatic, and they hesitate to embrace risk. Data and facts are baseline requirements for them, and details matter. Guardians think it makes sense to learn from the past.
- **Drivers** value challenge and generate momentum. Getting results and winning count most. Drivers tend to view issues as black-and-white and tackle problems head-on, armed with logic and data.
- **Integrators** value connection and draw teams together. Relationships and responsibility to the group are paramount. Integrators tend to believe that most things are relative. They're diplomatic and focused on gaining consensus.[8]

How you put this knowledge to work is by first identifying your own work style and then identifying the work style of those with whom you'll be working. To create a hunch or a hypothesis regarding someone's work style, you can register at the Deloitte website and complete a free twenty-question survey.[9] Together with your own results, a hunch can help you flex your work and communication style to improve the effectiveness of your interactions with others.

Understanding your personal working preferences and how they may differ from others will provide you with some astounding insights about how best to approach people. Remember, you are entering a new world here, a different environment populated with people with far different experiences than yours. These people speak, think, and act differently than you do. Having some basic guideposts regarding how to act may come in handy. Have you ever been in a foreign country where you didn't speak the language? I'll bet you have. And I'll bet you would agree that in such instances a translator—someone from the local area who could help you understand the local customs, culture, and communications—was heaven-sent. Well, the same is true here. You would be wise to put this tool to use.

Up to now, we've been talking about transmitting information. Perhaps even more important, and a skill you will likewise need to adjust, is active listening. According to Get in Front Communications:

- We listen at a rate of 125–250 words per minute, but think at 1000–3000 words per minute.
- Fewer than 2 percent of people have had any formal education on how to listen.[10]

And so, even though you may have had zero training in it, the numbers tell us you can fully absorb what another person is saying, but you need to be fully focused on the conversation for its meaning to sink in. Just as our questioning needs to be purposeful, our listening needs to be active. Being an active listener entails:

- Fighting the urge to monopolize conversations even when you have a strong point of view.
- Not interrupting.
- Eliminating distractions.
- Using both verbal ("uh-huh") and nonverbal (nodding, eye contact) cues to indicate interest.
- Acknowledging what was said and reflecting it back to confirm understanding and test assumptions.

Actively listening shows respect for other people and will help you greatly in building relationships in your new environment.

INFLUENCING OTHERS

Since 1999, *Time* magazine has published an annual list of the one hundred most influential people in the world. It is often one of their best-selling issues. Influential people are captivating. They make an impact on the world, for better or for worse. But you don't need to make this list to have influence. Influence is a competency that is required for success in the civilian world. You can hone this skill with practice, just as you did with giving orders in the military. But you're no longer giving orders and potentially not in a position of authority, so you need to be able to persuade others in different ways.

Influence represents the ability to persuade others to act, to coalesce stakeholders around a point of view, to generate support for an idea. It involves acting in a way that is always consistent with your purpose and priorities (it is not situational). It involves verbal and nonverbal communication and is measured by results. It is necessary in the matrix-type environments in which you will likely be working.

Robert Cialdini, a professor at Arizona State University and a noted researcher in influence, has identified six principles of influence that translate into specific actions (see Table 11-2). These principles can effectively act as tactics you might leverage to influence others in your new role.

Strategy	Principle	Application
Reciprocity	• People repay in kind. • People are more willing to comply with requests for information, services, etc., from those who have provided such things first.	Give generously and share openly with others.
Commitment and Consistency	• People align with their clear commitments. • People are more willing to be moved in a particular direction if they see it as being consistent with an existing or recently made commitment.	Encourage commitments that are active, public, voluntary, and gradual.
Social Proof	• People follow the lead of similar others. • People are more willing to take a recommended action if they see evidence that many others, especially similar others, are taking it.	Share peer examples when available.
Liking	• People like those who like them. • People prefer to say yes to those they know and like.	• Uncover real similarities and offer genuine praise. • Build rapport and trust.
Authority	• People defer to experts. • People are more willing to follow the direction or recommendation of someone to whom they attribute relevant authority or expertise.	• Expose your expertise; do not assume it is self-evident. • Dress and act the part.
Scarcity	• People want more of what they can have less of. • People find objects and opportunities more attractive to the degree that they are scarce, rare, or dwindling in availability.	Highlight unique benefits and exclusive information.

Table 11-2. Principles of influence.[11]

As mentioned in the cultural awareness section above, you will want to adjust your personal leadership style in your new civilian environment. A leader's style refers to their manner and approach to planning, providing direction, and prompting others to action. Most leaders tend to adopt a style that suits their personality and then flex that style to meet the needs of specific situations. In adjusting your own style to suit a civilian environment, you should recognize there exists a spectrum of leadership styles, with transactional styles on one end and transformation styles on the other end (see Figure 11-2).

This figure is not intended to imply there is a right or wrong style. Your personal style likely falls somewhere within this spectrum. The point is that you may not be used to flexing your style, and this will become more of a need in your new civilian environment. To be

Transactional ←—————————————————→ **Transformational**

• Primarily concerned with maintaining normal flow of day-to-day operations
• Focus on the present
• Rely on discipline and rewards to motivate others
• Exchange rewards for performance (i.e., a "carrot and stick" approach)
• Common style in the military

• Look beyond the day-to-day operations to develop strategies for achieving goals
• Serve as role models for desired behaviors and emphasize team building and collaboration
• Tend to be charismatic and motivate others through coaching, growth opportunities, and involvement in decision making
• Preferred style in most civilian organizations

Figure 11-2. Leadership styles spectrum.

most effective, you need to adapt your leadership style based on the specific situations you encounter. To give you a better sense of the range of styles and the circumstances in which they may work best, see Table 11-3, which highlights six common leadership styles.

Style	Coercive	Authoritative	Affiliative	Democratic	Pacesetting	Coaching
Summary	Demands immediate compliance "Do what I say"	Mobilizes others toward a vision "Come with me"	Creates harmony and emotional bonds "People come first"	Forges consensus through participation "What do you think?"	Sets and models high standards for performance "Do as I do"	Develops others for the future "Consider this"
Characteristics and Risks	• Factual about consequences. • Lavishes praise when goals are met. • Can have a negative impact on climate by inhibiting flexibility and dampening motivation.	• Explains the overall goal but gives others the freedom to choose their own means of achieving it. • Lets others see their personal impact.	• Takes a genuine interest in others and ensures regular contact. • Heavy focus on praise can allow poor performance to go unchecked. • Tends to avoid offering advice, which can leave others stuck.	• Solicits team contributions, uses the ideas quickly, and visibly praises involvement. • Builds organizational flexibility and a sense of responsibility and helps to generate fresh ideas. • Danger of endless meetings and confused team members who feel leaderless.	• Expects clarity, excellence, and self-direction. • Employs facts and reasoning to call teams to action. • Demand for excellence can be overwhelming and cause resentment in team members who are not highly driven or skilled.	• Uncovers concerns and needs, then helps to resolve them. • Spends one-on-one time. • Listens actively, with empathy. • Focuses more on longer term talent development than immediate work goals.
Works Best . . .	• In a crisis. • To kickstart a turnaround. • With problem team members.	• When changes require a new vision. • When a team is adrift and clear direction is needed.	• To heal rifts in a team and improve morale. • To motivate others during stressful circumstances.	• To build buy-in or consensus. • To gather input from valuable team members.	• To get quick results from a highly motivated and competent team.	• To help a person improve performance or leverage strengths.

Table 11-3. Six common leadership styles.[12]

Depending on the situations you encounter in your new environment, you will want to apply several of these at varying turns. This may seem uncomfortable or contrived initially, but time, practice, and patience will produce the beneficial results you seek and make you a more effective leader in your new world.

ENGAGING WITH OTHERS

Interfacing with others will take on new dynamics in the civilian world as well. Let's take meeting facilitation as an example, since meetings drive progress in organizations. The military is known for having lots of meetings. They tend to follow a well-established cadence, whether it is an after-action review or a monthly unit training meeting. While some are organized on an as-needed basis, most were predictable, structured, and routine. In contrast, meetings in your new civilian environment will likely be more dynamic and less predictable. You will surely have some recurring meetings, but most will be scheduled as needed and the format, topics, and participants will vary.

The first step to running a great meeting is knowing whether to call for one at all. Do not call for a meeting if:

- Another method of communicating, such as email, would work as well or better.
- The group is upset and needs time apart before being able to address the source of the conflict or frustration.
- You don't have time to prepare.

If you do call for a meeting, consider the various types of meetings and whether one would better suit your cause:

- In-person meetings are best for sensitive topics and driving high levels of engagement and participation.
- Virtual meetings can be more economical, time efficient, and easier to organize, especially when a team is geographically dispersed.

Regardless of format, you should begin each meeting with an agenda, respect people's time by inviting only those who must attend, and detail responsibility for specific action items before the meeting is over. You will need to work a bit harder to facilitate meetings in the civilian world. They tend to be more collaborative and interactive and will thus require a different style of facilitation. Table 11-4 provides some helpful facilitation techniques whose application can help you be a more effective leader in your new role.

Technique	Description	Supporting Tactics	
Create Process Awareness	Provide clear direction about how the meeting will proceed. Gain agreement from participants as new facilitation processes are introduced during the meeting.	• Define roles (e.g., note taker). • Explain objectives and desired outcomes. • Confirm participant expectations.	• Set ground rules. • Review agenda.
Manage Discussion Flow	Keep participants focused on the same content, using the same process, at the same time.	• Refer back to meeting objectives and agenda. • Monitor time.	• Use a parking lot or idea bin for off-topic points.
Increase Engagement	Encourage high levels of active participation from everyone. Control dominators. Break silences.	• Precede open discussion with silent idea generation. • Lead a spontaneous free-form discussion.	• Use a round-robin to give everyone a chance to contribute. • Brainstorm to generate ideas.
Build Agreement	Achieve small agreements throughout the meeting in order to reach consensus by the end.	• Build agreement on both process and content.	• Use a poll to assess how close participants are to agreement.
Manage Strategic Moments	Recognize and address pivotal points in a meeting when a conflict or problem arises or the group requires redirection to get back on track.	• Clearly state the problem. • Accept and legitimize the issue. • Reach agreement on how to move forward (e.g., address it now or defer it)	• Refer back to the ground rules. • Don't be defensive.
Capitalize on Energy and Creativity	Look for opportunities to tap into the energy and creativity of the group in order to maximize productivity and innovation.	• Leverage visuals and encourage visual thinking (e.g., use a flip chart). • Use creativity toys (e.g., putty).	• Use energizers and brainteasers. • Change the seating arrangement during the meeting.
Conclude with Clarity	Wrap up by summarizing what has been accomplished and what will happen next.	• End on time. • Recap action items and owners.	

Table 11-4. Sample civilian meeting facilitation techniques.[13]

Next, let's revisit the topic of networking, which we first introduced in chapters 5 and 6. We just discussed the importance of veteran support networks. While important, those now become just part of your ever-increasing network that should include friendlies and targets within your new organization and surrounding community. The importance of this network increases, as your personal situation has changed dramatically. Networking continues to be about building relationships, and as we discussed above, this is one of the key ways in which you must adjust your personal approach in the civilian world. Even more important, networking helps you feel you are part of something greater than yourself and helps prevent you from feeling isolated. As before, networking should be purposeful and strategic. To avoid wasting anyone's time, make sure your ongoing networking efforts bear these hallmarks:

- They are mutually supportive or beneficial.
- They involve others purposefully, not randomly.
- They consider future possibilities rather than focusing only on the present.
- They consider relationship quality, not just network size.
- They enable professional growth.
- They help you achieve your career goals.
- They increase your impact.

★   ★   ★

TROOPS IN THE TRENCHES

"Find multiple mentors both in and out of the military. Create your own board of advisors, your Jedi council. People are usually willing to give you their time. Go after successful people in the industry in which you have an interest. Learn as much as you possibly can."

JON SANCHEZ, FORMER NAVY SEAL

Let's revisit the network organization chart we produced in chapter 5 (see Figure 11-3). Let's update the content and the corresponding database with your updated list of friendlies and targets. Among them, think of building a personal board of advisors, mentors and guides whom you can call upon for advice throughout your career.

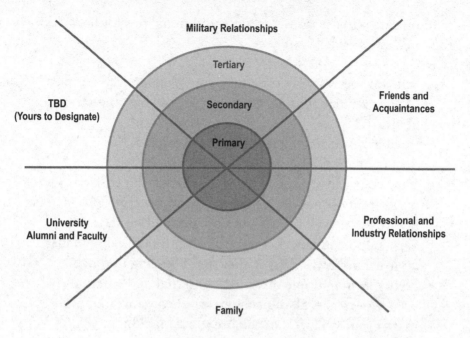

Figure 11-3. Network organization chart.[14]

Don't forget to track your activity and follow up on all your commitments. The relationship tracker noted in Figure 11-4 will likewise remain a useful tool throughout your career.

Name	Date of Last Contact	Meeting Objectives	Meeting Outcomes	Next Steps and Action Items

Figure 11-4. Relationship tracker.[15]

In putting it to use, consider these additional tips for networking in your new world:

- Schedule networking time on your calendar. Make it part of your regular routine. Make it part of your annual goals.
- Regularly update your network and related documentation.
- Vary your networking activities. Take advantage of any opportunity—meals, coffee breaks, drinks, airport layovers, at work or not—to connect with others.
- Seize opportunities to congratulate and thank others in your network. It's a great excuse for staying in touch.
- Network in multiple directions: internal and external to your workplace, all dimensions of the organizational matrix, and all levels of the organizational hierarchy.
- Be proactive and generous. Figure out what can benefit the other person first rather than wait to ask for something that might benefit you.
- Do what makes sense for you.

A final networking topic to address is the way in which we engage with leaders in the organization. In the hierarchical, authoritative, command-and-control environment that is the military, engagement with senior leaders tended to be infrequent and indirect. Leaders in the military are not supposed to be your friend. Depending on the nature of your civilian role, however, engagement with senior leaders may be more direct, more frequent, and perhaps even a necessary part of your job. In doing so, you may need to learn how to manage up, which entails:

- Working purposefully to obtain the best results for you and the organization. This is intentional, not accidental.
- Building relationships based on mutual trust, respect, and support. This does not involve manipulation or playing office politics.

- Collaborating to solve problems, manage risks, and achieve common goals.

If this is new to you, consider the following tips for engaging with civilian leaders:

- Be authentic. Don't force it.
- Know their work style (i.e., business chemistry) and tailor your communications accordingly.
- Follow the Platinum Rule: Treat others as they want to be treated.
- Smile, use their name, use a firm handshake, and maintain eye contact.
- Be courteous but not too formal. A higher value is normally placed on interacting with warmth and friendliness.

Interacting with civilian leaders can be daunting, especially when there is no formal protocol or structure to drive the interaction. But business is propelled by relationships, and to be successful in your new role, you will need to nurture connections with people at all organizational levels, including leaders.

★

PASSING ON LESSONS LEARNED AND CONTRIBUTING TO THE VETERAN NETWORK

Mahatma Gandhi supposedly said, "The best way to find yourself is to lose yourself in the service of others."[16] And so it must be with you. By successfully transitioning into the civilian world, you have overcome innumerable hurdles and personal challenges that have tripped up many a veteran who came before you. It should now be our collective goal to eliminate false starts and failed transitions for all future transitioning veterans.

★   ★   ★

TROOPS IN THE TRENCHES

"Seek ways to give back to the military. There are opportunities all over the place. Mentor, be an asset to veterans, and you'll never feel that far away from the service. It makes you feel like you're still serving."

BRIAN HANKINSON, FORMER ARMY LIEUTENANT COLONEL

Assuming you've diligently followed the steps in the transition process enumerated over these past eleven chapters, you've undoubtedly learned some lessons along the way. Some may reinforce the thinking noted herein. Some may run counter to what is stated. Some may well go beyond the text. This is all good. In the spirit of the Center for Army Lessons Learned, let's get this information out. Let it be free and open for public consumption and subject to public debate. If it helped you, chances are it may help someone else. Just as in the military, lives are at stake here, and your contribution may well save one. Here is one person's story, and I'd ask you to share the same:

★   ★   ★

TROOPS IN THE TRENCHES

What was the most difficult part of your transition?
"Finding and developing specific opportunities that fit within my overlapping criteria of industry, location, and position. My approach for this challenge began in earnest six months before I accepted a position, and I'll share this as an example to reinforce this one point: I worked just as hard at this as I did my day job, and I relentlessly committed myself to a steady course of planning, preparation, and execution. I was under no illusions and quickly came to the realization that no one owed me anything, and no one was going to

hand me anything on a platter. This was a journey all about finding how I can add value to a company and then convincing the right folks in that company that I could deliver that value.

"My planning activities included days, nights, and weekends of careful reflection and study on what was important to me and my family. I talked constantly about this with my wife, who, as my best friend, served as my coach, editor, and cheerleader through it all. We turned my home office into a war room with a whiteboard and bulletin board that allowed us to map out goals, options, and evolving priorities and opportunities. To prepare, I started tracking contacts, prospects, and specific position openings using OneNote and Excel to keep a progress log of what to do next. I steadily dedicated myself to several hours of nightly research after a full day in a demanding role, subscribing to job lists and targeting companies I was interested in. I read company mission statements, learned about their products, and read annual reports to gauge the big picture while exploring the particulars of the jobs posted. Whenever possible, I sought out information using LinkedIn and other sources to explore as much as I could about the company and the folks working there. I probably wrote over forty versions of different résumés, each tailored to each role for which I applied. This may seem ridiculously detailed and overboard for some, but for me it fixed my goals in time and gave me concrete to-do activities that drove me on a path to make my own opportunities. I took the mind-set that I'd begin a second career with the attitude, work ethic, and energy of a twenty-two-year-old but the benefit of twenty-five additional years of experience.

"Most important, I networked in person/telephonically/electronically, and methodically tracked every conversation and email while giving myself a deliverable suspense to update résumés and conduct follow-on activity. I made it a point to meet or talk to/email at least someone new every day. I reached out to some folks who in turn referred me to others and explored possibilities with an open mind as I was determined to reinvent myself with a renewed sense of enthusiasm. I was given only a few opportunities to interview. Of the seventy-five positions for which I applied, I was given the opportunity to interview for four. Once this happened, my execution plan unfolded. I dove deep into interview preparation by immersing myself in learning all I could about the company and the products and the services I'd soon get a chance to interview for. I mapped out an even closer level of detail in my daily and nightly efforts."

What was the best part of your transition?

"Getting an offer from a company I respected and in a place I had ranked high on my family's wish list, with the news that a position was available at precisely the time I had hoped to start. This drove the detailed execution planning that allowed me to fill in the many blanks I'd hoped to finalize for several months: timelines that included everything to make a new life—from transitioning beyond the military, to selling a home, moving our daughters to new schools in a new state, and lining up the logistics of a cross-country family move. There was tons to do, and without my wife fully committed, I'd never have succeeded in any of this."

Did you have any particularly good or bad stories about the experience you would be willing to share?

"The joy of making the transition successfully is truly rewarding, although it takes a lot to keep the faith when you are facing the unsettling prospect of the unknown and questioning your own abilities and pathways. You've got to keep the faith as you plunge into the unknown, realizing you may not have all the answers, but you do know you have the right stuff to ask the right questions, ask for help, and navigate through the haze. I'd been through a post-military career move once before as a young captain, but now, with a family, it changed the complexities and consequences completely. My wife and I prayed every night that God would guide us in the right path, and we're convinced He did. We've got so much to be thankful for, particularly the support of our incredible friends and family."

**What advice would you offer those currently going
through or about to go through the transition experience?**

"Take the time to reflect on what you truly want, and pour yourself
relentlessly into planning, preparing, and executing this in a way
that opens up pathways. Be dauntless in your curiosity and be willing to take chances! Without risk, there is no reward."

JIM NUGENT, FORMER ARMY COLONEL

Please do two things:

1. Share your additional thoughts, along with this book, with
   your veteran affinity or support groups.
2. Post your additional lessons learned to my website (www
   .matthewjlouis.com).

I wish you, the veteran, and your families the peace and pros-
perity you deserve. I wish your employers the productivity and
profitability I know you will provide.

Thank you. God's speed. And until next time—

KEYS TO SUCCESS

★ Your first role in the organization solidifies a reputation. Make it a
good one. Get ahead and stay ahead.

★ Dedicate yourself to a professional reading program. Use the
best ideas to continuously improve your new organization.
Remember this:

  Good—Better—Best
  Never Let It Rest
  'Til Your "Good" Gets Better
  And Your "Better" Gets Best[17]

★ Adjust your leadership, work, and communication styles to your new environment.

★ Be an active participant in one or more veteran support networks or affinity groups.

★ Continue building and maintaining your professional network. Consider creating your own board of advisors.

★ Share your lessons learned with the broader veteran network.

★ Pay it forward. Once you complete this book, you will effectively be trained in this career change process. Share this with your peers who are going through or about to go through the same transition. This is not about furthering this book; this is about helping other people be successful and our nation be successful as a result.

★ Your personal value is not determined by where you start but by where you finish.

★ You are the next greatest generation in waiting. You have much left to do in life. Service doesn't stop when you take off your uniform. The world needs you. The world awaits. Do not disappoint.

APPENDIX A

SUGGESTED TRANSITION PLAN TIMING

★ = Attend SFL-TAP, including career track classes

Activity	M1	M2	M3	M4	M5	M6	M7	M8	M9	M10	M11	M12	M13	M14	M15	M16	M17	M18	M19	M20	M21	M22	M23	M24
Identify your strengths.	★	█	█																					
Identify personality type and related careers.	█	█	█																					
Explore typical career options and skill requirements.			█	█	█																			
Identify industry, geographic, role preferences.			█	█	█																			
Recognize lifestyle factors.			█	█	█																			
Define personal brand.			█	█	█																			
Document and translate past performance.					█	█	█																	
Create tailored résumés.					█	█	█																	
Solicit feedback from friendly civilians in the know.					█	█	█																	
Identify target employers and decision makers.							█	█	█															
Define your network.							█	█	█															
Create stories to highlight your strengths, skills, and experience.									█	█	█	★	█	█										
Research your targets and decision makers.									█	█	█	█	█	█										
Engage the network: Conduct informational interviews, job shadowing, internships, career-skills program.									█	█	█	█	█	█										
Execute social media strategy.									█	█	█	█	█	█										
Practice interviews.														█	█	█								
Assemble wardrobe.														█	█	█								
Conduct interviews and follow up.														█	█	█								
Understand your financial needs.																█	█							
Research salary ranges.																█	█							
Research support networks at the organization.																█	█							
Negotiate opportunity and follow up.																█	█							
Seek onboarding resources and support networks.																	█	█	█	█	█	█	█	█
Adopt your new culture.																	█	█	█	█	█	█	█	█
Refine your approach and style as needed.																	█	█	█	█	█	█	█	█
Find new meaning in your work.																	█	█	█	█	█	█	█	█
Pass on your lessons learned and contribute to the veterans network.																	█	█	█	█	█	█	█	█

APPENDIX B

ACTION CHECKLIST

CHAPTER ONE
UNDERSTAND WHO YOU ARE

- ☐ Have you identified your personal strengths?
  - ☐ What clues do your strengths provide regarding your potential career paths?
- ☐ Have you taken at least two of the personality tests suggested?
  - ☐ What career paths did those tests suggest?
  - ☐ Did you further research those career paths?
  - ☐ Do you have the skill sets required for those career paths?
    - ☐ If not, what is your plan to attain those skills?

CHAPTER TWO
UNDERSTAND WHO YOU WANT TO BE

- ☐ Have you researched all practical career alternatives?
- ☐ Have you considered which could be a possible fit based on your strengths and personality type?
- ☐ Have you prioritized your potential career paths?

CHAPTER THREE
DEFINE YOUR CAREER PREFERENCES AND PERSONAL BRAND

☐ What are your industry, geographic, and role preferences?

☐ Have you considered internships or rotational programs?

☐ What lifestyle factors may influence your career path choices?

☐ What is your personal brand?

☐ Can you recite your elevator speech?

CHAPTER FOUR
GET YOUR RÉSUMÉ INTO FIGHTING SHAPE

☐ Have you collated all the necessary documentation for building your résumé?

☐ Did you . . .

    ☐ Quantify your accomplishments?

    ☐ Customize your résumé?

    ☐ Address every required qualification?

    ☐ Use keywords?

    ☐ Include a cover letter?

☐ If applying for a federal role, did you . . .

    ☐ Open a USAJOBS account?

    ☐ Build or upload a résumé?

    ☐ Use keywords in the job announcement?

☐   Make your résumé searchable?

☐   Have someone review it?

☐   Document your veteran's preference?

☐   If applying for a civilian role, did you . . .

    ☐   Identify how what you do impacts the income statement?

    ☐   Thoroughly translate your skills and experiences?

    ☐   Select the appropriate résumé type (chronological, function, or combination) for the type of role for which you are applying?

    ☐   Review your résumé with multiple experienced people in that industry?

☐   Have you taken advantage of the services of veteran collaboratives or American Job Centers around the country?

CHAPTER FIVE
DOCUMENT YOUR NETWORK

☐   Have you documented your network?

☐   Have you identified specific networking targets in light of your chosen career path?

☐   Have you identified some friendly contacts or networking venues for meeting your networking targets?

CHAPTER SIX
ENGAGE THE NETWORK

- ☐ Have you documented an action plan for engaging with your networking targets?

- ☐ Have you thoroughly researched your targets and their organizations before engaging with them?

- ☐ Have you created stories that highlight your strengths, skills, and experience?

- ☐ Did you follow up on all action items assumed during your discussions?

- ☐ Did you send a thank-you note?

- ☐ Have you established a LinkedIn profile?

- ☐ Have you procured a set of business cards for use in networking?

CHAPTER SEVEN
APPLY FOR ROLES

- ☐ If applying for a federal role, did you . . .

  - ☐ Prepare your application in USAJOBS for those job announcements for which you were interested and qualified?

  - ☐ Have someone familiar with the hiring agency proofread your application?

  - ☐ Submit your application to the hiring agency?

- ☐ If applying for a civilian role, did you . . .

  - ☐ Attempt to find job opportunities via networking that avoid the application process?

☐ Diligently follow all instructions on the application?

☐ Translate all military terms into something a civilian can understand?

☐ Handle sensitive questions (salary, criminal charges, etc.) with tact?

☐ Have someone familiar with the employer proofread your application?

☐ Complete all assessments, tests, and checks?

CHAPTER EIGHT
INTERVIEW FOR ROLES

☐ In preparing for interviews, did you . . .

  ☐ Document specifics from all past roles?

  ☐ Thoroughly research the role, the organization, its culture, and the interviewers themselves?

  ☐ Thoroughly rehearse answers to likely questions?

  ☐ Acquire the appropriate wardrobe for the interview?

  ☐ Ensure your grooming is appropriate?

  ☐ Arrive early and reconnoiter the objective?

☐ In conducting interviews for federal roles, did you . . .

  ☐ Bring a copy of your DD-214?

  ☐ Bring a prepared list of references?

  ☐ Bring a portfolio of completed work samples?

☐ In conducting interviews for civilian roles, did you . . .

☐ Show up on time with a positive attitude and respectful disposition?

☐ Bring a copy of your tailored résumé?

☐ Bring a pad, pen, and your business cards?

☐ Ask questions about the role and the organization?

☐ Close with confidence?

☐ Send a thank-you note?

☐ Follow up appropriately?

CHAPTER NINE
CLOSE THE DEAL

☐ Have you identified your financial needs . . .

    ☐ For retirement?

    ☐ For annual cash flow purposes?

☐ Do you understand the differences between your total military compensation and benefits and your prospective civilian compensation package?

☐ Have you thoroughly planned your job offer negotiation with the prospective employer using a win-win approach?

☐ Did you send a thank-you note after finalizing the terms and accepting the role?

☐ Have you completed an annual budget for your family?

☐ Have you taken advantage of all veterans benefits for which you are eligible?

CHAPTER TEN
ACCLIMATE TO YOUR NEW CULTURE

☐ Have you recognized the culture of your new organization and acclimated to it?

☐ Have you refined your approach and working style accordingly?

☐ Have you found new meaning in your work?

CHAPTER ELEVEN
ASSIMILATE AND PAY IT FORWARD

☐ Have you taken advantage of all available onboarding resources and support networks?

☐ Have you continued to build your network internally and externally?

☐ Have you committed to a professional reading program that ensures continuous improvement?

☐ Have you passed on your lessons learned to the broader veteran network?

OVERALL

☐ Have you taken advantage of my website (www .matthewjlouis.com) and all its available materials and additional resources?

ACKNOWLEDGMENTS

The process of writing this book has been a long, hard effort and would not have been possible without the many contributions of a multitude of others. I'll start with my wife, Michelle, and my boys—Jack, Nick, and Will—who have been incredibly supportive, kind, and patient. Their love has sustained me over many trying days.

Next come the professional servicemen, servicewomen, and veterans who have contributed their time and talent to this effort: Julia Aldrich, David Anderson, James Auvil (COL, USA), Matt Baringhaus, Kevin Berry (COL, USA Retired), Matt Birck, John W. Boerstler, Gordon Brown, Bob Carruthers (COL, USA), Chip Colbert (LTC, USA Retired), Joe DePinto, Anthony DeToto, Brian Dickinson (Col, USAF Retired), Joe Dziezynski (BG, USA), Peter Fontana, Malissa Gallini, Andrew Hall (COL, USA), Brian Hankinson (LTC, USA Retired), Greg Hardewig, Sal Herrera (COL, USA Retired), Grant Heslin, Dan Hodne (COL, USA Retired), Perry Jefferies (1SG, USA Retired), Dan Knowles, Dominic Lanzillotta, Jeff LeRoy (COL, USA), Norm Litterini (COL, USA Retired), Travis Long, Jim Lorraine, Robert Louderback, Lara Louis, Doug McCormick, Brian Melton, Harris Morris (COL, USA Retired), Brian Niswander, Jim Nugent (COL, USA Retired), Nate Pelletier, Dave Raymond (LTC, USA Retired), Ted Russ, Jon Sanchez, Don Seifert, Guy Swan (LTG, USA Retired), Dave Tomasi, Dave Uslan (SMSgt, USAF Retired), Martha VanDriel (COL, USA Retired), and Scott Williams (LTC, USA Retired).

Thanks also to many individuals outside the service who provided much needed feedback and perspective: Mark Faust, Pio Juszkiewicz, Brian Klems, Scott Mautz, Keith O'Brien, Diana Rau, Julie Anna Ring, and Paul Smith.

Thanks as well to my colleagues at Deloitte who provided encouragement, insight, and feedback: Kurt Babe, Terry Bickham, Heath Clayton, Mark Cotteleer, Bill Eggers, Katy Hollister, Terry Horton, Leslie Knowlton, Jack Midgley, and John Powers.

To my editing and publishing team, whose collective efforts have greatly improved the final product: Tim Burgard and Sara Kendrick at HarperCollins and Bob Babcock.

To my agent, Rita Rosenkranz, whose guidance to an impatient author had a huge impact.

To my website team: Kevin LeMasters at PixelParade, Kim Post at Kim Post Design, and Ben Yee at The Camera Department.

To all veterans, caregivers, and support organizations: Thank you for your service and the ongoing impact you have in our communities all around the country.

Thanks to the Department of Defense, the Department of Labor, and the Veterans Administration for what they have done to improve the Transition GPS curriculum in recent years. While the current product needs improvement (and is a reason for this book), it does better by the transitioning veteran than it has in the past. This work is intended to augment, not replace, what they do. My hope is they may adopt many of the elements herein to further strengthen their offering.

My apologies to anyone I may have missed. I recognize this is by no means a singular act, and I go forth with an attitude of gratitude for the contributions of all.

NOTES

★

FOREWORD

1. John Maxwell, "Caring for Your Corporate Family," *John C. Maxwell*, accessed July 25, 2018, http://www.johnmaxwell.com/blog/caring-for-your-corporate-family.

★

INTRODUCTION

1. Dwight D. Eisenhower, "Order of the Day," Eisenhower Presidential Library and Museum, June 6, 1944, accessed August 4, 2017, https://www.eisenhower.archives.gov/research/online_documents/d_day/Order_of_the_Day.pdf.
2. US Department of Veterans Affairs, VetPop 2007 Data, "Table 2S: Separations by State, Period, Age Group, Gender 2000–2036," 2007.
3. US Department of Defense, "2015 Demographic Profile of the Military Community," 2015, 55, accessed December 31, 2016, http://download.militaryonesource.mil/12038/MOS/Reports/2015-Demographics-Report.pdf.
4. Bruce Drake, "On Memorial Day, public pride in veterans, but at a distance," Pew Research Center, May 24, 2013, accessed January 2, 2017, http://www.pewresearch.org/fact-tank/2013/05/24/on-memorial-day-public-pride-in-veterans-but-at-a-distance-2/.
5. Gretchen Livingston, "Profile of US veterans is changing dramatically as their ranks decline," Pew Research Center, November 11, 2016, accessed January 2, 2017, http://www.pewresearch.org/fact-tank/2016/11/11/profile-of-u-s-veterans-is-changing-dramatically-as-their-ranks-decline/.
6. Efraim Benmelech and Carola Frydman, "Military CEOs," *Journal of Financial Economics* 117, no. 1 (2015): 43–59, accessed on July 2, 2017, http://www.nber.org/papers/w19782.pdf.

7. Vanessa Fuhrmans, "Generals Bring Battlefield Expertise to the Business World: Employers are tapping military leaders to develop leadership talent, provide corporate governance and oversee cybersecurity strategy," *Wall Street Journal*, August 29, 2017, accessed August 31, 2017, https://www.wsj.com/articles/generals-bring-battlefield-expertise-to-the-business-world-1504008002?shareToken=st0173955a9a9e4f4d9d7c2056ac1f3e19&reflink=article_email_share&mg=prod/accounts-wsj.

8. Fuhrmans, "Generals Bring Battlefield Expertise to the Business World," https://www.wsj.com/articles/generals-bring-battlefield-expertise-to-the-business-world-1504008002?shareToken=st0173955a9a9e4f4d9d7c2056ac1f3e19&reflink=article_email_share&mg=prod/accounts-wsj.

9. Rosalinda V. Maury et al., "Workforce Readiness Alignment: The Relationship Between Job Preferences, Retention, and Earnings," Workforce Readiness Briefs, no. 3, Institute for Veterans and Military Families, Syracuse University, August 2016, accessed October 27, 2017, https://ivmf.syracuse.edu/wp-content/uploads/2016/08/USAA_paper3_8.30.16_REVISED_digtial.pdf.

10. US Department of Veterans Affairs, "2015 Veteran Economic Opportunity Report," accessed October 30, 2017, http://www.benefits.va.gov/benefits/docs/veteraneconomicopportunityreport2015.pdf.

11. Maury et al., "Workforce Readiness Alignment," https://ivmf.syracuse.edu/wp-content/uploads/2016/08/USAA_paper3_8.30.16_REVISED_digtial.pdf.

12. Maury et al., "Workforce Readiness Alignment," https://ivmf.syracuse.edu/wp-content/uploads/2016/08/USAA_paper3_8.30.16_REVISED_digtial.pdf.

13. US Government Publishing Office, "United States Code 2011, Title 38 Section 101," accessed October 30, 2017, https://www.gpo.gov/fdsys/pkg/USCODE-2011-title38/pdf/USCODE-2011-title38-partI-chap1-sec101.pdf.

14. Drake, "On Memorial Day, public pride in veterans, but at a distance," http://www.pewresearch.org/fact-tank/2013/05/24/on-memorial-day-public-pride-in-veterans-but-at-a-distance-2/.

15. Deborah A. Bradbard, Nicholas J. Armstrong, and Rosalinda Maury, "Work After Service: Developing Workforce Readiness and Veteran Talent for the Future," Workforce Readiness Briefs, no. 1, February 2016, Institute for Veterans and Military Families, Syracuse University, accessed October 30, 2017, https://ivmf.syracuse.edu/wp-content/uploads/2016/05/USAA_Report_Jan27FINAL.pdf.

16. US Department of Veterans Affairs, "Veterans Employment Toolkit: Common Challenges During Re-adjustment to Civilian Life," accessed January 3, 2017, https://www.va.gov/VETSINWORKPLACE/docs/em_challengesReadjust.asp.

17. See: Elisabeth Kübler-Ross and David Kessler, *On Grief and Grieving: Finding the Meaning of Grief Through the Five Stages of Loss*, August 12, 2014, accessed on January 2, 2017, http://grief.com/the-five-stages -of-grief/.

18. Bradbard, Armstrong, and Maury, "Work After Service," https://ivmf .syracuse.edu/wp-content/uploads/2016/05/USAA_Report_Jan27 FINAL.pdf.

19. CareerOneStop, US Department of Labor, "Competency Model Clear-inghouse," accessed January 2, 2017, https://www.careeronestop.org /competencymodel/.

20. Bradbard, Armstrong, and Maury, "Work After Service," https://ivmf .syracuse.edu/wp-content/uploads/2016/05/USAA_Report_Jan27 FINAL.pdf.

21. Corri Zoli, Rosalinda Maury, and Daniel Fay, "Missing Perspectives: Servicemembers' Transition from Service to Civilian Life— Data-Driven Research to Enact the Promise of the Post-9/11 GI Bill," November 2015, Institute for Veterans and Military Families at Syra-cuse University, accessed October 30, 2017, https://ivmf.syracuse.edu /article/missing-perspectives-servicemembers-transition-from-service -to-civilian-life/.

22. Bradbard, Armstrong, and Maury, "Work After Service," https://ivmf .syracuse.edu/wp-content/uploads/2016/05/USAA_Report_Jan27 FINAL.pdf.

23. Chris Andrew Cate et al., "National Veteran Education Success Tracker: A Report on the Academic Success of Student Veterans Using the Post-9/11 GI Bill," Student Veterans of America, Washington, DC, 2017, 32, accessed August 18, 2017, http://nvest.studentveterans.org /wp-content/uploads/2017/03/NVEST-Report_FINAL.pdf.

24. J. Michael Haynie, "Revisiting the Business Case for Hiring a Veteran: A Strategy for Cultivating Competitive Advantage," Workforce Readiness Briefs, no. 2, April 2016, Institute for Veterans and Military Families, Syracuse University, accessed October 30, 2017, https://ivmf.syracuse .edu/wp-content/uploads/2016/06/IVMF_WorkforceReadinessPaper2 _April16_Report2.pdf.

25. Institute for Veterans and Military Families, "The Business Case for Hiring a Veteran: Beyond the Clichés," Institute for Veterans and Mil-itary Families, March 5, 2012, accessed October 30, 2017, https://ivmf .syracuse.edu/article/the-business-case-for-hiring-a-veteran-beyond-the -cliches/.

26. Amy Shafer et al., "Onward and Upward: Understanding Veteran Re-tention and Performance in the Workforce," Center for a New Ameri-can Security, November 2016.

27. Bradbard, Armstrong, and Maury, "Work After Service," https://ivmf .syracuse.edu/wp-content/uploads/2016/05/USAA_Report_Jan27 FINAL.pdf.

28. The Conference Board Inc. et al., "Are They Really Ready to Work: Employers' Perspectives on the Basic Knowledge and Applied Skills of the New Entrants to the 21st Century US Workforce," 2006, accessed March 20, 2019, https://archive.org/details/ERIC_ED519465.

29. Conference Board Inc. et al., "Are They Really Ready to Work," https://archive.org/details/ERIC_ED519465 .

30. Zoli, Maury, and Fay, "Missing Perspectives," https://ivmf.syracuse .edu/article/missing-perspectives-servicemembers-transition-from -service-to-civilian-life/.

★

CHAPTER ONE
UNDERSTAND WHO YOU ARE

1. Angela Duckworth, *Grit: The Power of Passion and Perseverance* (New York: Scribner, 2016), 8.

2. Maury et al., "Workforce Readiness Alignment," https://ivmf.syracuse .edu/wp-content/uploads/2016/08/USAA_paper3_8.30.16_REVISED _digtial.pdf.

3. © 2016 Deloitte Services LP.

4. See: Marcus Buckingham, *Go Put Your Strengths to Work: Six Powerful Steps to Achieve Outstanding Performance* (New York: Free Press, 2007).

5. See: Marcus Buckingham and Donald O. Clifton, *Now, Discover Your Strengths* (New York: Free Press, 2001).

6. See: Buckingham, *Go Put Your Strengths to Work*, 85–109.

7. "Career Leader Home Page," Career Leader, accessed March 29, 2019, https://www.careerleader.com/.

8. "Myers-Briggs® Career Test Online," Discoveryourpersonality.com, accessed March 29, 2019, http://www.discoveryourpersonality.com /myers-briggs-career-report-1.html.

9. "Self-Directed Search® Home Page," Self-directed-search.com, accessed March 29, 2019, www.self-directed-search.com/Who-uses-it /Veterans-Service-Members.

10. "iStartStrong™ Report," Career Assessment Site, accessed March 29, 2019, https://careerassessmentsite.com/tests/strong-tests/istartstrong -report/.

★

CHAPTER TWO
UNDERSTAND WHO YOU WANT TO BE

1. Maury et al., "Workforce Readiness Alignment," https://ivmf.syracuse
   .edu/wp-content/uploads/2016/08/USAA_paper3_8.30.16_REVISED
   _digtial.pdf.
2. Percentages are from: "Transition Survey Results, 2017 Veteran Survey,
   Page 9," Military-Transition.org, accessed March 20, 2019, http://
   www.military-transition.org/dashboard.html. Percentages do not add
   to 100 percent because roughly 4 percent of respondents chose not to
   answer this question.
3. "Transition Survey Results," http://www.military-transition.org
   /dashboard.html.
4. A listing of all federal governmental agencies is found at: "A-Z Index
   of U.S. Government Departments and Agencies," usa.gov, accessed
   March 29, 2019, https://www.usa.gov/federal-agencies/a.
5. "Veteran Employment Program Offices (VEPO) Directory," FedsHire-
   Vets®, accessed March 29, 2019, https://fedshirevets.gov/Agency
   Directory/index.aspx.
6. "Professional Occupations," USAJOBS, US Office of Personnel Management, accessed on January 30, 2017, https://www.usajobs.gov
   /Help/how-to/search/advanced/occupational-series/.
7. For a list of occupational families and a description of what types of
   positions are included in each, see: "Professional Occupations," USA-
   JOBS Help Center, accessed March 29, 2019, https://www.usajobs.gov
   /Help/how-to/search/advanced/occupational-series/.
8. For details, see: "Veterans' Preference Advisor," US Department of Labor,
   accessed March 29, 2019, http://webapps.dol.gov/elaws/vetspref.htm.
9. Arthur Kaff, "Job Hunting? These post-government employment restrictions might apply to you," Army Echoes, June–September 2017,
   accessed March 19, 2019, http://soldierforlife.army.mil/Documents
   /echoes/Army_Echoes_2017_Jun_printerfriendly.pdf. See also: "Post
   -Government Employment Guidance from the Department of the Air
   Force General Counsel," accessed July 8, 2017, http://www.safgc
   .hq.af.mil/Organizations/GCA/Ethics/Post-Government-Employment/;
   "Rules on Job Hunting and Post-Government Employment," Fort Knox
   Office of the Staff Judge Advocate, accessed July 8, 2017, https://www
   .knox.army.mil/Garrison/supportoffices/sja/docs/papers/adminlaw
   /Post_Gvt_Employment.pdf.
10. "Transition Survey Results," http://www.military-transition.org
    /dashboard.html.
11. For a list of all state government agencies, see: "State, Local, and Tribal
    Governments," usa.gov, accessed March 29, 2019, https://www.usa
    .gov/state-tribal-governments.

12. "Transition Survey Results," http://www.military-transition.org
    /dashboard.html.

13. See: "University Studies for Student Veterans," Columbia University
    Center for Veteran Transition and Integration, accessed March 30,
    2019, https://veterans.columbia.edu/content/university-studies-student
    -veterans.

14. For details on eligibility, see "Education and Training: Post-9/11 GI
    Bill," US Department of Veterans Affairs, accessed December 11, 2018,
    https://www.benefits.va.gov/gibill/post911_gibill.asp.

15. "Post-9/11 GI Bill: General Information," Department of Veteran Af-
    fairs, accessed March 29, 2019, https://www.benefits.va.gov/BENEFITS
    /factsheets/education/Post-911_General_info.pdf.

16. "Financial Aid for Veterans and their Dependents," FinAid.org Smart-
    Student™ Guide to Financial Aid, accessed March 29, 2019, http://
    www.finaid.org/military/veterans.phtml.

17. "State Veteran Education Benefits," Military.com, accessed March 29,
    2019, http://www.military.com/education/money-for-school/state
    -veteran-benefits.html.

18. For specific requirements in each state, see: "In-State Tuition and State
    Residency Requirements," FinAid.org SmartStudent™ Guide to Fi-
    nancial Aid, accessed March 29, 2019, http://finaid.org/otheraid/state
    residency.phtml.

19. "Ten Suggestions for Returning Veterans Thinking About Going to
    College," National Association of Veterans' Programs Administrator
    (NAVPA), accessed February 17, 2017, http://www.benefits.va.gov
    /GIBILL/docs/factsheets/NAVPA_Tips.pdf.

20. "Military Friendly® Schools," Militaryfriendly.com, accessed March
    29, 2019, https://militaryfriendly.com/schools/.

21. For the latest Military Times rankings of colleges and other
    veteran-related items, see: "Best For Vets Rankings," Military Times
    Reboot Camp, accessed March 29, 2019, https://rebootcamp.military
    times.com/rankings/.

22. "Licensing and Certification," Department of Veterans Affairs—
    Education and Training, accessed March 29, 2019, https://benefits
    .va.gov/gibill/licensing_certification.asp?_ga=2.173586017.315457607
    .1553882831-36901272.1536538515.

23. "Non-VA Resources for Student Veterans and School Administrators,"
    Department of Veterans Affairs—Education and Training, accessed
    March 29, 2019, http://www.benefits.va.gov/gibill/non_va_resources.asp.

24. Amy Shafer et al., "Onward and Upward: Understanding Veteran Re-
    tention and Performance in the Workforce," Center for a New Ameri-
    can Security, November 2016.

25. "Management Analysts," Bureau of labor Statistics—Occupational
    Outlook Handbook, accessed March 29, 2019, https://www.bls.gov
    /ooh/business-and-financial/management-analysts.htm#tab-1.

26. Kaff, "Job Hunting?" http://soldierforlife.army.mil/Documents/echoes /Army_Echoes_2017_Jun_printerfriendly.pdf.; see also: "Post-Government Employment Guidance from the Department of the Air Force General Counsel," http://www.safgc.hq.af.mil/Organizations/GCA/Ethics /Post-Government-Employment/; "Rules on Job Hunting and Post-Government Employment," http://www.knox.army.mil/Garrison/support offices/sja/docs/papers/adminlaw/Post_Gvt_Employment.pdf.

27. "Transition Survey Results," http://www.military-transition.org /dashboard.html.

28. See: Moshe Schwartz and Joyprada Swain, "Department of Defense Contractors in Afghanistan and Iraq: Background and Analysis," Congressional Research Service, accessed January 30, 2017, https://fas.org /sgp/crs/natsec/R40764.pdf.

29. "Top 100," *Defense News*, accessed March 29, 2019, http://people .defensenews.com/top-100/.

30. "Competency Model Clearinghouse," Careeronestop, accessed March 29, 2019, https://www.careeronestop.org/CompetencyModel/competency -models/pyramid-home.aspx.

31. "Survival of private sector establishments by opening year," Bureau of Labor Statistics, accessed February 1, 2017, https://www.bls.gov/bdm /us_age_naics_00_table7.txt.

32. "Frequently Asked Questions," US Small Business Administration Office of Advocacy, June 2016, accessed February 1, 2017, https://www .sba.gov/advocacy/frequently-asked-questions-about-small-business.

33. "John Adams Quotes," Goodreads, accessed March 22, 2019, https:// www.goodreads.com/author/quotes/1480.John_Adams.

34. "Thinking about self-employment? You can get help from a Small Business Development Center," Careeronestop Veteran and Military Transition Center, accessed March 30, 2019, https://www.career onestop.org/veterans/jobsearch/findjobs/start-a-business.aspx?ES=Y& EST=entreprenuer.

35. "Office of Veterans Business Development | Resources," Small Business Administration, accessed March 30, 2019, https://www.sba.gov/offices /headquarters/ovbd/resources/1548576.

36. "Veteran Entrepreneur Portal," Department of Veterans Affairs Office of Small & Disadvantaged Business Utilization, accessed March 30, 2019, https://www.va.gov/osdbu/entrepreneur/index.asp.

37. "Office of Veterans Business Development | Resources," Small Business Administration, accessed March 30, 2019, https://www.sba.gov/offices /headquarters/ovbd/resources/1354361. See also: "Center For Women Veterans (CWV)," Department of Veterans Affairs, accessed March 30, 2019, https://www.va.gov/womenvet/resources/index.asp.

38. See: "Set-asides for government contracting programs," Small Business Administration, accessed March 31, 2019, https://www.sba.gov /federal-contracting/contracting-guide/types-contracts. See also: "VA

Small and Veteran Business Programs," Department of Veterans Affairs —Office of Small & Disadvantaged Business Utilization, accessed March 30, 2019, https://www.va.gov/osdbu/programs/index.asp.

39. "Franchising 101," International Franchise Association, accessed February 3, 2017, http://www.franchise.org/franchising-101.

40. "What are the advantages and disadvantages of owning a franchise?" International Franchise Association, accessed March 30, 2019, www.franchise.org/what-are-the-advantages-and-disadvantages-of-owning-a-franchise.

41. "Introduction to Franchising," Small Business Administration, accessed March 30, 2019, www.sba.gov/tools/sba-learning-center/training/introduction-franchising.

42. "America's Best & Worst Franchises to Buy," *Forbes*, accessed March 30, 2019, www.forbes.com/best-worst-franchises-to-buy/#4a2dee 631a03.

43. "Franchises, Business Opportunities, and Investments," Federal Trade Commission, accessed March 30, 2019, www.ftc.gov/tips-advice/business-center/selected-industries/franchises%2C-business-opportunities%2C-and-investments.

44. "Company Directory," VetFran®, accessed March 30, 2019, https://www.vetfran.org/company-directory/.

45. "What Are the Keys to Franchise Success?" International Franchise Association, accessed March 30, 2019, https://www.franchise.org/faqs/resources/what-are-the-keys-to-success.

46. "Franchise Businesses," US Small Business Administration, accessed February 3, 2017, https://www.sba.gov/starting-business/how-start-business/business-types/franchise-businesses.

47. Helen Stone Tice, Lester M. Salamon, and Regina A. List, "Finding a Sacred Bard: Portraying the Global Nonprofit Sector in Official Statistics," Center for Civil Society Studies Working Paper, Series 19, 2001, accessed February 9, 2017, http://ccss.jhu.edu/wp-content/uploads/downloads/2011/09/CCSS_WP19_2001.pdf.

48. "Overview," Troops To Teachers, accessed March 30, 2019, https://www.proudtoserveagain.com/About/Overview.

49. "Transition Survey Results," http://www.military-transition.org/dashboard.html.

50. Note that consulting is not portrayed as an option in the small cap space. The reality is that all companies pose the potential to be a client of a consultant, and small cap companies are served by consultants to some degree. But this alternative does not pose a realistic possibility for a transitioning veteran in commercial industry (as opposed to governmental contractors or consultants, where it is a realistic possibility). The skill sets required and the support infrastructure available to ensure success are typically not present.

51. For the full NAICS, see: "North American Industry Classification System," United States Census Bureau, accessed March 30, 2019, http://www.census.gov/eos/www/naics/index.html.

52. "Competency Model Clearinghouse," Careeronestop, accessed March 30, 2019, https://www.careeronestop.org/CompetencyModel/competency-models/pyramid-home.aspx.

53. "Building Blocks Model," US Department of Labor, accessed February 20, 2017, https://www.careeronestop.org/CompetencyModel/competency-models/building-blocks-model.aspx.

54. "Large Cap–Big Cap," Investopedia.com, accessed February 17, 2017, http://www.investopedia.com/terms/l/large-cap.asp.

55. "S&P 500; Ticker: SPX," S&P Dow Jones Indices, accessed December 11, 2018, https://us.spindices.com/indices/equity/sp-500/.

56. "Large Cap–Big Cap," http://www.investopedia.com/terms/l/large-cap.asp.

57. Bureau of Labor Statistics, US Department of Labor, "Job growth at small businesses, 1992–2013," TED: The Economics Daily, May 12, 2014, accessed August 11, 2017, https://www.bls.gov/opub/ted/2014/ted_20140512.htm.

58. "Table of Size Standards," US Small Business Administration, accessed December 11, 2018, https://www.sba.gov/contracting/getting-started-contractor/make-sure-you-meet-sba-size-standards/table-small-business-size-standards.

59. "Occupational Outlook Handbook, Management Analysts," Bureau of Labor Statistics—US Department of Labor, accessed March 30, 2019, https://www.bls.gov/ooh/business-and-financial/management-analysts.htm.

60. "IMC Certification," Institute of Management Consultants, accessed March 30, 2019, http://www.imcusa.org/.

61. "America's Largest Private Companies," Forbes, accessed March 30, 2019, https://www.forbes.com/largest-private-companies/list/.

★

CHAPTER THREE
DEFINE YOUR CAREER PREFERENCES AND PERSONAL BRAND

1. Maury et al., "Workforce Readiness Alignment," https://ivmf.syracuse.edu/wp-content/uploads/2016/08/USAA_paper3_8.30.16_REVISED_digtial.pdf.

2. Maury et al., "Workforce Readiness Alignment," https://ivmf.syracuse.edu/wp-content/uploads/2016/08/USAA_paper3_8.30.16_REVISED_digtial.pdf.

3. Sharon P. Brown, "Business Processes and Business Functions: A new way of looking at employment," *Monthly Labor Review*, December 2008, 55–56, accessed August 11, 2017, https://www.bls.gov/opub/mlr/2008/12/art3full.pdf.

4. The federal government sponsors several: Post-9/11 GI Bill Apprenticeship Program (http://www.doleta.gov/oa/veterans.cfm), where eligible veterans receive a monthly housing allowance in addition to their apprenticeship wages; the Department of Labor (https://www.apprenticeship.gov/); the US Chamber of Commerce Foundation Fellows program, also known as the Hiring Our Heroes Corporate Fellowship Program (https://www.hiringourheroes.org/fellowships/); Army Career Skills Program, whose participating companies are unique to each post. Contact your local SFL-TAP center (https://home.army.mil/imcom/index.php/customers/career-skills-program). Details on the Marine Corps' version are at https://www.marines.mil/News/Messages/Messages-Display/Article/1559310/marine-corps-skill bridge-employment-training-program/. The Navy's is at https://www.navy.mil/ah_online/deptStory.asp?issue=3&dep=5&id=91366. The Air Force's version is at https://www.afpc.af.mil/Separation/CSP/. VA benefits that cover costs associated with on-the-job training and apprenticeships (https://www.vets.gov/education/work-learn/job-and-apprenticeship/).

5. To find local short-term training opportunities, visit: "Local Training Finder," Careeronestop, accessed March 30, 2019, https://www.careeronestop.org/toolkit/training/find-local-training.aspx.

6. For details, see: "Preparing Veterans for Careers at Top Companies," BreakLine, accessed March 30, 2019, https://breakline.org/; "CORE Leadership Program," Deloitte, accessed March 30, 2019, https://www2.deloitte.com/us/en/pages/about-deloitte/articles/join-deloitte-core-leadership-program.html.

7. US Census Bureau, "North American Industry Classification System," accessed October 31, 2017, http://www.census.gov/eos/www/naics/.

8. See: "North American Industry Classification System," US Census Bureau, accessed March 30, 2019, https://www.census.gov/eos/www/naics/.

9. Bureau of Labor Statistics, US Department of Labor, "Table 5: Employed persons 18 years and over by industry, class of worker, sex, veteran status, and period of service, 2017 annual averages," Labor Force Statistics from the Current Population Survey: Employment Situation of Veterans, accessed September 9, 2018, https://www.bls.gov/news.release/vet.t05.htm.

10. "2018 Cost of Living Calculator: Houston, Texas vs Los Angeles, California," Sperling's Best Places, accessed December 12, 2018, https://www.bestplaces.net/cost-of-living/houston-tx/los-angeles-ca/114000.

11. Shafer et al., "Onward and Upward."

12. "National Center for Veterans Analysis and Statistics," Department of Veterans Affairs, accessed March 30, 2019, https://www.va.gov/vet data/Veteran_Population.asp.

13. See the most recent "Best for Vets: Employers" rankings here: "Best For Vets Rankings," Military Times Reboot, accessed March 30, 2019, https://rebootcamp.militarytimes.com/rankings/.

14. For more on your legal rights concerning ongoing employment, voting, or financial/housing matters, see: the US Department of Justice's Servicemembers and Veterans Initiative (https://www.justice.gov/service-members/servicemembers-veterans-and-military-family-members, accessed January 23, 2018) or the Department of Defense's Employers Support of the Guard and Reserve (ESGR) agency (https://www.esgr .mil, accessed January 23, 2018).

15. See: "Best Companies," *Working Mother*, accessed October 31, 2017, http://www.workingmother.com/best-companies.

16. See: Alison Doyle, "Employee Benefits Questions to Ask," The Balance, December 24, 2018, accessed March 30, 2019, https://www.the balance.com/employee-benefits-questions-to-ask-2060431.

17. See: Albert Mehrabian, *Silent Messages* (Belmont, CA: Wadsworth, 1981), 76–77.

18. © 2016 Deloitte Services LP.

★

CHAPTER FOUR
GET YOUR RÉSUMÉ INTO FIGHTING SHAPE

1. Based on Kathryn Troutman, *Military to Federal Career Guide*, 2nd ed. (Baltimore: Résumé Place, 2010), 22.

2. You would find this among your military transition program paperwork at https://www.dodtap.mil/log`in.html (login required).

3. Based on Troutman, *Military to Federal Career Guide*, 35.

4. Troutman, *Military to Federal Career Guide*, 22.

5. "What should I include in my federal resume?" USAJOBS, US Office of Personnel Management, accessed March 10, 2017, https://www.usa jobs.gov/Help/faq/application/documents/résumé/what-to-include/.

6. "How to make your resume and profile searchable," USAJOBS, US Office of Personnel Management, accessed March 13, 2017, https://www .usajobs.gov/Help/how-to/account/documents/résumé/searchable/.

7. "What should I leave out of my resume?" USAJOBS, US Office of Personnel Management, accessed March 10, 2017, https://www.usajobs .gov/Help/faq/application/documents/résumé/what-to-leave-out/.

8. Institute for Veterans and Military Families, "The Business Case for Hiring a Veteran: Beyond the Clichés," Institute for Veterans and

Military Families, March 5, 2012, accessed October 30, 2017, https://ivmf.syracuse.edu/article/the-business-case-for-hiring-a-veteran-beyond-the-cliches/.

9. "Crosswalk Search," O*NET Online, accessed March 30, 2019, https://www.onetonline.org/crosswalk.

10. See: "Competency Model Clearinghouse," Careeronestop, accessed March 30, 2019, https://www.careeronestop.org/CompetencyModel/competency-models/pyramid-home.aspx.

11. "Military Skills Translator," Military.com, accessed March 30, 2019, http://www.military.com/veteran-jobs/skills-translator/.

12. See: "Google Resources for Veterans and Families," Accelerate with Google, accessed March 30, 2019, https://accelerate.withgoogle.com/veterans.

13. See: "Essential Skills Service Members Gain During Professional Military Training," Rand.org, accessed March 30, 2019, http://www.rand.org/content/dam/rand/pubs/tools/TL100/TL160z3-1/RAND_TL160z3-1.pdf.

14. "Get Past Resume Robots," Jobscan, accessed March 30, 2019, https://jobscan.co/#.

15. Register at: "A.Word.A.Day," Wordsmith.org, accessed March 30, 2019, http://wordsmith.org/awad/index.html.

16. "American Job Centers," Careeronestop, accessed March 30, 2019, https://www.careeronestop.org/localhelp/americanjobcenters/american-job-centers.aspx.

17. "Employment Initiatives & Resources for Veterans," Department of Labor Veterans' Employments & Training Service (VETS), accessed March 30, 2019, https://www.dol.gov/vets/goldcard.html.

★

CHAPTER FIVE
DOCUMENT YOUR NETWORK

1. See: Mark Granovetter, *Getting a Job* (Chicago: University of Chicago Press, 1995). See also: Malcolm Gladwell, *The Tipping Point* (New York: Back Bay Books, 2013), 54.

2. Try also: "iSABRD; A Networking Resource for Alumni of Service Academies," isabrd.com, Accessed March 30, 2019, www.isabrd.com.

3. See the most recent "Best for Vets: Employers" rankings here: "Best For Vets Rankings," Military Times Reboot, accessed March 30, 2019, https://rebootcamp.militarytimes.com/rankings/.

4. See: "Military Friendly® Employers," Militaryfriendly.com, accessed March 30, 2019, http://www.militaryfriendly.com/employers/; "Military Friendly® Schools," Militaryfriendly.com, accessed March 29, 2019, https://militaryfriendly.com/schools/.

5. See: "VetJobs™ – The Leading Military Job Board," vetjobs.com, accessed March 30, 2019, https://vetjobs.com/.
6. Concept © 2016 Deloitte Services LP.

★

CHAPTER SIX
ENGAGE THE NETWORK

1. © 2016 Deloitte Services LP.
2. © 2016 Deloitte Services LP.
3. See: "EDGAR | Company Filings, " US Securities and Exchange Commission, accessed March 30, 2019, https://www.sec.gov/edgar/search edgar/companysearch.html.
4. For potential internships or volunteer roles, see: "Land the Perfect Job or Internship," Internships.com, accessed March 30, 2019, https://www.internships.com/; "Volunteering in America," Corporation for National and Community Service, accessed March 30, 2019, https://www.nationalservice.gov/serve/via; "VolunteerMatch," Impact Online Inc., accessed March 30, 2019, https://www.volunteer match.org/.
5. For viable temporary agencies within your area, see: "Best of Staffing Award Winning Staffing Agencies," Clearlyrated, accessed March 30, 2019, https://www.clearlyrated.com/staffing.
6. Submit your request for a free year of Premium service at: https://linked inforgood.linkedin.com/programs/veterans. Once you have access, see useful ways to use LinkedIn at: https://www.linkedin.com/pulse /how-veterans-can-make-most-out-linkedin-daniel-savage/?trackingId =kYTPKFFaQDuutKZmFDc11w%3D%3D.
7. See: "Removal Policies," Google, accessed March 30, 2019, https:// support.google.com/websearch/topic/9173608?hl=en&ref_topic =3180360.
8. "Remove information from Google," Google Search Help, Google .com, accessed April 14, 2017, https://support.google.com/websearch /troubleshooter/3111061.

★

CHAPTER SEVEN
APPLY FOR ROLES

1. See: "Classification & Qualifications—Classifying General Schedule Positions," Office of Personnel Management, accessed March 30, 2019, https://www.opm.gov/policy-data-oversight/classification -qualifications/classifying-general-schedule-positions/#url=Overview.

2. "How does the application process work?" USAJOBS, US Office of Personnel Management, accessed April 20, 2017, https://www.usajobs .gov/Help/faq/application/process/.

3. Troutman, *Military to Federal Career Guide*, 39.

4. See also: Ronald L. Krannich, *Military-to-Civilian Success for Veterans and Their Families* (Manassas Park, VA: Impact, 2016), 177–180.

5. Krannich, *Military-to-Civilian Success for Veterans and Their Families*, 177–180.

6. "I-9, Employment Eligibility Verification," US Department of Homeland Security, accessed April 20, 2017, https://www.uscis.gov/i-9.

7. Roger Cameron with Chuck Alvarez and Joel Junker, *PCS to Corporate America* (Fredericksburg, TX: Shearer Publishing, 2012), 119–120.

★

CHAPTER EIGHT
INTERVIEW FOR ROLES

1. See: Ron Fry, *101 Great Answers to the Toughest Interview Questions* (Wayne, NJ: Career Press, 2016), 46–49.

2. See: "United States Government Manual," Govinfo.gov, accessed March 30, 2019, https://www.gpo.gov/fdsys/browse/collection.action ?collectionCode=GOVMAN.

3. See: "Occupational Outlook Handbook," Bureau of Labor Statistics, accessed March 30, 2019, https://www.bls.gov/ooh/.

4. See: "Business Websites," Stanford Graduate School of Business, accessed March 30, 2019, https://www.gsb.stanford.edu/library/conduct -research/business-websites.

5. See: F. John Rey, "Understanding a Company's Culture," TheBalance .com, February 10, 2019, accessed March 30, 2019, https://www.the balance.com/company-culture-2275155.

6. See: Lily Zhang, "The Ultimate Guide to Researching a Company Pre-Interview," TheMuse.com, accessed March 30, 2019, https://www .themuse.com/advice/the-ultimate-guide-to-researching-a-company -preinterview. See also: Heather Huhman, "7 Things to Research Before Any Job Interview," Glassdoor, July 14, 2018, accessed March 30, 2019, https://www.glassdoor.com/blog/7-research-job-interview/.

7. See: "How to Answer the 31 Most Common Interview Questions," TheMuse.com, accessed March 30, 2019, https://www.themuse.com /advice/how-to-answer-the-31-most-common-interview-questions. See also: Alison Doyle, "Top 10 Job Interview Questions and Best Answers," TheBalance.com, March 15, 2019, accessed March 30, 2019, https://www.thebalance.com/top-interview-questions-and-best-answers -2061225.

8. See: John T. Molloy, *John T. Molloy's New Dress for Success* (New York: Warner Books, 1988). See also: Kim Johnson Gross and Jeff Stone, *Dress Smart Women: Wardrobes That Win in the New Workplace* (New York: Warner Books, 2002).
9. See: Lizzie Post and Daniel Post Senning, *Emily Post's Etiquette: Manners for Today,* 19th ed. (New York: William Morrow, 2017).

★

CHAPTER NINE
CLOSE THE DEAL

1. "The Eleventh Quadrennial Review of Military Compensation," Department of Defense, June 2012, accessed November 1, 2017, http://militarypay.defense.gov/Portals/3/Documents/Reports/11th_QRMC_Main_Report_FINAL.pdf?ver=2016-11-06-160559-590.
2. See: "Financial Coaching Initiative," Consumer Financial Protection Bureau, accessed March 30, 2019, https://www.consumerfinance.gov/practitioner-resources/financial-coaching/financial-coaching-initiative/. See also: "Office of Servicemember Affairs (OSA)," Consumer Financial Protection Bureau, accessed March 30, 2019, https://www.consumerfinance.gov/servicemembers/).
3. Roger Fisher and William Ury, *Getting to Yes: Negotiating Agreement Without Giving In* (New York: Penguin Books, 2011), 11.
4. Fisher and Ury, *Getting to Yes,* 105.

★

CHAPTER TEN
ACCLIMATE TO YOUR NEW CULTURE

1. Pat Clifford, "4C Veteran Transition Survey: Pretest results and recommendations," Tristate Veterans Community Alliance, 2016. See also: "Tristate Veteran Community Report: Progress, Outlook, and Recommendations," Tristate Veterans Community Alliance, July 2016, 21, accessed March 19, 2019, http://www.tristatevca.org/wp-content/uploads/2017/08/20160711_Tristate-Veteran-Community-Report_PDF-min.pdf.
2. For the values of each individual service, see: "The Army Values," Army.mil, accessed June 30, 2017, https://www.army.mil/values/; "Who We Are: Our Values," Marines.com, accessed June 30, 2017, https://www.marines.com/who-we-are/our-values.html#; "Honor, Courage, Commitment," United States Navy, accessed March 19, 2019, https://www.navy.mil/navydata/nav_legacy.asp?id=193 "Our Principles: Core Values," AirForce.com, accessed June 30, 2017, https://www

.airforce.com/mission/vision; "Senior Coast Guard Leadership," USCG. mil, accessed March 19, 2019, https://www.uscg.mil/seniorleadership/.

3. Michael Abrams, "Mission Critical: Unlocking the Value of Veterans in the Workplace," Center for Talent Innovation, 2015, 5, accessed July 1, 2017, http://www.talentinnovation.org/_private/assets/MissionCritical _ExecSumm-Nov2015-CTI.pdf.

4. Dan Witters, "Active Duty Military Leads U.S. in Well-Being; Veterans Lag," Gallup, June 30, 2010, accessed July 1, 2017, http://www.gallup .com/poll/141089/active-duty-military-leads-well-being-veterans-lag .aspx.

5. Witters, "Active Duty Military Leads U.S. in Well-Being," http://www .gallup.com/poll/141089/active-duty-military-leads-well-being-veterans -lag.aspx.

6. © 2017 Deloitte Services LP.

7. John R. P. French Jr. and Bertram Raven, "Bases of Social Power," Value Based Management.net, 1959, accessed July 4, 2017, http://value basedmanagement.net/methods_french_raven_bases_social_power .html.

8. "The Age Discrimination in Employment Act of 1967," US Equal Op- portunity Employment Commission, accessed November 1, 2017, https://www.eeoc.gov/laws/statutes/adea.cfm.

9. See: "Handbook No. 15-6: Military Decision-Making Process (MDMP): Lessons and Best Practices," Center for Army Lessons Learned, March 2015, accessed July 3, 2017, http://usacac.army.mil/sites/default/files /publications/15-06_0.pdf.

10. For a free management library that focuses on this topic, see: "Personal Wellness," Free Management Library™, accessed March 30, 2019, http://managementhelp.org/personalwellness/index.htm.

11. Other quotes attributed to Eisenhower include, "These are nothing more than sturdy, down-to-earth rules that, in the busy life of high of- ficials who seem to be always compelled to deal with the urgent ahead of the truly important, can, by their availability in the mental reference library, often point the way to satisfactory solutions" ("Now that I am a Private Citizen . . . ," *Saturday Evening Post*, May 13, 1961); "Espe- cially whenever our affairs seem to be in crisis, we are almost compelled to give our first attention to the urgent present rather than to the im- portant future" (Address to the Century Association, December 7, 1961); "We need to feel a high sense of urgency. But this does not mean that we should mount our charger and try to ride off in all directions at once" (Radio and Television Address to the American People on Science in National Security, November 7, 1957, Mary Burtzloff, Archivist, Ei- senhower Presidential Library and Museum, August 4, 2017).

12. Maxwell Wessel, "Why Big Companies Can't Innovate," *Harvard Busi- ness Review*, September 27, 2012, accessed July 3, 2017, https://hbr .org/2012/09/why-big-companies-cant-innovate.

13. George K. Pitchford, "An Examination of the At-Will Employment Doctrine," ALA Allied Professional Association, August, 2005, accessed January 15, 2018, http://ala-apa.org/newsletter/2005/08/17/an-examination-of-the-at-will-employment-doctrine/. Also see: Charles J. Muhl, "The Employment-At-Will Doctrine: Three Major Exceptions," *Monthly Labor Review*, January 2001, accessed July 3, 2017, https://www.bls.gov/opub/mlr/2001/01/art1full.pdf.

★

CHAPTER ELEVEN
ASSIMILATE AND PAY IT FORWARD

1. Nate Scott, "The 50 Greatest Yogi Berra Quotes," *USA Today*, September 23, 2015, accessed November 12, 2017, http://ftw.usatoday.com/2015/09/the-50-greatest-yogi-berra-quotes.
2. See also: Tom Wolfe, *Out of Uniform* (Lincoln: University of Nebraska Press, 2012), 223–225; and Emily King, *Field Tested: Recruiting, Managing, and Retaining Veterans* (New York: Amacom, 2012), 133–136.
3. Sebastian Junger, *Tribe: On Homecoming and Belonging* (New York: Twelve Books, 2016), 101–103.
4. H. A. Lyons, "Civil Violence: The Psychological Aspects," *Journal of Psychosomatic Research* 23, no. 6 (1979): 373–393.
5. © 2017 Deloitte Services LP.
6. © 2017 Deloitte Services LP.
7. Suzanne M. Johnson Vickberg and Kim Christfort, "Pioneers, Drivers, Integrators, and Guardians," *Harvard Business Review*, March–April 2017, accessed July 7, 2017, https://hbr.org/2017/03/the-new-science-of-team-chemistry.
8. Vickberg and Christfort, "Pioneers, Drivers, Integrators, and Guardians," https://hbr.org/2017/03/the-new-science-of-team-chemistry.
9. See: "Welcome to Business Chemistry®," Deloitte, accessed March 30, 2019, https://businesschemistry.deloitte.com/Login/Index?ReturnUrl=%2f#/.
10. "Infographic: Insights into our communication," Get in Front Communications, accessed March 30, 2019, https://getinfrontcommunications.com/uncategorized/infographic-insights-into-our-communication/.
11. Based on Robert B. Cialdini, *Influence: Science and Practice* (Boston: Pearson/Allyn & Bacon, 2009).
12. Based on Daniel Goleman, *Leadership That Gets Results* (Boston: Harvard Business School Publishing, 2017), 64–66.
13. © 2017 Deloitte Services LP.
14. Concept © 2016 Deloitte Services LP.
15. © 2016 Deloitte Services LP.

16. Mahatma Gandhi, "Meaningful Quotes About Helping Others," Keep Inspiring.Me, accessed November 12, 2017, http://www.keepinspiring .me/helping-others-quotes/.

17. Attributed to Saint Jerome, "St. Jerome Quotes," BrainyQuote, accessed March 19, 2019, https://www.brainyquote.com/authors/st _jerome.

INDEX